THE PARAMETERS OF MILITARY ETHICS

Edited by

Lloyd J. Matthews

and

Dale E. Brown

Published under the auspices of the
U.S. Army War College Foundation, Inc.

Introduction by

Col. Harry G. Summers, Jr., U.S. Army (Ret.)

Selected by the Institute of Land Warfare
Association of the U.S. Army

PERGAMON-BRASSEY'S
International Defense Publishers, Inc.

WASHINGTON · NEW YORK · LONDON · OXFORD · BEIJING
FRANKFURT · SÃO PAULO · SYDNEY · TOKYO · TORONTO

U.S.A. (Editorial)	Pergamon-Brassey's International Defense Publishers, Inc., 8000 Westpark Drive, Fourth Floor, McLean, Virginia 22102, U.S.A.
(Orders)	Pergamon Press, Inc., Maxwell House, Fairview Park, Elmsford, New York 10523, U.S.A.
U.K. (Editorial)	Brassey's Defence Publishers Ltd., 24 Gray's Inn Road, London WC1X 8HR, England
(Orders)	Brassey's Defence Publishers Ltd., Headington Hill Hall, Oxford OX3 0BW, England
PEOPLE'S REPUBLIC OF CHINA	Pergamon Press, Room 4037, Qianmen Hotel, Beijing, People's Republic of China
FEDERAL REPUBLIC OF GERMANY	Pergamon Press GmbH, Hammerweg 6, D-6242 Kronberg, Federal Republic of Germany
BRAZIL	Pergamon Editora Ltda, Rua Eca de Queiros, 346, CEP 04011, Paraiso, São Paulo, Brazil
AUSTRALIA	Pergamon-Brassey's Defence Publishers Pty Ltd., P.O. Box 544, Potts Point, N.S.W. 2011, Australia
JAPAN	Pergamon Press, 5th Floor, Matsuoka Central Building, 1-7-1 Nishishinjuku, Shinjuku-ku, Tokyo 160, Japan
CANADA	Pergamon Press Canada Ltd., Suite No. 271, 253 College Street, Toronto, Ontario, Canada M5T 1R5

First edition 1989

Library of Congress Cataloging-in-Publication Data

The Parameters of military ethics/edited by Lloyd J. Matthews and Dale E. Brown: introduction by Harry G. Summers, Jr.—1st ed.
p. cm. - (An AUSA book)
"Published with the Institute of Land Warfare, Association of the U.S. Army."
1. Military Ethics. 2. War—Moral and ethical aspects.
I. Matthews, Lloyd J. II. Brown, Dale E. III. Institute of Land Warfare (Association of the United States Army) IV. Series.
U22.P36 1989 172'.42—dc19 88–28969

British Library Cataloguing in Publication Data

The Parameters of military ethics.—(An AUSA book)
Military service. Ethical aspects
I. Matthews, Lloyd II. Brown, Dale E.
174.'9355

ISBN 0–08–036717–8 Hardcover
ISBN 0–08–036718–6 Flexicover

An AUSA Institute of Land Warfare Book

THE Association of the United States Army, or AUSA, was founded in 1950 as a not-for-profit organization dedicated to education concerning the role of the U.S. Army, to providing material for military professional development, and to the promotion of proper recognition and appreciation of the profession of arms. Its constituencies include those who serve in the Army today, including Army National Guard, Army Reserve, and Army civilians, and the retirees and veterans who have served in the past, and all their families. A large number of public-minded citizens and business leaders are also an important constituency. The Association seeks to educate the public, elected and appointed officials, and leaders of defense industry on crucial issues involving the adequacy of our national defense, particularly those issues affecting land warfare.

In 1988 AUSA established within its existing organization a new entity known as the Institute of Land Warfare. Its purpose is to extend the educational work of AUSA by sponsoring scholarly publications, to include books, monographs and essays on key defense issues, as well as workshops and symposia. Among the volumes chosen for designation as "An AUSA Institute of Land Warfare Book" are both new texts and reprints of titles of enduring value which are no longer in print. Topics include history, policy issues, strategy, and tactics. Publication as an AUSA Book does not indicate that the Association of the United States Army and the publisher agree with everything in the book, but does suggest that the AUSA and the publisher believe this book will stimulate the thinking of AUSA members and others concerned about important issues.

Contents

Acknowledgments

Writing acknowledgments is like eating dessert; we save it for last because it is the most enjoyable part of putting together a book.

Foremost among those we wish to acknowledge here are the authors of the 17 essays comprising *The Parameters of Military Ethics*, essays that originally appeared in *Parameters: U.S. Army War College Quarterly*. Many observers of the military scene are prone to quick and easy judgments concerning the path of righteousness in our nation's deliberations upon war and are equally prone to declaim with certitude on the ethical norms that should inform the soldier's professional behavior. But few are inclined to record their views in a truly reflective and analytical way so that the world can judge the cogency of their arguments, the clarity of their vision, and the extent of their contribution to a genuinely constructive dialogue. Our 17 authors, however, accepted this challenge without flinching, and for their courage and sacrifice, we are grateful.

The groundwork had been well laid. Lieutenant General DeWitt C. Smith, Jr. (U.S. Army, Retired), U.S. Army War College commandant in 1974–77 and 1978–80, strove with notable success to transform the college into a leading center for contemporary military thought. General Carl E. Vuono, Army Chief of Staff, Major General Howard D. Graves, Army War College commandant, and Brigadier General Stephen Silvasy, Jr., Army War College deputy commandant, have labored in the same enlightened tradition. Further, they have taken decisive steps to emphasize the ethical dimensions of strategy and military command within today's War College curriculum. We should mention, too, the vigilant efforts of Colonel Donald E. Lunday, director of academic affairs at the War College, in preserving an educational environment marked by the twin precepts of free intellectual inquiry and unfettered expression of ideas.

Thanks go as well to the Army War College Foundation, Inc., which has served as a solicitous godfather not only to the present *Parameters*-based volume, but to three earlier ones as well—*The Parameters of War*, *Assessing the Vietnam War*, and *The Challenge of Military Leadership*. Colonel LeRoy Strong (U.S. Army, Retired), executive director of the foundation, has been a ready source of wise counsel and generous support.

Finally, we remember with gratitude past *Parameters* editors—Colonels Alfred J. Mock, Roland R. Sullivan, and William R. Calhoun, Jr.—all now retired, who labored anonymously but always with invigorating effect in the vineyards of service journalism. And we remember with special affection and appreciation present *Parameters* staffers—Assistant Editor Gregory N. Todd and Editorial Assistants Mrs. Lisa A. Ney and Miss Jennifer L. Cunningham—who in ways large and small have advanced the cause of *Parameters* in general and the present volume in particular.

The Editors

Introduction

Ethics may well be America's secret weapon. As the late Air Force Major General Edward Geary Lansdale—the prototype for William J. Lederer and Eugene Burdick's Colonel Hillandale in the *Ugly American* (Hillandale was, in case you've forgotten, one of the good guys)—wrote,

> The most pragmatic course [for Americans is] to heed the idealism of our country's political tenets and make them the basis for our actions. . . . The back rooms of Washington policymakers are too full of articulate and persuasive practitioners of the expedient solution to daily problems, of the hoary art of power politics, and of the brute usages of our physical and material means. They can scarcely comprehend the pragmatism of sticking to the ideal of having a government "of the people, by the people, for the people" as the strongest defense any country could have against the Communists. . . . If we are to succeed, impatient Americans will have to remember our own heritage.

An important part of that heritage is the unique relationship existing between the American people and their armed forces. As former Army Chief of Staff General Fred C. Weyand said in his examination of America's performance in Vietnam, "The American Army really is a people's army in the sense that it belongs to the American people, who take a jealous and proprietary interest in its involvement."

At one time that was well understood, but that understanding has eroded, as has an appreciation for the importance of ethics in general. "The fact of the matter is that those who serve the nation in a military capacity no longer can assume any dominant moral consensus in the United States," writes Professor Donald Atwell Zoll in the present collection *The Parameters of Military Ethics.* "Such a lack of ethical homogeneity may be tolerable in the nation as a whole," he continues, "but ethical incongruities are simply not feasible in a military establishment. That organism must be knit by a relatively tight ethical code—and perhaps one that must now be formally postulated."

Postulating that ethical code in particular and the morality of American military force in general is what this book is all about. As the title suggests, the purpose is to lay out the ethical parameters of the military universe. Drawing from the cornucopia of professional reflections that over the years have appeared in the pages of *Parameters*, the professional journal of the Army War

College, *The Parameters of Military Ethics* examines the many facets of that universe.

One of the touchstones of that universe is the just-war tradition. As Princeton University Professor James Turner Johnson explains in this volume's lead article, two characteristic facts encompass this tradition. First, a moral response to the question of forcible defense of values "has often found expression . . . in codification and theories of international law [and] in military manuals on how rightly to conduct war." More importantly, it reflects "the judgments and reactions of common people." This tradition, he states, "encapsulates something of how we in this culture respond morally to the question of protection of value by force."

The second characteristic fact about the just-war tradition is that it "preserves two kinds of moral responses to the question of value and force, not merely one: limitation always accompanies justification . . . what has come to be known as the *jus ad bellum* has to do with the question of justification, while that of limitation is addressed by the *jus in bello*." But there is the possibility of "the transgression of value in the service of value" (i.e., the "we had to destroy the town in order to save it" syndrome), which poses the question, "Do the values constituting the *jus ad bellum* have priority over those of the *jus im bello*?"

Addressing that dilemma in the context of nuclear war is Dr. Stephen M. Millett. As he puts it, "The fundamental American moral dilemma of nuclear deterrence is how the United States can prevent one evil (communist expansion of power at the expense of Western interests) by threatening to unleash another evil (nuclear destruction and radioactive contamination)." While Millett notes "some students of international relations will immediately reject the moral dilemma of deterrence by asserting that concepts of morality and evil are irrelevant in modern secular macropolitics," he goes on to quote approvingly Henry Kissinger's comment that "morality without security is ineffectual; security without morality is empty. To establish the relationship and proportion between these two goals is perhaps the most profound challenge before our government and our nation."

In chapter three, Professor John W. Coffey concentrates his attention on the Catholic bishops' pastoral letter on war and peace, finding that "the bishops ground their discussion of nuclear policy in the 15-century-old just-war tradition. . . . In the nuclear age, the critical conditions are proportionality and discrimination." And there's the rub. "Recognizing the inexact nature of discrimination in practice, the bishops admit that 'concise and definitive answers' still appear to be wanting," Coffey tells us. And when it comes to the principle of proportionality, the fact is that it cannot "be reduced to some crude material calculus."

"Were the preservation of the Union and the end of slavery worth one million dead and wounded Americans?" Coffey asks. "Was the defeat of Nazism commensurate with the loss of 55 million lives?" Rather than resolve these types of dilemmas, the bishops' proposals to promote peace "range from a feckless endorsement of the United Nations as a step toward world government to a perverse recommendation to create a global political body [what Coffey labels "a monstrous totalitarianism"] that would maintain surveillance over the earth and have the power to prevent any nation from bellicose preparations."

Colonel James L. Carney also addresses the nuclear dilemma, but comes to quite different conclusions. Asking "Is it ever moral to push the button?" he returns to the arguments posed by just-war theory and concludes that "the two just-war principles most jeopardized by nuclear weapons are discrimination (noncombatant immunity) and proportionality."

"There appear to be only three ways out of this box we have created for ourselves," Carney concludes. "One is to find another means of defense. The Strategic Defense Initiative offers a glimmer of hope, but only a glimmer. . . . A second way out of our nuclear dilemma is arms control. . . . A third way, the most radical but also the most promising as a long-term solution, is the establishment of some kind of world authority with enough power to enforce the renunciation-of-force doctrine in the United Nations Charter." Carney believes that "whether we like it or not the time is approaching when we must move on to a more effective, less-dangerous governance than that embodied in the nation-state system."

Although not directly attacking Carney's reasoning, Professor William Barrett nevertheless calls it into question by bringing the moral argument down to earth. "All philosophical and moral questions are carried out in the context of our actual situation," he writes. "When the actuality is benign, we tend to forget it, and we seem free for a while to spin our hypothetical and contrafactual cases in the thin air of abstraction."

"Two predominant conditions define our present situation in the world today," he continues. "First is the fact that the United States is confronted with an implacable enemy in the form of the Soviet Union. . . . The second overriding fact in our actual situation is the presence of nuclear weapons." But when it comes to reconciling these two facts, "tactical complexities of a moral as well as a military nature tend to becloud our sense of the basic imperative. . . . Kant remarked that the honest citizen, the decent citizen, knows what his duty is—he does not have to learn it through the dialectic of philosophers. If this were not so, the moral life of mankind could not be carried on and the race would have long since floundered."

"My main point comes back to that of Kant," Barrett concludes. "We can know our moral duty in a certain situation without having resolved antecedently all the difficulties or complexities that may attend it, and we cannot let the deliberation upon the latter weaken our primary resolves."

With Telford Taylor bridging the way with a useful examination of the link between law and morality, the discussion turns from the grand issues of nuclear morality in chapters two through five to the more prosaic but nonetheless vital issue of individual military responsibility. "Who is responsible to whom and for what?'' asks Professor Michael Walzer. Not surprisingly, he finds that an officer is responsible upward to his military and civilian commanders and through them ''to the sovereign people, whose 'officer' he properly is and to whose collective safety and protection he is pledged.'' His obligation is ''to win the battle that he fights . . . and he is responsible up the chain . . . to the ordinary citizens of his country who are likely to suffer for his failures.''

As every officer knows, he is also responsible downward to the soldiers he commands. ''He is bound to minimize the risks his soldiers must face, to fight carefully and prudently, and to avoid wasting their lives, that is, to not persist in battles that cannot be won, to not seek victories whose costs overwhelm their military value, and so on. And his soldiers have every right to expect all this of him and to blame him for every sort of omission, evasion, carelessness, and recklessness that endangers their lives.''

But beyond these hierarchical responsibilities, Walzer lays out yet a third responsibility: as a moral agent the officer has outward responsibility for ''the civilian casualties of the battles he fights.'' My Lai is horrible confirmation that this is more than just a moral abstraction. In conclusion, Walzer quotes General MacArthur's comments at the time of the Yamashita trial: ''The soldier . . . is charged with the protection of the weak and unarmed. It is the very essence and reason of his being . . . [a] sacred trust.''

Examining this ''sacred trust,'' Chaplain Kermit D. Johnson finds ''four pressing ethical issues for leaders in the military establishment to consider.'' The first is ethical relativism, where right and wrong have been replaced by a ''no-fault'' society. The second is the loyalty syndrome—''the practice wherein questions of right and wrong are subordinated to the overriding value of loyalty to the boss.'' Then there is the third ethical trap—image. ''Instead of acting upon what is right, we often hear: 'You know, if we do this, it'll be embarrassing to the Army's image.' '' Finally there is ''the drive for success'' or ''the masochistic whip by which, sometimes, we punish ourselves and by which we sometimes are beaten sadistically by others.''

Homing in on the issue of ethical relativism, Lieutenant Colonel James L. Narel notes that ''although military officers may not recognize the contradiction between ethical relativism or egoism and the nature of the military profession, the consequences of holding inconsistent convictions are anything but trivial. Like so many other social institutions, the military profession suffers at times from a spiritual malaise that undercuts our collective confidence, saps our energy, and produces a cynicism that seems to feed on itself.''

With ''a firsthand appreciation of various ethical tensions that confront senior Army officers,'' retired Major General Clay Buckingham ''explores the foundation of our ethical system, offers some thoughts about how this ethical system should apply specifically to the military profession, and finally takes an empirical look at the tensions in the military society that provide fertile ground for ethical abuses.''

"The one tension that will be most consistently with you involves the ethical use of authority," he writes, especially "the exploitation and degradation of subordinates." The second great tension "involves the use of military force. . . . When should it be used? Under what circumstances? In what strength? In defense of U.S. territory only? Or in defense of U.S. interests? Or in defense of our allies?"

Turning from the ethical dimension of professionalism in general, Professor Arthur J. Dyck focuses discussion more squarely on a codified professional ethic. "A traditional approach to professional responsibilities in the military consists of emphasizing the three central concepts: duty, country, and honor," he writes. "Duty implies not only the obligation to do one's job conscientiously, but to do so within ethically acceptable norms . . . [including an understanding of and an adherence to] just-war theory."

When it comes to country, "the military professional's clients are the people of the country. Strictly speaking, faithfulness to one's fellow citizens is expressed appropriately as a vow to uphold the Constitution. . . . But the ethics of military professionals must go beyond fidelity to law and its legal underpinnings. No constitution or law is obeyed and understood without the cultivation of moral consciousness and moral sensitivity. That is why every professional ethic, including the military's, also includes concern for honor."

Continuing in the vein of the professional ethic, Professor Donald Zoll notes that "the conduct of war has generally reflected prevailing moral attitudes in a number of ways." These include "prohibitions against the violation of *a universal moral order*" as well as violations of what he labels *class attitudes*, which were derived from the traditions of chivalry. Other limiting factors were a *philosophically derived social ethic* and a *concern for the maintenance of professional self-interest.*

"What must a professional military ethic be?" he asks. "Conceived of at its most rudimentary level, a professional ethic must be built upon two basic considerations: first, the maximum attainment of objectives for which the profession itself exists, and, second, a reconciliation with the precepts of humane values that have been manifested in the course of human history."

"I believe there are five principal elements that form the base for a contemporary military ethic," he writes: "Personal honor; obedience and limits of moral freedom; relationships to the society as a whole; relationships to existing political institutions and forces; and the moral implications of command responsibility."

This military ethic must hold not only on the nuclear and conventional battlefield, but in combatting terrorist activity as well, writes Colonel Anthony E. Hartle. As he sees it, the fundamental principles of the professional ethic demand that professional soldiers "always do their duty"; "conduct themselves as persons of honor"; "develop and maintain the highest possible levels of professional skill and knowledge"; "take full responsibility for their orders"; "strictly observe the principle that the military is subject to civilian authority''; ''promote the welfare of their subordinates [; and] adhere to the laws of war.''

Colonel Hartle goes on to tell us that ''the American professional military ethic provides a comprehensive reinforcing structure rooted in cultural and social values that limit in principle what is permissible in any activity that the military undertakes, including counterterrorist activities. . . . [The leader] must ensure that our responses to terrorism do not injure the moral fabric of our society. A clear understanding of the moral structure within which we operate constitutes the most effective means to that end.''

Lieutenant General Sir James Glover reinforces Colonel Hartle's argument with his discussion of a soldier's conscience. ''A soldier is trained to kill,'' he points out. ''He may be ordered to, or he may order others to, break the Sixth Commandment. . . . He is not protected by that shell of remoteness that shields the sailor in his ship and the airman in his aircraft. In simple terms this—the act of killing—poses the soldier's ultimate moral predicament.''

General Glover then examines the *quieters of conscience:* ''leadership by persuasion which silences the soldier's misgivings''; ''the soldier's loyalty to, and pride in, his own outfit which convinces him that he is part of something bigger than himself''; ''the very presence of others who are doing the same thing as he without funk or complaint, whom he just cannot let down''; and ''the last and most disputable of the moral pressures, the mandate that the end justifies the means.''

Turning to the antidote—the military virtues and their impact—General Glover lists professionalism, judgment, willpower, courage (especially including moral courage), and integrity. ''I submit that a man of character in peace is a man of courage in war,'' he concludes. ''As Aristotle taught, character is a habit, the daily choice of right and wrong. . . . The conflict between morality and necessity is eternal. But at the end of the day the soldier's moral dilemma is resolved only if he remains true to himself.''

In American military history, one of the main protagonists in the struggle between morality and necessity was Union General William Tecumseh Sherman. Examining the roots of that struggle, Chaplain John W. Brinsfield finds that ''Sherman's problem throughout the Civil War was how to reconcile the brutal nature of modern war with the ethical values he had learned as a West Point cadet, as an Army officer, in his intermittent study of the law from 1839 to 1859, and as a practicing attorney.''

''The genesis of Sherman's conversion from a proponent of warfare by the rules of courtesy to warfare by the rules of survival . . . was not the result of a deliberate policy rooted in intellectual theory. It was a reaction to the conditions he encountered in the field. . . . With constitutional interpretation replaced by congressional law and the principle of military necessity, Sherman was free to suppress rebellion with almost any amount of force necessary. . . . He was not the author of either the theory or the ethic of total war, but, in his generation, he may have been the leading intellectual apologist for both.''

It is most fitting that this volume concludes with an essay by retired Vice Admiral James Bond Stockdale. A prisoner of war in Hanoi for eight years, honored for his travail with the Medal of Honor, and later named President of the Naval War College, Admiral Stockdale found underlying truth in Aristotle's remark that "education is an ornament in prosperity and a refuge in adversity." From the writings of Epictetus in *The Enchiridion* to the Greek historian Polybius to Homer's *The Iliad* to Cervantes, Dostoyevski, Koestler, and Solzhenitsyn, Stockdale drew the strength that would carry him through his adversity.

As Carl von Clausewitz remarked, anyone can command when things are going well, but it is only when disaster strikes that the character of the commander is really tested. During his prison experiences, Admiral Stockdale came to the same conclusion: "The challenge of education is not to prepare a person for success, but to prepare him for failure. It is in disaster, not success, that the heroes and the bums really get sorted out." Thus his admonition that "always striving for true education—with its emphasis on moral reflection—is the best insurance against losing your bearings, your perspective, in the face of disaster, in the face of failure."

One of the most poignant experiences of my military career was talking with Vietnam-era Army Chief of Staff General Harold K. Johnson shortly before he died. An intensely moral man who not only kept a Bible and a Boy Scout manual on his desk but lived by their precepts, General Johnson was also a most distinguished soldier. A battalion commander of the Philippine Scouts at the outbreak of World War II, he survived the Bataan Death March and imprisonment by the Japanese. During the Korean War he commanded the 8th Cavalry Regiment and bore the initial brunt of the Chinese invasion. He confided to me that at one point during the Vietnam War, he had become so disgusted with how the war was being conducted that he left for the White House to tell the president the United States had no strategy worth the name in Vietnam, that all the principles of war were being violated, and that American soldiers were being killed needlessly. On the way there, however, he thought better of it and convinced himself that he could do more by staying on than he could by resigning. "And now," he said, "I will go to my death with that lapse in moral courage."

Everyone knows that taking a moral and ethical stand may have disastrous consequences for one's career ambitions. But General Johnson's comments are testimony that the consequences of not taking such a stand may be far worse.

Colonel Harry G. Summers, Jr.
U.S. Army, Retired

I. DEFINING THE JUST IN MODERN CONFLICT

1

Does Defense of Values by Force Remain a Moral Possibility?

By JAMES TURNER JOHNSON

Two deep and broad streams of moral reflection on war run through Western history. These streams have their thematic origin in a single fundamental question: Is it ever morally allowable to employ force in the protection and preservation of values? The moral tradition of pacifism has resulted from a negative response to this question, given in various ways under various historical circumstance. A positive answer, given in ways no less conditioned by historical circumstance yet with a similar depth of underlying consistency and wholeness, has produced the other moral tradition on force and violence, which it is both convenient and proper to call by a familiar name: just war tradition. We should note two characteristic facts about this tradition.

First, it is a moral response to the question of value and force that is not only historically deep but is a product of reflection and action across the whole breadth of this culture's experience. It is not a moral doctrine in the narrow sense, reflecting the attitudes only of those sectors of the culture, like religion, often conceived as having a specialized function of moralizing cut off from the rest of human existence. This tradition has often found expression, to be sure, in church law and theological reflection; yet it also appears in codifications and theories of international law, in military manuals on how rightly to conduct war, and, as Michael Walzer has shown in *Just and Unjust Wars*, in the judgments and reactions of common people.[1] In short, this tradition encapsulates something of how we in this culture respond morally to the question of protection of value by force; it is not the only response, for pacifist rejection of force parallels it through history, but it is a fundamental one, revealing how we characteristically think about morality and war and defining the terms for our reflections in new or changing circumstances.

The second characteristic fact about just war tradition is that it preserves two kinds of moral response to the question of value and force, not merely one: limitation always accompanies justification. The response that says, yes, here are some conditions in which it is morally right to use force to protect value goes on to set limits to what may rightly be done toward that end. This second element in the response is determined by the nature of the value or values to be protected; thus the need for limitation is built into the need to protect value as a necessary correlate. This means in general that unlimited or even disproportionately large amounts of force are not what is justified when the use of force to protect values is itself justified. Just war tradition, as recognized by such contemporary commentators as Paul Ramsey, William V. O'Brien, and, as already mentioned, Walzer,[2] is a moral tradition of justifiable and limited war. What has come to be known as the *jus ad bellum* has to do with the question of justification, while that of limitation is addressed by the *jus in bello*. These are interconnected areas, but the priority, logical as well as historical, is with the former: only after the fundamental question is answered about the moral justification of employing force to protect value does the second question, about the morally requisite limits governing the use of that force, in turn arise. Problems arising in the *jus in bello* context may cause us to want to reflect further about the nature of the values we hold, the threat against them, and the means we may use to defend them; yet such further reflection means only that we must again enter the arenas of the "war decision,"[3] the *jus ad bellum*.

It is often claimed that the development of nuclear weapons has made this traditional way of thinking about morality and war obsolete and irrelevant.[4] From what I have said, it should be clear that I think this is not the case. Indeed, my claim is that we naturally think in the same terms that are encountered in the tradition, whether we want to or not: a pacifist critic like James Douglass employs one part of the tradition to reject the whole of it,[5] while no sooner has another critic, Stanley Hoffmann, rejected it than he reinvents it point by point.[6] Such phenomena should be instructive. We do not do well to repudiate this tradition of moral reflection from the past; doing so merely isolates us from the wisdom of others surely no less morally or intellectually acute than we, who in their own historical context have faced problems analogous to our own about whether and how to employ force in the defense of values. It is thus better to use this tradition consciously, trying to learn from it and with it, even in the nuclear age, than it is to forget it and then have to reinvent it.

Defense of Values by Force as a Moral Possibility

To protect and preserve values is the only justifying cause for the use of force that is admitted in Western moral tradition. Classically the use of force in response to a threat to values was justified in four ways: to protect the innocent, to recover something wrongly taken, to punish evil, and to defend against a wrongful attack in progress. Let us look briefly at each of these and inquire what we may derive from them in our present context.

Defense of the innocent is an idea that can be traced at least as far as Augustine in Christian thought,[7] but it also has a history in military traditions back through the code of chivalry into the customs of pre-medieval Germanic societies.[8] By itself it implies an interventionist model of the justified use of military force and, more broadly, of national power. This not only flies in the face of much contemporary moralizing but also challenges such neo-isolationists as Laurence Beilenson[9] who argue for a retreat from foreign involvement by this country and the creation of a new "fortress America." It is also at odds with the individualistic ethics fostered domestically in our society with the demise of close ties of community,[10] an ethic that implies "not getting involved" perhaps even in extreme cases like mugging or rape. Granted that it is extremely dangerous to throw military power around in a world that has the capability of destroying itself by global war; granted also that national *hubris* if unrestrained[11] could use defense of others as an unwarranted excuse for a new round of imperialistic conquests; there still, I submit, remain in the contemporary world cases in which a limited and proportionate use of force may be the appropriate means to preserve the value referred to in the phrase "defense of the innocent." The case of Grenada was not morally the same as that of Afghanistan; intervention in Hungary by the West at the time of the 1956 uprising would not have been the moral equivalent of the Soviet invasion that did in fact occur; intervention in Uganda by neighboring Tanzania to depose Idi Amin and put an end to his bloodthirsty and self-aggrandizing rule was not the same as would have been an invasion aimed simply at increasing Tanzanian territory. Clearly not every case where the rights of innocent persons need to be protected should become an occasion for military intervention; the case of Hungary offers a clear instance when following out this line of implication from just war tradition to the exclusion of other considerations would have led to the wrong decision. But my point is that the moral distinctions assumed by the classical formulation of just war tradition still remain. The necessity to tread warily (which was no less an obligation in any previous age of human history) does not remove the moral outrage that comes from violation of the innocent,[12] the obligation to prevent or stop such violation if at all possible,[13] and the possibility that among all the means available, military ones may be the best.

The recovery of something wrongly taken is a necessary counterpart to the idea of defense against aggression in progress.[14] If such after-the-fact reaction were not allowed, the result would be that expansionist or other aggressive acts would, if speedy and effective, be tacitly accepted. There must be, of course, some consistent and agreed-upon means of identifying what belongs to one society or one polity and what to another, but even in the absence of complete consensus on this it is not necessary to reduce everything to a matter of different ideological or national perspective, so that what is one's own is simply whatever one says is one's own. The Falklands conflict provides an instructive contemporary example of the relevance of such reflection. The Argentine claim to the islands was not without some merit, but this was hardly of sufficient value to justify military invasion and occupation against the will of the inhabitants. The principle of self-determination, often cited to protect weak nations against military and other forms of aggression by stronger ones, while not the only meaningful principle here, was certainly violated by Argentina's action. If only defense against an aggression in progress were justified, then Britain and the British inhabitants of the islands would have had no recourse, after the failure of the intensively pursued negotiations, but to accept the newly established status quo of Argentine military rule. The allowance of the after-the-fact use of force to regain something wrongly taken is the source of moral justification for Britain's military actions in the Falklands war.

The punishment of evil is, in my judgment, the least useful of the classic formulations[15] of just cause in the present context. One reason for this is the prevalence of ideological divisions in the contemporary world. This line of justification for the use of force to protect value is all too easily changed into a justification for ideological warfare by one's own "forces of light" against the "forces of darkness" with their different ideological beliefs. This problem is not as acute among the superpowers as it once was, though it still exists and might still be fanned back to its former heat; more pressing immediate instances are to be found in the conflicts of the Middle East and Northern Ireland. Yet classically the punishment of differences of *belief* was not what was implied by this idea of just cause; what was to be punished was the kind of *action* identified in the other three kinds of justifying cause.[16] What is unique to this concept of punishment taken alone is that it implicitly allows going beyond what these other concepts justify to further action aimed at insuring that the same thing does not happen again. Such an allowance can easily be pushed too far, and so we should be cautious in citing this reason to justify force for the protection of value in the present age. Nuclear deterrence depends on the threat of punishment above all else; yet the use of current types of strategic nuclear weapons kept for deterrence purposes could itself threaten the very values such use would ostensibly seek to preserve. This is, of course, the heart of the nuclear dilemma, and I will return to it. For the present my only point is that the justification of force as punishment for wrong done must not be allowed to become isolated from the general question of the protection of value or from the other justifying moral reasons for the use of force to protect value. Yet even with this caveat, if the goal of permitted military action is, as another part of just war tradition insists, the end of peace, then it is not proper to rule out the morality of punishment entirely.

If we had begun with 20th-century international law and some other aspects of contemporary moral, political, and legal thought, we would have started with the justification of *defense against aggression in progress*—and perhaps got no further.[17] By keeping this classic idea of justifying cause for the use of force until last, I mean to symbolize that this idea is not as fundamental over the whole history of Western moral reflection on war as it has become in contemporary thought. Indeed, when we set this justification for the use of force alongside the others identified and discussed above, then we discover that the right of self-defense is not in fact a moral absolute. One may oneself be in the wrong in a particular conflict. Rather than to exalt one's own righteousness and well-being over that of others, the better moral cause is to deflate somewhat this allowance of self-defense to more appropriate proportions alongside the other *jus ad bellum* provisions. In short, self-defense may therefore not be limited; there are other values to consider than the integrity of the self or one's own national polity. It is this consideration from just war tradition that points to the wrongness of schemes of national defense based on a threat of catastrophic annihilation, even if that threat is mutual. The irony of the present situation is that the very legal and moral efforts that attempt to restrict the incidence of the use of force by allowing only its defensive use—I am thinking of the Kellog-Briand Pact of 1928 and Article 2 of the United Nations Charter, as well as current ostensibly moral arguments that the more terrible the deterrent threat, the less likelihood there will be of war—have the effect of insuring that should war come, despite these efforts, it will be of the most immoral and value-destructive kind attainable through military technology. That is, concentrating solely on the rightness of defense against aggression, while admittedly a moral justification for the use of force, has led us to think of strategic nuclear deterrence by threat of catastrophe as morally right, while ruling out lesser levels of force as possible responses to threats to value, even when these latter are more justifiable from the broader perspectives of just war tradition.[18]

In short, we would do well to remember what many in our present debate have either forgotten or systematically ignored: that circumstances may come into being in human history in which the use of force, at appropriate levels and discriminatingly directed, may be the morally preferable means for the protection and preservation of values. In forgetting or ignoring this, sometimes in the name of ostensibly moral considerations, those who would reject such a use of force are in fact choosing a less moral course than the one historically given form in the tradition which says that just war must also be limited war.

The Question of Values

May values ever be defended by forceful means? Answering this question requires us to think, first, about the nature of the values to be protected and the interrelation among values. We do this normally not by reflection but by affirmation. Hence the following from John Stuart Mill:

> War is an ugly thing, but not the ugliest of things. The decayed and degraded state of moral and patriotic feeling which thinks nothing *worth* a war, is worse. . . . A man who has nothing which he cares about more than he does about his personal safety is a miserable creature who has no chance of being free, unless made and kept so by the exertions of better men than himself.[19]

Mill in this context alludes to the values from which he speaks, but the salient fact about this statement is his ranking of relative values. He does not deny the value of personal safety; yet it is not for him the *highest* value. He does not deny the ugliness of war; he only affirms that in the ranking of priorities it is not the *worst* evil. Mill was, of course, a utilitarian in ethics; yet such priority ranking of values is not a feature unique to utilitarianism and to be dismissed by all non-utilitarians. Such ranking is indeed a feature of *any* ethic, for the service of one value often conflicts with the service of another, and there must be some way of deciding among them. Consider the following from Erasmus, a figure who was anything but a utilitarian:

> Think . . . of all the crimes that are committed with war as a pretext, while "good lawes fall silent amid the clash of arms"—all the instances of sack and sacrilege, rape, and other shameful acts, such as one hesitates even to name. And even when the war is over, this moral corruption is bound to linger for many years. Now assess for me the cost—a cost so great that, even if you win the war, you will lose much more than you gain. Indeed, what realm . . . can be weighed against the life, the blood, of so many thousand men?[20]

This passage is replete with priority ranking of values. Erasmus begins by identifying war rhetorically with criminal activity, thus locating it at the bottom of the value scale, then turns explicitly to proportional counting of relative costs: "even if you win the war, you will lose much more than you gain"; "what realm . . . can be weighed against the life, the blood, of so many thousand men?" Such comparative weighting of goods is as central to the ethics of Erasmian humanism as to Mill's utilitarianism; indeed, it appears as a core feature of moral argument as such. There is ultimately no way to get to the truth or falsity of various perceptions of value. This is why, finally, there can be no real argument between absolute pacifists, who reject all possibility of the use of force to protect value, and those who accept some possibility of such use of force.[21] But this is not a problem in most of the current defense debate, which is a debate over ranking of values among persons who weight their values as differently as do Mill and Erasmus.

Recognizing values where they exist and sorting them according to priorities where there are conflicts among them is the function of moral agency, an art learned in one's community of moral discourse.[22] Without going into a full theory of moral agency, which is far beyond the scope of this essay, the most we can say here is that affirmations like those of Mill and Erasmus allow us to glimpse the structure of relative values held by each participant in a moral debate and relate those structures of value both to a larger normative conception of common life and to our own personal rankings of value. For present purposes this is enough.

One interesting thing about Erasmus and Mill on war is how contemporary they sound; by thinking about them we may learn something about ourselves. Erasmus counted costs both great and small in his rejection of war. A glimpse of the latter appears elsewhere in the letter quoted above,[23] where he complains that preparations for war have dried up the sources of patronage on which he depended for support. This was purely personal injury, but the complaint is not unlike contemporary arguments against military spending as subtracting from resources available for feeding the hungry, healing the sick, and—in direct continuity with Erasmus—supporting humanistic scholarship. The value ranking is obvious. The real meat of Erasmus' objection to war was, however, in his idealistic vision of world community,[24] which he conceived as both good in itself beyond the goods of any national community and achievable by the right kind of human cooperative interaction. Again, this way of thinking has parallels in current debate, where rejection of force to protect values associated with the nation-state is coupled to a new vision of world order in which the nation-state system has no place.[25] The preservation of peace among nations, both in Erasmus and in contemporary debate, appears as the highest instrumental value, on which the maintenance of all other values depends. This is a different sort of reasoning from that of the pacifism of absolute principle, but even the latter may engage in priority ranking, as in these words of Mennonite theologian John Howard Yoder: " 'Thou shalt not kill' . . . is an absolute . . . immeasurably more human, more personalistic, more genuinely responsible than the competitive absolute, 'Thou shalt not let Uncle Sam down' or 'Thou shalt fight for freedom' or 'Never give up the ship.' "[26] What we may note here is the tendency to diminish rhetorically the values being downgraded; similarly, Erasmus in all his works against war represents warmaking as nothing more than the result of frivolous and misguided rivalry among sovereigns. War, Yoder and Erasmus alike suggest, may never be anything more than frivolous and misguided; the possibility that it might be an instrumental means of protecting value is dismissed out of hand. Contemporary examples of such reasoning abound, centering around the dismissal of any form of military preparedness as "militarism" and rejection of "war-fighting" strategic planning as opposed to deterrence strategy.[27]

The influence of Erasmian humanistic pacifism on contemporary debate runs deep, and I cannot here chart its full extent, but one more example of this presence must be noted for what it is. Erasmus rejects war as the *summum malum*, assimilating it to criminality; in contemporary debate the counterpart is the assimilation of all war to the evil of catastrophic nuclear holocaust. Erasmus cites "sack, sacrilege, and rape"; Jonathan Schell, in the idiom of our own age, cites "the biologic effects of ultraviolet radiation with emphasis on the skin"[28] while piling up evidence of "the likely consequences of a holocaust for the earth"[29]—as if anyone had to be reminded that a holocaust is, by definition, evil.

It should be clear that Erasmus, Schell, and Yoder are simply moving in a different sphere from Mill and the main line of just war thinking (which I also share). It is simply impossible, given the assimilation of war to criminality and holocaust, for Erasmus and Schell to share Mill's judgment that "war is an ugly thing, but not the ugliest of things." Neither could Yoder, for whom the use of force is trivialized into the maxim, "Never give up the ship," or persons who regard war as the result of frivolous self-assertion by political leaders or, in the current phrase, "militarism." Between these and the position represented by Mill there would seem to be an impassable gulf. Yet it is possible at least to see across that gulf, if not to bridge it or remove it. And from the perspective of just war tradition there is something fundamentally wrong with the perception of value found on the other side.

First, while there is no need to deny the charm of an idealistic vision of world community, such a conception of an ideal that is not yet a reality (and may never become one) should not subtract from the quite genuine value to be found in the nation-state system or, more particularly, in a national community like our own. Historically the roots of the nation-state system are in the need to organize human affairs so as to minimize conflict while preserving the unique cultural identities of different peoples. It can be argued plausibly that it still fulfills these functions—imperfectly, to be sure, but with nothing better currently at hand. Likewise, the personal security, justice, freedom, and domestic peace provided in a liberal democratic nation-state like the United States are not to be dismissed lightly by reference to a utopian vision in which these and other values would all be present in greater measure. We must always, as moral beings, measure reality against our ideals; yet to reject the penultimate goods secured by the real because they do not measure up to the ultimate goods envisioned in the ideal is to ensure the loss of even the penultimate goods that we now enjoy. The ultimate would certainly be better; yet in the meantime, we have the obligation to hold as fast as possible to the value at hand, even though doing so must inevitably incur costs. A positive response to the original just war question recognizes this, as did Mill; Erasmus and his contemporary idealistic descendants have not.

Second, if force is to be used to protect values, it is not trivia that are to be protected but values of fundamental worth. Mill's allusion to the value of "being free" is on a quite different level from Yoder's maxim, "Never give up the ship," or Erasmus' collapsing of all reasons for war into the venality of princes. Equally, I believe, not to be reduced to the trivial or frivolous is Walzer's perception, expressed throughout *Just and Unjust Wars*, that the justification for fighting lies in the recognition of evil and revulsion against it.[30] Walzer's negative way of putting the matter is important for another reason: it reminds us that we do not have to be able to give an extensive and comprehensive listing of all values that may be protected and in what ranking in order to know *that there are* such values; they will be apparent when they are violated or threatened with violation.

Third, knowing that some wars have resulted from the aggressively self-assertive characters of rulers does not mean that war may never be anything else. It is doubtful that Erasmus was right even about the rulers of his own time. In our own age we must surely make a distinction between, for example, the war made by Hitler and that made by Churchill; nor is it particularly useful to reduce the rise and fall of relations between the United States and the Soviet Union to the personalities of a Carter and a Brezhnev, an Andropov or Chernenko and a Reagan. A manichaean dismissal of everything military as "militaristic" is also an uncalled-for reductionism that makes military preparedness itself an evil, not an instrument for good or ill in ways to be determined by human choices.

Finally, neither in Erasmus' time nor in our own is it right to represent war as the irreducible *summum malum*. I have already suggested why I think Erasmus was wrong in making this claim; more important for our current context is the wrongness of assimilating all contemporary war to catastrophic nuclear war. Let us dwell on this for a moment.

Who would want a nuclear holocaust? Yet the effort to avoid such a catastrophe is not itself justification for rejection of the possibility that lower levels of force may justifiably be employed to protect value. This is, nonetheless, the clear import of the argument when limited conventional war is collapsed into limited nuclear war by reference to the threat of escalation and nuclear war of any extent is collapsed into catastrophic holocaust on a global scale.[31] Such an argument has the effect of making any contemporary advocate of the use of force to protect values an advocate instead of the total destruction of humankind or even of all life on earth. It should hardly need to be said that such rhetorical hyperbole is unjustified; no one who argues from just war tradition, with its strong emphasis on counting the costs and estimating the probability of success of any projected military action, should be represented as guilty of befriending the idea of nuclear holocaust.

Yet this collapsing of categories is also wrong historically. War in the nuclear age has not been global catastrophe but a continuation of conventional warfare limited in one or several ways—by geography, goals, targets, means. This arena of contemporary limited warfare is one in which traditional moral categories for judging war are very much at home, as such different writers as William V. O'Brien and Michael Walzer have, in their respective ways, both recognized. The issue, then, is not of the prohibition of all means of defense in the nuclear age, because the assimilation of all contemporary war to the *summum malum* of nuclear holocaust is invalid; it is rather the perennial question of when and how force may be used for the defense of values.[32] We will return to this question below.

The Problem of Threats to Values

For there to be a need to defend values, there must be a threat to those values. To anyone with a modicum of objectivity, though, it must be apparent that in the current defense debate there is no argument about the nature of the threat, and so there can be little hope of agreement about the means of preserving values in the face of the menace identified. Speaking broadly, I find in the present debate three distinctively different identifications of the threat to values that must be met. For some, there is no danger worth mentioning beyond that of nuclear holocaust, which is defined as threatening everything that is of value; for others the principal challenge to the values that matter for them is the arms race as such, with its diversion of resources to military ends and a perceived transformation of values toward those of "militarism"; finally, a third perspective identifies the principal threat to values in the rivalry between the United States and the Soviet Union, West and East, two different and competing social, economic, political, and moral systems. This last is the most easily identifiable in terms of traditional interstate political analysis and in terms of just war tradition. All three perspectives have many forms and are somewhat fluid, so that in painting them with broad strokes of the brush I cannot render the inner details of each. Yet the broadly painted pictures of these different perspectives are themselves interesting morally, and it is on these that I will focus in this brief context.

Let us begin by exploring what is distinctive about each of the first two positions I have identified. These clearly overlap, but their emphases are importantly different, as are their respective histories and implicit value commitments. One way of recognizing this quickly is by noting that the anti-nuclear-holocaust position can be expressed in a commitment to increased military spending for an enhanced deterrent, quite contrary to the anti-arms-race position, which finds typical expression in the nuclear freeze movement and support for disarmament programs. Similarly, part of the historical case for tactical and theater nuclear weapons has been that they cost less to provide than equivalent conventional forces, thus tending to free economic and manpower resources for non-military purposes; yet many from the anti-nuclear-holocaust position view such "war-fighting" weapons as inherently destabilizing and dangerously likely to lead to catastrophic nuclear war.[33] Within the anti-nuclear-holocaust position opposition to the arms race and military spending is but an instrumentality, while within the anti-arms-race position opposition to nuclear arms is only an instrumentality; when there is convergence between these two positions (as there has been in the most recent stage of the defense debate), it is a mixed marriage that is as likely to end in divorce as in conversion of one or both partners.

These two positions also have different historical and ideological roots. The anti-nuclear-holocaust position is, of course, a product of the nuclear age and specifically of the period when the United States and the Soviet Union have practiced strategic nuclear deterrence against each other. It is thus the child of nuclear deterrence theory and finds a characteristic expression in one such theory, the "deterrence only" position. Clearly, though, there has been a transformation of values from parent to offspring. Thus when Philip Green wrote *Deadly Logic* in the mid-1960s, he cited "resistance to Communism" as the fundamental "ethical root of deterrence theory,"[34] but the ethical root of the contemporary "deterrence only" position is the perception of *nuclear warfare*, not the menace to values posed by a totalitarian political system, as the evil to be avoided by the possession of a nuclear deterrent.[35]

The historical roots of the anti-arms-race position are at least a century old; they lie in opposition to the increasing practice in 19th-century European states of sustaining a standing army built up by universal or nearly universal conscription, and in opposition to the social and economic costs of sustaining such armies. Religious groups have been the chief enunciators of this position; they are so today. A direct line runs between the *Postulata* on war prepared for Vatican Council I in 1870, which deplored the "intolerable burden" of defense spending and the social costs of "huge standing and conscript armies,"[36] and the 1983 pastoral of the American Catholic bishops with its deploring of the "economic distortion of priorities" due to the "billions readily spent for destructive instruments"[37] or, to take a Protestant example, the 1980 statement on the arms race by the Reformed Church in America decrying "the devastating social and personal consequences of the arms race."[38] Two ethical roots of this position are visible in the sources cited: an opposition to war and weapons as contrary to the biblical vision of peace and an identification with the needs of the poor as best expressing Christian conformity to Christ. Both themes have secular counterparts in contemporary debate, and the first obviously parallels the utopian vision of Erasmian humanism.

If nuclear holocaust is the danger against which values must be protected, then deterrence theory is one rational response, but so would be general nuclear disarmament. If the arms race itself is the menace to values that must be defended against, then a freeze on military expenditures followed by a general scaling down of military establishments is the clear implication. Both these perspectives on the contemporary threat to values incorporate truths about the present historical situation; both are rooted in important perceptions of moral value; each offers, in its own way, a response to the problem of threat to values as it perceives that threat. Yet neither of these perspectives is really about the question with which we began this paper, the fundamental question that is at the root of our moral tradition on war: when and how may force justifiably be employed for the defense of values. Rather than approaching seriously the problem of possible moral justification of force, each of these perspectives has, in its own way, *defined that possibility out of existence* in the search for a general rejection of the use of force as a moral option in the contemporary age. The reason is that neither of these perspectives is able to comprehend the possibility of significant threats to value alongside the one on which each of them is fixed.

The problem, however, is that what is thus ignored does not for this reason cease to exist. International rivalries persist, as they did in the pre-nuclear era; ideologies and realistic perceptions of national interest continue to influence the actions of nations, and these actions are often played out through projections of force. Terrorism, civil war, and international war continue to be plain realities of our present era, and there is no reason to suppose either that aggression will no longer take place in human history or that it can effectively be opposed by means other than military ones.[39] Indeed, prospective victims of aggression today might reflect with Clausewitz: "The aggressor is always peace-loving; he would prefer to take over our country unopposed."[40] The just war perspective, the third perspective in the contemporary debate, views the problem of threats to value in this light, in continuity with the main line of statecraft over history, and conceives the problem of defense against such threats also in terms continuous with that historical experience.

Let it be clear: the rivalry between the Soviet Union and the United States is not the only source of danger to American values; yet it would be blindness to wish away the existence of this rivalry, which is rooted in more than common possession of mutual annihilative power, more than competing ideologies, more than national interest, more than global competition for friends, allies, and trading partners—and yet all of these. And this rivalry is more than simply a product of adverse perceptions; it is real. Where it takes military form, as for example most unambiguously along the NATO-Warsaw Pact border, thinking about the menace to values must go beyond efforts to avoid catastrophic nuclear war and to end the arms race to include efforts to define and mount a credible, effective, and moral defense against the particular military threat manifest there.

At the same time, though, potential military defense of values is not limited to this confrontation nor to the global East-West rivalry; it may be a matter of attempting to secure a weak Third World nation against the power of a nearby predator, deterring or responding to terrorist attacks, or maintaining the traffic of oil tankers through the Strait of Hormuz. All these possible uses of force involve the defense of value; all are, in general terms, the kind of resort to force regarded as justified in just war tradition. This third perspective on the threat to values, then, is the one I wish to address in my concluding section.

The Problem of Defense against Threats to Value

I wish now to take us back to a reflection with which this essay began, that in general the nature of values to be protected and the threats against them are such that unlimited or even disproportionate amounts of force are not what is justified when the use of force to defend values is justified. When defense of values by force appears to require transgressing the boundaries set by the *jus in bello* concepts of proportionality and discrimination, this necessitates that we look again to see whether this is an occasion when the defense of values by force is morally justified. The answer may be no; yet it may also be yes, and this is the possibility I wish to explore in this section.

In fact there are two directions of thought, not one, which lead toward a renewal of the justification of value-protection by force in such a situation. The first drives toward restructuring the application of force and beyond that to the creation of new kinds of force capabilities suited to limited application in the defense of value. The second leads into the far more dangerous consideration whether values may ever be protected by means that themselves violate important values. I will discuss these in turn.

Clausewitz in his time understood well the difference between "absolute war," war pushed to the limits of the destructive capacities of the belligerents, and "real" wars carried on by less than absolute means for limited purposes as an extension of politics; in the 20th century many others have forgotten or ignored this difference.[41] Typically the values threatened by war are less than ultimate, and so is the threat; it is wrong to defend these values against such challenges by totalistic means disproportionate to both the values to be defended and the evil that menaces them. When we add that total war implies also the indiscriminate targeting of noncombatants, a violation of the fundamental idea of protection of the innocent, the indictment of such use of force in response to threats against values grows yet more damning.

But the problem of limitation of force in contemporary warfare is different from that which existed earlier. Today limitation must be accomplished first and foremost by human choice; in previous ages such limitation was also a product of the nature of weapons available, the restraints imposed by the seasons of the year, and the economic and social bases on which war was waged. Limitation in the use of force was relatively easy when the means were battle-axes or smooth-bore muskets, when three-quarters of the year was closed to military actions, and when soldiers were themselves units of economic production who could not be in arms year-round.

Today the problem is more complex: the structuring of force capabilities to defend against possible menaces to value must at the same time provide an effective deterrent and an effective means of active defense while still honoring the moral identity manifest in the society or culture in which the threatened values are known and maintained. Among recent nuclear strategies that did not meet this dual test is massive retaliation, conceived as a strategy for use, since it allowed "brush-fire wars" to erupt unchecked and threatened disproportionate and indiscriminate nuclear devastation as a response to aggression on a much lower scale. Nor does contemporary mutual assured destruction doctrine, for reasons already given above. But the issue is not simply one of the disproportionateness of nuclear arms. The same moral problems exist with the strategic conventional air strikes against population centers of World War II, for example; similarly, in the context of current history one of the most acute problems is how to frame a moral response against terrorist activity without oneself being forced into the characteristic patterns of terrorism.

Complicated this problem is; yet it is not insoluble. If the use of force is justified in response to threats against value, but the only means of force available are such that they contravene important values themselves, then the preferred moral alternative is the development of different means of force. If tactical and theater nuclear weapons are judged too destructive to use or deemed too likely to result in escalation to all-out nuclear war if employed, then the moral choice is to devise non-nuclear defenses to replace them and pay the costs, economic and social, of such defenses.[42] If the strategic nuclear deterrent is deemed immoral to employ, the right response is not to engage in the self-deception of "deterrence-only" reasoning but to explore possible means of defense against nuclear strikes that would not require a preemptive first strike by this nation or a possibly indiscriminate and disproportionate punitive second strike.[43] The justification of using force to defend value certainly means, as I have said earlier, more than "defense" in its narrow sense, the warding off of attacks in progress; yet it certainly also means at least that, and to claim the moral high ground for a rejection of steps toward creating such defense is simply to twist moral reasoning out of shape.

Finally, though, there remains the possibility that protection and preservation of values must be by force, and must be by force that contravenes at least some of the values it intends to protect and preserve. This is the possibility that, at the extreme, has been called by the term "supreme emergency,"[44] and it is only at this extreme that it is a morally unique case. Must one fight honorably and die, even when knowing that one's ultimate moral values will thus die also? Or may one sin for the moment in order to defeat the evil that threatens, hoping for time to repent later and making the commitment to pass on undiluted to future generations the values that have in the emergency been transgressed?[45] Some of the lines of argument already advanced bear on this dilemma. I have suggested that ideological claims ought not to be inflated to the point of seeming to justify unlimited warfare; I have argued against disproportionate and indiscriminate warfare as morally evil in themselves; and I have suggested that part of the trouble in responding to an immoral form of warfare like terrorism is that in making such a response one's own humanity may be diminished to the level of that of the terrorist. In short, I tend to be dubious of "supreme emergency" claims and I am inclined to hold the moral line for preservation of value in the means chosen as well as in the decision to offer a defense. Even so there remains a possibility of a genuine "supreme emergency" situation. What is to be said about this?

First, it is not a newly recognized kind of situation. In the early Middle Ages Christian soldiers were required to do penance after participating in war because of the possibility that they might have acted sinfully in that war, killing perhaps out of malice toward the enemy rather than with feelings of regretful duty in the service of justice. Here we encounter a case in which the possibility is admitted that protection of values may involve violation of values. When in the 16th century Victoria considered what might be done in a just war, he allowed that a militarily necessary storming of the city could be undertaken even though this would inevitably result in violations of the rights of noncombatants in the city.[46] Such historical evidence suggests a moral acceptance of the possibility of preserving value by wrong means; yet this evidence also implies the limits on that acceptance.

Second, the transgression of value in the service of value must be approached through the general recognition that value conflicts are the stuff with which human moral agency has to deal. Every moral system provides means for handling such conflicts, and that a genuine "supreme emergency" might come to exist is by definition such a conflict, in which higher values must in the last analysis be favored over lower ones. The values constituting the *jus ad bellum*, having priority over those of the *jus in bello*, would on my reasoning have to be honored in such a case, even at some expense to the latter.

I have thus brought this discussion to the brink of morally admissible possibility so that we might look over and see what lies below. The view is not a pretty one. Having seen it, though, we may the more purposefully return to the other line of implication sketched before: the development of military capabilities suited to our moral commitments. We may still yearn—and work—for a world without war, for an end to the menace of catastrophic nuclear war, for an end to the arms race; yet with such military capabilities we would be the better prepared to meet morally the threats to value that may be expected to be inevitable so long as these ideals are not achieved.

NOTES

1. Michael Walzer, *Just and Unjust Wars* (New York: Basic Books, 1977).
2. See Paul Ramsey, *War and the Christian Conscience* (Durham, N.C.: Duke Univ. Press, 1961) and *The Just War* (New York: Charles Scribner's Sons, 1968); William V. O'Brien, *The Conduct of Just and Limited War* (New York: Praeger, 1981).
3. The term is O'Brien's and is meant by him to emphasize the difference in order of priority between the *jus ad bellum* and the *jus in bello*, which has to do with "war-fighting" once the initial decision to make war has been made. See O'Brien, especially chaps. 1-3.
4. Compare Stanley Hoffmann, *Duties Beyond Borders* (Syracuse, N.Y.: Syracuse Univ. Press, 1981), pp. 46-55, and James Douglass, *The Non-Violent Cross* (New York: Macmillan, 1968).
5. Compare Ramsey's criticism in *The Just War*, pp. 259-78.
6. Hoffmann, pp. 59ff.
7. For an example of such tracing in contemporary argument see Ramsey, *War and the Christian Conscience*, pp. 34-37.
8. For discussion see my *Just War Tradition and the Restraint of War* (Princeton: Princeton Univ. Press, 1981), pp. 131-50.
9. See Laurence Beilenson, *Survival and Peace in the Nuclear Age* (Chicago: Regnery and Company, 1980).
10. On the loss of community and its implications see James Sellers, *Warming Fires* (New York: Seabury Press, 1975), and Thomas Luckmann, *The Invisible Religion* (New York: Macmillan, 1967).
11. This is a familiar theme in the thought of Reinhold Niebuhr. Compare his *Christianity and Power Politics* (New York: Charles Scribner's Sons, 1940) and *The Structure of Nations and Empires* (New York: Charles Scribner's Sons, 1959).
12. Compare Walzer, pp. 133-35.
13. Compare Ramsey, *The Just War*, pp. 141-47.
14. This concept, taken over from Roman law by Augustine and Isidore of Seville, was central to the definition of just war given in medieval canon law. See *Corpus Juris Canonici*, Pars Prior, *Decretum Magistri Gratiani*, Pars Secunda, Causa XXIII, Quaest. II, Can. II.
15. This is another *jus ad bellum* criterion that came from Roman law through Augustine into church law; see ibid. But it had a more central place in the thought of Thomas Aquinas, who connected it to the words of Paul in Romans 13:4 "[The prince] is the minister of God to execute his vengeance against the evildoer." See Thomas Aquinas, *Summa Theologica*, II/II, Quest. XL, Art. 1.
16. I make this judgment cognizant of the minority tradition in Christian just war theory from Augustine forward that allowed some forms of war for religion; in Augustine's words, repeated for canon law by Gratian, "The enemies of the church are to be coerced even by war" (*Decretum Magistri Gratiani*, Quaest. VIII, Can. XLVIII). But in fact efforts to justify wars in Western cultural history, even those clearly involving some benefit or detriment to religion, have generally been justified by appeal to the other reasons already given:

protection of the innocent, retaking of something lost, punishment of evil. For discussion of this issue of religious war—and by extension ideological war—see my *Ideology, Reason, and the Limitation of War* (Princeton: Princeton Univ. Press, 1975), chaps. I-III.
17. See ibid., pp. 266-70.
18. An early version of this kind of argument undergirded massive retaliation strategy, which Robert W. Tucker in *The Just War* (Baltimore: The Johns Hopkins Press, 1960) regards as an expression of a general American moral attitude justifying all-out responses to injustice received rather than limited uses of force proportionate to harm done to American interests. But suppose that this opposition to limited warfare is retained while all-out retaliation is itself denied as immoral (though the use of deterrence as a *threat* continues to be accepted); then the argument changes shape, though its fundamentals remain. Such a new version of the moral argument for deterrence and against limited warfare can be found in the 1983 pastoral letter of the American Catholic Bishops (National Conference of Catholic Bishops, *The Challenge of Peace* [Washington: United States Catholic Conference, 1983]). The purpose of deterrence, as defined here, is "only to prevent the *use* of nuclear weapons by others" (paragraph 188, emphasis in text). "War-fighting strategies," including even *planning* for fighting nuclear war at a limited level over a protracted period, are explicitly rejected (paragraphs 184, 188, 189). The reason is the prudential judgment that limited nuclear warfare can be expected to escalate to "mass destruction" (paragraphs 151-61, 184). Though this suggests heavier reliance on conventional weapons (paragraph 155), even a conventional war "could escalate to the nuclear level" (paragraph 156). While the resultant position is not *explicitly* a "deterrence-only" one, it is difficult to find in the pessimism toward limited war and "war-fighting strategies" expressed in the bishops' letter any room for limited and proportionate responses to limited levels of harm done, such as the traditional *jus in bello* implies.
19. John Stuart Mill, "The Contest in America," pp. 208-09, in John Stuart Mill, *Dissertations and Discussions* (Boston: William V. Spencer, 1867). The full text of the passage in question, written to oppose England's siding with the Confederacy in the American Civil War, is as follows: "War is an ugly thing, but not the ugliest of things: the decayed and degraded state of moral and patriotic feeling which thinks nothing *worth* a war, is worse. When a people are used as mere human instruments for firing cannon or thrusting bayonets, in the service and for the selfish purposes of a master, such war degrades a people. A war to protect other human beings against tyrannical injustice; a war to give victory to their own ideas of right and good, and which is their own war, carried on for an honest purpose by their own free choice—is often the means of their regeneration. A man who has nothing which he cares about more than he does about his personal safety is a miserable creature who has no chance of being free, unless made and kept so by the exertions of better men than himself. As long as justice and injustice have not terminated their ever renewing fight for ascendancy in the affairs of mankind, human beings must be willing, when need is, to do battle for the one against the other."
20. Desiderius Erasmus, Letter to Antoon van Bergen, Abbot of St. Bertin, dated London, 14 March 1514; number 288 in *The Conference of Erasmus, Letters 142 to 297*, tr. by R. A. B. Minors and D. F. S. Thomson, annotated by Wallace K. Ferguson (Toronto and Buffalo: Univ. of Toronto Press, 1975), lines 47-63.
21. That is, for such pacifists the rejection of force has itself become a value or it is necessarily implied by some other value (e.g. Christian love in some forms of religious pacifism); in either case it is unassailable from outside the moral system in which this value is held. Other forms of pacifism, of course, reach their judgment against the use of force by argument based not on the evil of force as such but on the harm to some higher good that the use of force may entail. The contemporary position sometimes called "just-war pacifism," which is based on a prudential calculation of proportionality, is such a form of pacifism.
22. See further my "On Keeping Faith: The Uses of History for Religious Ethics," *The Journal of Religious Ethics* 7 (Spring 1979): 98-116.
23. Erasmus, lines 17-24.
24. See further Roland H. Bainton, *Christian Attitudes toward War and Peace* (New York and Nashville: Abingdon Press, 1960), p. 131, and Lester K. Born, *The Education of a Christian Prince by Desiderius Erasmus* (New York: Octagon Books, Inc., 1965), pp. 1-26.
25. See, for example, Richard A. Falk, *A Study of Future Worlds* (New York: Macmillan/The Free Press, 1975).

26. John Howard Yoder, *Nevertheless* (Scottdale, Pa., and Kitchener, Ont.: Herald Press, 1976), p. 33.
27. Condemnation of "militarism" has become a common feature of the public policy statements of many Protestant denominations. See, for example, the statements by The Christian Church (Disciples of Christ) and the Reformed Church in America in Robert Heyer, ed., *Nuclear Disarmament* (New York and Ramsey, N.J.: Paulist Press, 1982), pp. 245-46, 251-52, and 267. A prominent example of condemnation of "war-fighting" strategic planning is the American Catholic bishops' pastoral; see National Conference of Catholic Bishops, paragraphs 184-90. Such thinking is far more like the traditional pacifism represented by Yoder and Erasmus than it is like the reasoning of just war tradition.
28. Jonathan Schell, *The Fate of the Earth* (New York: Avon Books, 1982), p. 85.
29. Ibid., p. 78.
30. See, for example, the discussions of noncombatant immunity found in Walzer, chaps. 8-10. Despite the criticisms I have earlier directed at the American Catholic bishops' letter, it clearly embodies an understanding that the values that might be endangered by an enemy are not trivial: they include "those key values of justice, freedom and independence which are necessary for personal dignity and national integrity" (National Conference of Catholic Bishops, paragraph 175).
31. See, for example, Louis Rene Beres, *Mimicking Sisyphus* (Lexington, Mass., and Toronto: Lexington Books, 1983), pp. 15-24; compare the argument of the American Catholic bishops, note 18 above.
32. O'Brien, chap. 1.
33. Compare National Conference of Catholic Bishops, paragraphs 188, 190.
34. Philip Green, *Deadly Logic* (New York: Schocken Books, 1968), pp. 249-51.
35. Compare National Conference of Catholic Bishops, paragraphs 175, 188. This document, on my reading, is only a whisker away from the "deterrence only" position on nuclear weapons; that whisker is the ambiguity maintained in the threat of strategic nuclear retaliation, specifically in the possible difference between "declaratory policy" and "action policy" (paragraph 164). Paragraph 148 denies counterpopulation retaliation; paragraph 184 repeats this and also undercuts the possibility of counterforce strategic retaliation. These themes recur elsewhere in Section II of the document as well. Is the "conditional acceptance of nuclear deterrence" (paragraph 198) in this pastoral letter then anything more than a "conditional acceptance" of the *possession* of such weapons (not making any distinctions among types, purposes, or relative destructive power but treating all nuclear weapons the same), and does not the "no first use" position taken in the letter (paragraph 150 and *passim*) in practical terms collapse into a policy of "no use at all"?
36. See John Eppstein, *The Catholic Tradition of the Law of Nations* (Washington: Catholic Association for International Peace, 1935), p. 132.
37. National Conference of Catholic Bishops, paragraph 134.
38. Heyer, p. 266.
39. Compare Walzer, pp. 329-35.
40. Carl von Clausewitz, *On War*, ed. and trans. by Michael Howard and Peter Paret (Princeton: Princeton Univ. Press, 1976), p. 370.
41. See, for example, Paul Fussell's argument in his *The Great War and Modern Memory* (New York and London: Oxford Univ. Press, 1975), passim, that modern war is inevitably totalistic, chaotic, beyond human control, and disproportionately destructive of values.
42. Compare National Conference of Catholic Bishops, paragraphs 115, 215-26.
43. See further Sam Cohen, "Rethinking Strategic Defense," pp. 99-122 in Robert W. Poole, Jr., ed., *Defending a Free Society* (Lexington, Mass., and Toronto: Lexington Books, 1984).
44. Walzer, chap. 16.
45. See further my discussion of Walzer on this matter in *Just War Tradition*, pp. 24-28.
46. Franciscus de Victoria, *De Jure Belli*, section 37, in Franciscus de Victoria, *De Indis et De Jure Belli Relectiones*, ed. by Ernest Nys (Washington: Carnegie Institute, 1917). Victoria makes clear, however, that he thought few wars meet the test of an unambiguous conflict of justice against injustice.

This article originally appeared under the title "Threats, Values, and Defense: Does Defense of Values by Force Remain a Moral Possibility?" in the spring 1985 issue of *Parameters*.

2

The Moral Dilemma of Nuclear Deterrence

By STEPHEN M. MILLETT

Reviewing the highlights of past American foreign policy, former Secretary of State Henry A. Kissinger observed in an address in London on 25 June 1976:

> We must therefore conduct a diplomacy that deters challenges if possible and that contains them at tolerable levels if they prove unavoidable—a diplomacy that resolves issues, nurtures restraint, and builds cooperation based on mutual interest.[1]

Kissinger may have been referring just to the policy of Soviet-American detente that he had championed since 1969, but his comments generally hold true for the goal of American relations toward Moscow since 1945.

The two principal concepts of American policy toward the Soviet Union have been deterrence and containment. The first seeks to avoid a military confrontation with the Soviets by threatening the use of nuclear retaliation in response to grievous Soviet provocations. The logic of deterrence (a theoretical logic without conclusive empirical verification) has been that if the possible retaliatory strength is great enough and the fear of such retaliation is repugnant enough, the potential aggressor will refrain from a direct challenge. Since nuclear arms are indeed of great destructiveness and repugnance, the U.S. can keep the Soviets at bay, so the logic goes.

The concept of deterrence went hand-in-glove with that of containment, which sought to girdle Soviet territory and geopolitical power within the postwar status quo of 1945. As originally expounded by George F. Kennan in 1947, containment asserted that the paradoxes of the Soviet system could not be solved without continued attempts on the part of the Soviets to expand their system. Therefore, the U.S. had to meet and repel Soviet aggrandizement, especially in the critically important industrial regions of Western Europe and Japan.[2]

Kennan later argued that he perceived Soviet political threats as more serious to the security of the West than military ones.[3] However, regardless of the evolution of his thinking, certain influential American policymakers (Clark Clifford, Paul Nitze, and John Foster Dulles, to name just three) came to identify containment with military deterrence to prevent Soviet expansion. Indeed, after the Korean War erupted in 1950, American authorities increasingly assumed that the most serious communist threat to the West was military aggression, often drawing a historical analogy between Sino-Soviet provocations and the aggressions of Nazi Germany and Fascist Italy during the 1930s.[4]

The objective of both deterrence and containment was Western security with peace—the avoidance of a catastrophic World War III, which was popularly feared as the war that would end all civilization, East and West, socialist and capitalist. Along with peace, the objective was the preservation of the Western democratic social and political way of life; war was tolerable only as the last desperate defense of the West against Soviet military and ideological power. Of course, war itself, regardless of the cause, was expected to be devastating to the West, if not absolutely fatal. American foreign policy worldwide also sought to prevent drastic internal political changes in individual countries as effected by military coercion from without. Deterrence and containment, therefore, were perfectly consistent with American ideology as expressed in the Atlantic Charter (1941), the United Nations Declaration (1942), the Declaration of Liberated Europe (1945), the Truman Plan (1947), and the Marshall Plan (1947).

However, the doctrine of deterrence, especially as applied in its broadest context with containment, posed a disturbing dilemma for the U.S. The principal instruments of deterrence were nuclear weapons, which could inflict far-reaching damage to the Soviet Union. Americans hoped that the spectre of nuclear retaliation alone would frustrate Soviet challenges to Western interests. Yet, the same nuclear weapons, if used (the ultimate credibility for deterrence), would cause the very World War III, with all its horrendous consequences, that the U.S. was trying to prevent. Deterrence was thus a two-edged sword: it had to deter both the deterred and the deterrer from embarking into confrontations that would lead to total war.

The extensive literature on deterrence has tended to concentrate on how the American nuclear arsenal should affect Soviet behavior. It has also emphasized the technical and operational aspects of nuclear strategy. This literature, however, has neglected to give due attention to the self-restraints associated with the use of nuclear weapons. A common assumption has been that the nation that possessed nuclear weapons is free to use them whenever it so chooses. The thesis of this paper, however, is that the possession and deployment of operational nuclear weapons place significant restraints on the nation possessing and deploying them. And of these restraints, moral inhibitions play a significant role.

The fundamental American moral dilemma of nuclear deterrence is how the U.S. can prevent one evil (communist expansion of power at the expense of Western interests) by threatening to unleash another evil (nuclear destruction and radioactive contamination). Likewise, the logic of deterrence may require ever more weapon systems, warheads, and megatonnage to preserve its doctrinal integrity. That is, nuclear deterrence by two, in turn creating an arms competition which in itself raises the fear of war by accident, miscalculation, or insanity. The question thus becomes: Can a nation preserve peace by amassing huge nuclear forces and threatening a war which it so desperately seeks to avoid?

Some students of international relations will immediately reject the moral dilemma of deterrence by asserting that concepts of morality and evil are irrelevant in modern, secular macropolitics. The so-called "realists" will argue that national interests and power rather than idealism motivate political behavior in the world. They will point out that there have been few examples of explicitly moral behavior among Western nations since the erosion of Judeo-Christian religious standards of conduct among sovereigns. But beyond that, some would argue that the U.S. cannot afford the luxury of a moral foreign policy in relations with the atheist Marxist-Leninist countries that embrace an ideology so radically different from and inimical to American ideology.

On the other hand, arguments can be made that morality does indeed play an important role in international relations even today and even among nations with variant religious and political faiths (after all, Marxism is a product of Western culture). Some of the arguments appear esoteric and theoretical, but others, especially those that emphasize the political consequences of alienating world public opinion, seem pragmatic and relevant to present circumstances.[5] This article, however, will not explore this line of thinking. Rather, the contention here is that the American people, decisionmakers, and opinion-makers hold certain beliefs deeply rooted in American political ideology and historical experience that do indeed place moral restraints on American deterrence.

For example, one hears the question, Why did the U.S. not hit the Soviets with nuclear weapons in the 1940s before the Soviets had them? Certainly the Soviets provoked the U.S. sorely with the Berlin blockade, the communist coup in Prague, the communization of Eastern European countries, encroachments upon Iran, and support for the Communists in the Chinese civil war. Even if the U.S. had the operational abilities and the political impulse to devastate the Soviet Union with nuclear weapons, morality prevented it from doing so. President Harry S. Truman, the only man ever to have authorized the dropping of atomic bombs on enemy targets, felt deeply that nuclear armaments were too brutal and too indiscriminately destructive to use in less than the most extreme situation. "The destruction at Hiroshima and Nagasaki was lesson enough to me," he recorded in his memoirs; "The world could not afford to risk war with atomic weapons."[6]

Indeed, Truman's aversion to nuclear weapons caused Secretary of Defense James Forrestal to wonder during the Berlin blockade of 1948 whether the U.S. would even use them in an actual war with the Soviets. The president assured Forrestal that he would use them if it were absolutely necessary. Forrestal next questioned whether the American people would support the president in the use of nuclear weapons. A gathering of 20 newspaper publishers unanimously agreed that the public would *expect* the president to employ atomic bombs in a war with Soviet Russia.[7] The secretary, however, did not pursue the next logical question: Would the people support the use of atomic bombs in a situation short of full-scale, declared war? Former Secretary of State James Byrnes asserted in 1947 that they would not: "No President in the absence of a declaration of war by Congress could authorize an atom bomb [to be dropped on an enemy target] without running the risk of impeachment."[8]

The argument for a "preventive" nuclear war has never been seriously argued by a responsible decisionmaker; after all, it advocates the very war that the U.S. is trying to avoid. As Bernard Brodie observed in 1959:

> Only by adopting a rigid dictatorship within could American leaders shut out reports from abroad of the unimaginable horror of their own creation [nuclear war]. It argues some want of imagination to assume . . . that the American people could acquiesce in such a deed and then go about their usual business of pursuing happiness, free of guilt as well as fear.[9]

If one can dismiss preventive war as morally outrageous, one has more difficulty dismissing massive retaliation. John Foster Dulles, the secretary of state from 1953 to 1959, advocated the threat of large-scale nuclear retaliation against Soviet or Communist Chinese threats to the interests of the Western World, even in situations not of first importance to the security of the U.S. What Dulles wanted was a deterrent that discouraged the entire spectrum of Soviet mischief, not merely overt Soviet attacks. The problem was that massive retaliation never enjoyed sufficient credibility to work successfully. It was unlikely, then as now, that the American people would tolerate "nuclear blackmail" in ambiguous or even marginally important circumstances deemed unworthy of risking war. As Professor Henry Kissinger of Harvard observed in 1957:

> The notion of a nuclear stalemate under present conditions is more a testimony to the fears and conscience of the non-Soviet world than to actual Soviet power. In the short-term the stalemate, if it exists, will be a balance between our unwillingness to use all-out war to achieve our goals and the Soviet inability to do so.[10]

From the moral perspective, perhaps the most troublesome issue is the preemptive nuclear strategy: striking an enemy just before he himself is expected to strike you. Self-defense certainly has moral justification. A nation has the political duty as well as the abstract right to prevent harm to itself, even if it requires inflicting harm upon others. In the 16th and 17th centuries, jurists Francis de Victoria and Hugo Grotius, who were deeply rooted in humanist and Christian values, espoused the concept of just cause for war, including self-defense, avenging harm, and recovery of property.[11] By crippling the enemy forces poised to attack, the preemptive strike may limit the anticipated damage he can inflict. The moral justification, however, must be in the supreme confidence that the enemy does indeed intend to strike and is not merely posturing. There is always uncertainty in the preemptive strategy. The anticipatory first strike will surely lead to war, whereas waiting for the enemy to attack first, even when the consequences might be devastating, may result in avoiding the conflagration altogether. There is thus a fine distinction, not easily discernible morally, between the preemptive strike in self-defense and vicious aggression.

To avoid the dilemmas of the preemptive strategy, the Kennedy Administration in the early 1960s adopted the nuclear strategy of the second-strike deterrent. After fortifying ("hardening") and diversifying its nuclear forces, the U.S. could absorb an all-out first strike by the Soviet Union and still have enough surviving weapons to destroy the enemy. The logic was that if the Soviets knew that the U.S. could indeed endure an all-out attack and still provide a cataclysmic response, then the Soviets would have no incentive to attack in the first place.

The moral dilemma of deterrence seemed solved in this second-strike strategy, although the strategy in fact raised other moral questions. What if the Soviets attacked American troops or allies with conventional forces alone in distant theaters? What if the Soviets maneuvered the U.S. into using nuclear weapons first? At what point in an escalating crisis would the American people support the use of nuclear weapons as morally justifiable? Fortunately, these difficult questions were never put to the test, since the U.S. had sizable conventional forces to supplement its nuclear arsenal. Indeed, General Maxwell Taylor has argued that the diplomatic triumph of the U.S. over the Soviets in the Cuban missile crisis of 1962 was due primarily to American superiority of conventional weapons in the area of crisis rather than to superiority of nuclear weapons.[12]

Another moral problem of the second-strike strategy revolved around the concept of "assured destruction." The Kennedy Administration set as a theoretical objective the ability to kill 20 to 25 percent of the Soviet people and destroy 50 percent of Soviet industrial capacity to achieve "assured destruction"—the level of punishment that would be unacceptable, and therefore deterring, to the Soviets. In reality, the U.S. force structure by 1968 could have eliminated at least 50 percent of the Soviet population and 80 percent of its industrial capacity.[13] The moral question that followed was, should the U.S. hold half of all Russians hostage when in fact they were not responsible for the actions of their own leaders? The objective of assured destruction required counter-value targeting analogous to strategic bombing of civilians. As one expert remarked:

> I cannot see how a city-targeting strategy can possibly be reconciled with principles of the just employment of armed force, even though to threaten destruction of millions of noncombatants is by no means as evil as would be their actual destruction, and though the threat may deter war.[14]

The counterforce strategy of targeting military targets alone avoids some of the moral questions of counter-value, but it raises moral problems of its own. Nuclear weapons often produce lethal fallout that can kill and sicken people and animals far away from the area of blast. The surface burst required to knock out a missile silo or any other hardened target can spew radioactive debris hundreds of miles. Millions of civilians could be killed or incapacitated downwind from a nuclear counterforce attack.[15]

It is purely wishful thinking to contemplate a world without nuclear weapons. Perhaps it is an idle dream even to speculate about nuclear strategies that conform ideally to moral standards. Yet morality is a factor that must be considered in nuclear strategy. Even if there were no universal moral standards, American leaders are restrained by the moral sensitivities of the American people. Ultimately, the power of the U.S. rests not upon technology and weapon systems but upon the resolution and conviction of the American people. Clausewitz argued that public support for the policies of the state are vital for any military success: "One might say that the physical seem little more than the wooden hilt [of the sword], while the moral factors are the precious metal, the real weapon, the finely honed blade."[16]

The anti-war protest movement in the U.S. during the Vietnam War demonstrated that many Americans have deep feelings toward what is "right" and "wrong," what is "just" and "evil," in American foreign policy, though we will not pretend that all protesters acted from moral imperatives. There is every reason to expect a great public outcry if Washington employed nuclear weapons in such a way that alienated its moral sensitivities. Henry Kissinger, who himself was the object of moral protest while he directed American foreign policy, observed in 1977: "Our tradition and the values of our people ensure that a policy that seeks only to manipulate force would lack all conviction, consistency, and public support."[17]

The central question is whether nuclear deterrence itself is moral. One might be tempted to argue a priori that deterrence is moral simply because deterrence has been the proclaimed strategy and there has not been a nuclear war. But such thinking is superficial. One needs to ask whether deterrence has a moral objective and moral means to achieve that objective. In the narrowest of terms, the objectives of deterrence are morally acceptable to the American people. There is little doubt that the American government would use nuclear weapons, and the people would fully support it, in retaliation for an attack upon the U.S. or its principal allies. Even in the absence of a military attack, nuclear retaliation for grave damage to U.S. interests would be accepted in certain dire situations. But the use of nuclear weapons for convoluted political purposes, especially in politically and morally questionable circumstances, would likely not be acceptable to most Americans. The collateral objective of deterrence is peace; Americans not only approve of peace but crave it.

If the objectives of deterrence are moral, then it is the means of achieving those objectives that are often morally questioned. How can one justify the brutal killing of millions of innocent people and the possible contamination of the earth by nuclear weapons? For obviously the potential *use* of nuclear weapons is the logically derived consequence of deterrence. The only comfortable answer is to accept as an article of faith that nuclear weapons are so horrendous that peace will be preserved by the threat alone that they will be used. Yet the doubts are nagging: Can war be prevented by threatening to wage it? Can the use of force be precluded by the threat of counter-violence? Can a moral objective be morally accomplished by immoral means, or the threat of using immoral means? Does the right justify the might?

Judging from the experience of the last 34 years, we can tentatively say in answer to the group of questions above that deterrence is moral when the deterrer exercises moral restraints. After all, the tools of power are inanimate with no inherent morality. It is man and society that have moral qualities, so it is in human behavior that the moral problem resides. The wise and restrained employment of force can indeed be moral, even when the force can inflict damage and pain to others. It is imperative, both from the perspective of morality and from that of physical survival, that the nations possessing nuclear weapons practice the utmost caution and self-inhibition. The threat of retaliation in kind, of course, is a powerful inhibitor, but external restraints are not enough to preclude nuclear confrontation. To be moral, and to be effective practically, the country that practices deterrence against other countries must also practice deterrence against itself.

Henry Kissinger rightfully observed:

> Morality without security is ineffectual; security without morality is empty. To establish the relationship and proportion between these two goals is perhaps the most profound challenge before our government and our nation.[18]

NOTES

1. Henry A. Kissinger, "The Western Alliance: Peace and Moral Purpose," *The Department of State Bulletin* 75 (26 July 1976): 110.
2. [George F. Kennan], "The Sources of Soviet Conduct," *Foreign Affairs* 25 (July 1947): 566-82.
3. George F. Kennan, *Memoirs, 1925-1950* (Boston: Little, Brown, 1967), pp. 354-67. Also see Paul Y. Hammond, "NSC-68: Prologue to Rearmament," in *Strategy, Politics, and Defense Budgets* by Warner R. Schilling, Paul Y. Hammond, and Glenn H. Snyder (New York: Columbia Univ. Press, 1962), pp. 267-387; and John Lewis Gaddis, "Containment: A Reassessment," *Foreign Affairs* 55 (July 1977): 873-87.
4. Les K. Adler and Thomas G. Paterson, "Red Fascism: The Merger of Nazi Germany and Soviet Russia in the American Image of Totalitarianism, 1930-1950's," *American Historical Review* 75 (April 1970): 1046-64; Ernest R. May, *Lessons of the Past* (New York: Oxford Univ. Press, 1973), pp. 19-51; John Lewis Gaddis, "The Cold War: Some Lessons for Policymakers," in *War, Strategy, and Maritime Power*, ed. B. Mitchel Simpson III (New Brunswick, N.J.: Rutgers Univ. Press, 1977), pp. 251-70, especially pp. 267-68.
5. Klaus Knorr, *On the Uses of Military Power in the Nuclear Age* (Princeton, N.J.: Princeton Univ. Press, 1966), pp. 43-72, 123, 126; Arthur Lee Burns, "Ethics and Deterrence," *Adelphi Papers*, No. 69 (London: International Institute for Strategic Studies, 1970); John Norton Moore, "Law and National Security," *Foreign Affairs* 51 (January 1973): 408-21; Charles F. Kriete, "The Moral Dimension of Strategy," *Parameters* 7 (No. 2, 1977): 65-73.
6. Harry S. Truman, *Memoirs*, Vol. I: *Year of Decisions* (Garden City, N.Y.: Doubleday, 1955), p. 524.

7. Walter Millis, ed., *The Forrestal Diaries* (New York: Viking Press, 1951), pp. 458, 462, 486-89.
8. James F. Byrnes, *Speaking Frankly* (New York: Harper, 1947), p. 275.
9. Bernard Brodie, *Strategy in the Missile Age* (Princeton, N.J.: Princeton Univ. Press, 1970), p. 237.
10. Henry A. Kissinger, *Nuclear Weapons and Foreign Policy* (New York: Harper, 1957), p. 111.
11. Quincy Wright, *A Study of War* (Chicago: Univ. of Chicago Press, 1942), I, 332-35; II, 886.
12. Maxwell Taylor, "The Legitimate Claims of National Security," *Foreign Affairs* 52 (April 1974): 577-94.
13. Alan C. Enthoven and K. Wayne Smith, *How Much is Enough?* (New York: Harper Colophon Books, 1971), pp. 175, 178, 194-95, 207-08.
14. Burns, p. 13.
15. Sidney D. Drell and Frank von Hippel, "Limited Nuclear War," *Scientific American* 235 (November 1976): 27-37; Kevin N. Lewis, "The Prompt and Delayed Effects of a Nuclear War," *Scientific American* 241 (July 1979): 35-47.
16. Carl von Clausewitz, *On War*, ed. and trans, by Michael Howard and Peter Paret (Princeton, N.J.: Princeton Univ. Press, 1976), p. 185. Also see Norman H. Gibbs, "Clausewitz on the Moral Forces in War," in Simpson, pp. 49-59.
17. Henry A. Kissinger, "Morality and Power," *The Washington Post*, 25 September 1977, p. C3.
18. Ibid.

This article originally appeared in the March 1980 issue of *Parameters*.

3

The American Bishops on War and Peace

By JOHN W. COFFEY

At a meeting in Chicago on the second and third of May 1983, the American bishops approved a pastoral letter on war and peace, "The Challenge of Peace: God's Promise and Our Response." Owing to pressure from the Vatican and European bishops, this final draft substantially improved on earlier versions and does not contain the meaning imputed to it by elements of the press and the peace movement. In order to understand the pastoral letter, one must therefore note certain changes required after a previous meeting at the Vatican.

Representatives of the National Conference of Catholic Bishops were summoned to Rome in January to discuss their second draft letter with representatives of European bishops' conferences and Vatican officials. Attending that meeting from America were Archbishop John Roach of St. Paul and Minneapolis, president of the NCCB; Cardinal Joseph Bernardin, Archbishop of Chicago and chairman of the ad hoc committee on war and peace; Monsignor Daniel Hoye, secretary of the NCCB; and Reverend Bryan Hehir, the principal author of the pastoral letter. The meeting on 18-19 January was closed, but a summary was made public by Reverend Jan Schotte, a secretary of the Pontifical Commission for Justice and Peace.

One important result of the Vatican meeting was a sharper distinction between the different levels of moral authority involved in a discussion of this issue, a differentiation which the second draft had obscured. As Roach and Bernardin later explained to their American colleagues,

> Perhaps the crucial point of the exchanges we have described has been to focus attention on the need to distinguish clearly between moral principles and their application to concrete realities—that is, between principles on the one hand and, on the other, specific applications of these principles via the assessment of factual circumstances. This is necessary to avoid attaching or seeming to attach an unwarranted level of authority to prudential, contingent judgments where the complexity of the facts makes possible a number of legitimate opinions.[1]

For one matter, a bishops' conference as such has no teaching authority. Only the Pope or the Whole College of Bishops with the Pope can proclaim morally binding principles for Catholics. Thus, the pastoral letter carried moral authority only when it reiterates the formal teaching of the universal Church or when it reaffirms natural law principles of the just war theory. Second, as the American bishops were compelled to admit in their final draft, "The applications of principles in this pastoral letter do not carry the same moral authority as our statements of universal moral principles and formal church teaching."[2] For example, natural law principles such as noncombatant immunity (noncombatant life must not be directly and intentionally taken) and proportionality (the good to be obtained must be proportional to the damage done) are binding, while the bishops' prudential judgments about specific policies, such as "no first use" of nuclear weapons or their proposals on how to secure peace do not possess a scintilla of authority. As we shall see, however, the practical application of even universally valid principles admits different conclusions. To the extent, then, that the American bishops uphold traditional Catholic just-war teaching, they have nothing to say; their own views about political policy, on the other hand, bear no moral weight.

A second significant result of the Vatican meeting was to force the U.S. bishops to employ Scripture more carefully in their treatment of war and peace. Those who read the bishops' second draft letter may recall Lincoln's response when importuned by a group of prophetic Christians about emancipation:

> I hope it will not be irreverent for me to say that if it is probable that God would reveal his will to others, on a point so connected with my duty, it might be supposed he would reveal it directly to me; for, unless I am more deceived in myself than I often am, it is my earnest desire to know the will of Providence in this matter. *And if I can learn what it is I will do it!* These are not, however, the days of miracles, and I suppose it will be granted that I am not to expect a direct revelation. I must study the plain physical facts of the case, ascertain what is possible and learn what appears to be wise and right. The subject is difficult, and good men do not agree.[3]

Warned at the Vatican meeting not to confuse this imperfect, earthly life with God's kingdom in eternal life, the bishops recognized finally that Revelation offers no political treatise and that God's Kingdom of peace and justice will never exist in this sinful world, which must settle for a rough justice that sometimes disrupts peace. An examination of the Scriptures, the bishops acknowledge, "makes it clear that they do not provide us with detailed answers to the specifics of the questions which we face today."[4] The final pastoral letter conforms to the sober realism of Pope John Paul II that "in this world a totally and permanently peaceful human society is unfortunately a utopia" and that any illusions otherwise "lead straight to the false peace of totalitarian regimes."[5]

At the Vatican meeting, furthermore, "it was clearly affirmed that only one Catholic tradition exists: the just-war theory."[6] The American bishops abandoned their earlier pretense that pacifist nonviolence holds equal standing in Church teaching and allowed pacifism as an option only for individuals, not states. The final pastoral letter reaffirms Pius XII's injunction that states have a moral duty to defend their people against aggression and that nations are obliged to assist one another in self-defense.

In the final pastoral letter the bishops ground their discussion of nuclear policy in the 15-century-old just war tradition and by doing so adhere to established Church teaching. Just war theory stipulates seven conditions for the *jus ad bellum* (when resort to war is permissible) and two conditions for the *jus in bello* (permissible conduct in war). In the nuclear age, the critical conditions are proportionality and discrimination. Proportionality applies to the *jus ad bellum* (the harm inflicted and suffered must be commensurate with the good to be obtained) and to the *jus in bello* (the response to aggression; hence, unlimited nuclear war would lack reasonable proportion). Discrimination applied to the *jus in bello* requires that innocent, noncombatant life may not be directly and intentionally taken.

Now, these prudential dictates of natural reason do not allow precise, definite application. Long ago Aristotle counseled that ethics is not geometry and that an educated man will look for the degree of certainty and exactness appropriate to a subject. Recognizing the inexact nature of discrimination in practice, the bishops admit that "concise and definitive answers still appear to be wanting."[7] Very great, although unintentional and indirect, loss of civilian life may occur without violating the standard of discrimination, and it is often not possible neatly to distinguish between military and nonmilitary targets. What are we to say, for instance, of a munitions factory located in a city? Moreover, in many forms of conflict, particularly in unconventional warfare, it may be exceedingly difficult to distinguish between combatants and noncombatants. This was the situation in Vietnam and, more recently, in the war in Lebanon. All that is morally required in such cases is a reasonable, good-faith effort.

Nor can the principle of proportionality be reduced to some crude, material calculus. Were the preservation of the Union and the end of slavery worth one million dead and wounded Americans? Was the defeat of Nazism commensurate with the loss of 55 million lives? The principle of proportionality cannot be quantified, and traditional Catholic teaching has never been marred by the vulgar hedonism of many contemporary peace activists who suggest that the greatest evil is physical pain and death. As the distinguished Jesuit theologian John Courtney Murray once explained,

> The comparison here must be between realities of the moral order, and not sheerly between two sets of material damage and loss. The standard is not a "eudaemonism and utilitarianism of materialist origin," which would avoid war merely because it is uncomfortable, or connive at injustice simply because its repression would be costly. The question of proportion must be evaluated in more tough-minded fashion, from the viewpoint of the hierarchy of strictly moral values. It is not enough simply to consider the "sorrows and evils that flow from war." There are greater evils than the physical death and destruction wrought in war. And there are human goods of so high an order that immense sacrifices may have to be borne in their defense.[8]

Earlier versions of the pastoral letter smacked of the kind of Hobbesian materialism against which Murray warned, but apparently the Vatican meeting helped clarify the hierarchy of moral values for the American bishops.

II

At the January meeting in Rome, Cardinal Casaroli, Vatican secretary of state, offered an informal commentary on John Paul II's 1982 message to the Second Special Session of the UN General Assembly on disarmament. Casaroli cautioned the U.S. bishops to stick to the level of moral principle that falls within their competence: "One must deal with true principles of the *moral order* without getting into questions of a technical, political, or any other nature that ultimately escape the competence of the ecclesiastical magisterium."[9] This the bishops do in their moral judgment of the general policy of deterrence.

On the fundamental strategy of nuclear deterrence, the bishops side with Pope John Paul II: Deterrence is still morally acceptable, not as an end in itself but as a step toward disarmament; the danger of nuclear war must be balanced against the protection of justice and freedom. Their concurrence with the Pope on deterrence leads the bishops nominally to support the maintenance of a balance of strategic forces: "Thus a balance of forces, preventing either side from achieving superiority, can be seen as a means of safeguarding both dimensions,"[10] that is, averting war and defending freedom. Contrarily, the bishops' specific policy recommendations preclude the maintenance of this balance.

The bishops condemn the particular policy of deliberate, direct counterpopulation warfare under any circumstances. "Under no circumstances," the pastoral letter emphatically states, "may nuclear weapons or other instruments of mass slaughter be used for the purpose of destroying population centers or other predominantly civilian targets."[11] At the January meeting in Rome participants agreed with this general prohibition, but the concrete application of even this principle is open to varied judgments: "Questions were raised though about the application of the principle to actual nuclear strategies or to the use of particular nuclear weapons. Such application entails a contingent judgment."[12] The summary of the Vatican meeting does not elaborate upon the contingent considerations participants may have contemplated, but we may perhaps assume that, for example, unintentional collateral damage arising from strikes against military targets proximate to urban areas would not violate the prudential standard of discrimination.

Dealing with the particular policy of flexible response entailing the possible first use of nuclear weapons by NATO, the final pastoral letter is much more qualified and cautious than earlier versions. First of all, the American bishops were required to clarify the morally nonbinding nature of their prudential judgment about the first use of nuclear weapons. Proximity to the Soviet threat has obviously concentrated the minds of the European prelates more powerfully than those of their American brethren. Consequently, according to the summary of the Rome meeting, participants believed that "clearer distinctions are called for in the text with regard to the question of first use in order to avoid any misunderstanding and ambiguity."[13] The final letter acknowledges the prudential character of the bishops' endorsement of no first use.

Because of the uncertainty in controlling escalation, the bishops profess that they do not see how "initiation of nuclear warfare on however restricted a scale can be morally justified."[14] Therefore, they urge NATO to renounce the option of first nuclear use against a conventional attack, relying instead on a conventional defense. Gone, however, is the bishops' earlier, bold endorsement of no first use. The final pastoral letter grants that development of an adequate conventional defense will take time, and although they do not explicitly approve the current strategy of flexible response, the bishops do lend it tacit assent:

> In the interim, deterrence against a conventional attack relies upon two factors: the not inconsiderable conventional forces at the disposal of NATO and the recognition by a potential attacker that the outbreak of large-scale conventional war could escalate to the nuclear level through accident or miscalculation by either side.[15]

The bishops cautiously hedge support of no first nuclear use by making it contingent upon concurrent creation of an adequate conventional defense: "We urge NATO to move rapidly toward the adoption of a 'no first use' policy, but doing so in tandem with development of an adequate alternative defense posture."[16]

For the bishops, "the first imperative is to prevent any use of nuclear weapons."[17] Over the question of whether it might be possible to conduct a limited nuclear war, the bishops register their doubt yet concede that the policy debate remains inconclusive. Contrary to the impression in some quarters, then, the final pastoral letter does not rule out the limited use of nuclear weapons. It is difficult to miss the influence on the final pastoral letter particularly of West German Catholic leaders, who have vigorously supported NATO's "two-track" decision of 1979 and who harbor no illusions about the threat they confront. As the Central Committee of German Catholics stated in 1981,

> Whenever a nation fails to visualize the extent to which life under a totalitarian system is devoid of human dignity, it becomes a breeding ground for active minorities that use the word peace and the longing for peace as a vehicle for asserting their own totalitarian or anarchistic goals—goals that are opposed to freedom. Where the fatal tendency to disregard history is combined with political ignorance, an insufficiently developed ability to make ethical distinctions, and the reluctance to fight for our common order, such minorities can gain an influence that far transcends their real importance.[18]

The bishops' general principles conform to established Church teaching, and their major pronouncements on the strategy of deterrence are largely unexceptionable. When they enter the area of concrete policy recommendations, however, where they lack authority and competence, they become hopelessly muddled and in the process reduce deterrence to an empty, dangerous bluff. Thereby the bishops also, against the Vatican's admonishment, diminish the teaching authority and influence of the Church in society.

The bishops' condemnation of direct, deliberate counterpopulation warfare under any circumstances accords with American strategy. U.S. nuclear strategy does not rest on the incredible threat of mutual extermination of civilians, but on the limited, flexible targeting of military forces. The Nixon Administration formulated the doctrine, reaffirmed by each subsequent administration, of limited nuclear options, whereby the United States would exercise a selective measured retaliation according to the scale and targets of a Soviet attack. President Carter lamentably delayed or canceled every new weapon system designed to give the United States that flexible, counterforce capability, but the Reagan Administration's strategic modernization program intends precisely to bring that capability into being in accordance with the nation's declared policy.

Although the bishops acknowledge U.S. deterrence strategy to be one of counterforce, not countervalue, targeting, they become entangled in a logical dilemma that renders deterrence a hollow threat. Unlike some nuclear freeze advocates who support the catastrophic doctrine of mutual assured destruction, realizing that in a crisis this doctrine would result only in U.S. self-deterrence, the bishops rightly reject the immoral, suicidal policy of attacks on Soviet cities. Conversely, they disapprove development of hard-target weapons that would give us the discriminate capability of hitting Soviet military targets. Since the bishops understand deterrence as preventing any use of nuclear weapons, they regard "sufficiency" to deter as an adequate strategy and oppose development of new counterforce weapons that might inspire fear of a first strike in the Soviets. But the bishops cannot logically have it both ways. Either they must embrace the suicidal doctrine of MAD, or they must favor the alternative of limited nuclear options; they cannot repudiate both and still purport to offer an intelligible strategic policy.

The bishops oppose the creation of a nuclear war-fighting capability along with the building of any new weapon system that would lower the nuclear threshold or blur the distinction between conventional and nuclear war. Though they do not say so, presumably the bishops have in mind a weapon such as the neutron bomb. Adoption of the strategy delineated by the bishops would present American decision-makers with an all-or-nothing response to Soviet aggression. Despite their rhetorical condemnation of the cataclysmic response to Soviet aggression, the bishops' position does not practically differ from the cynical endorsement of MAD by freeze advocates who know that in a confrontation this strategy would eventuate in American capitulation. Deterrence thus becomes for the bishops an incredible, dangerous bluff which we may not morally execute. Effective deterrence must be based on the ability to respond appropriately across the entire spectrum of conflict and on the credible intent to use nuclear weapons. By their rejection of a war-fighting capability and support of a nuclear freeze, the bishops undermine the flexible response that makes deterrence credible.

III

In their handling of arms control, the bishops exhibit the confusion that grips most members of the professional arms control community and most elected officials. The bishops at least are candid about their confusion. For them, as for most of its promoters, arms control has become an end in itself rather than one means by which we strengthen our national security. Security policy is geared toward the achievement of arms control for its own sake; arms control is no longer one instrument among others to bolster the nation's security. The bishops urge deep cuts in the nuclear arsenals of both superpowers and only grudgingly concede that the START and INF negotiations launched by President Reagan "are said to be designed to achieve deep cuts."[19] Why these proposals are merely "said to be designed to achieve" what they demonstrably call for, the bishops do not explain. But the bishops illustrate why we habitually wind up negotiating with ourselves in arms control talks. The United States, they admit, has already taken significant steps toward arms control, yet "additional initiatives are encouraged."[20] They have nothing to say about what the Soviets should do.

The bishops are candid about the source of their confusion, however, for their goal is not simply arms control or even reduction, but disarmament: "Nuclear deterrence should be used as a step on the way toward progressive disarmament. Each proposed addition to our strategic system or change in strategic doctrine must be assessed precisely in light of whether it will render steps toward 'progressive disarmament' more or less likely."[21] In this spirit the pastoral letter supports "immediate, bilateral, verifiable agreements to halt the testing, production, and deployment of new nuclear weapons systems."[22] A footnote in the pastoral letter disclaims support for any particular political initiative, but this statement effectively supplies aid and comfort to the nuclear freeze movement. Some of their newly found friends in the press and peace movement will, one suspects, be less enthusiastic about the bishops' call for opposition to direct war on innocent life in the womb as the first step toward a peaceful world. Nevertheless, the bishops show themselves captives of the hoary myth that weapons, not nations with conflicting vital interests in a fallen world, cause wars. And they can reconcile their support for maintenance of a strategic balance with their call for a nuclear freeze only by believing that deterrence is a static relation and that technology can be made to stand still. The bishops seem oblivious of the fact that the development of American nuclear weapons has made them less numerous and destructive and more discriminate in effect. Had we frozen our nuclear systems 20 years ago, we would have a third more warheads—with four times the megatonnage—than we have today.

With respect to substituting an adequate NATO conventional defense for the option of first nuclear use, the bishops seem unaware of some unpleasant realities, or perhaps they are simply less than forthcoming about the harsh alternatives. They are far from the first or sole proponents of enhancing NATO's conventional capability. From the alliance's beginning American leaders have exhorted European allies to do just so, and from the start the Europeans have resisted this course for economic and political reasons. European governments, encumbered with burgeoning welfare states, have never been willing to sacrifice butter for guns and to shoulder the much greater economic burden a robust conventional defense would impose. They have been unwilling to risk the political unpopularity with their electorates of a larger defense establishment, and they have always feared that a stronger conventional defense would decouple the link to the American nuclear umbrella. Yet even if our NATO partners substantially upgraded their conventional capability, a flat disavowal at any time of the possible first use of tactical nuclear weapons to repulse a Soviet attack would make a conventional war far more feasible. The uncertain scale of NATO's retaliation has in fact deterred the Soviets and sustained peace in Europe for 40 years. Moreover, the community of risk created by extended deterrence has buoyed European confidence in America and prevented the Finlandization of the continent. This was the message conveyed by a bipartisan group of German political leaders in reply to the argument for no first use made by George Kennan and others.[23]

Just as they reveal by their eschewal of both assured destruction and a war-fighting capability, the bishops want to have their cake and eat it, too. Conventional forces, unfortunately, cost more than nuclear weapons, and estimates for a sufficient NATO conventional defense range up to 10 percent beyond current expenditures. When we remember that our NATO allies have not even honored their agreement to a three percent increase made to President Carter, prospects for a reliable conventional defense look dim. Yet the bishops are disingenuous about the sacrifices conventional defense would demand. Sensing that a nuclear deemphasis would boost defense expenditures, the bishops shirk approving increased defense spending (to say nothing of conscription for America and Britain) by professing incompetence to judge the case: "We cannot judge the strength of these arguments in particular cases. . . . It is not for us to settle the technical debate about policy and budgets."[24] If the bishops plead incompetence to decide budgetary questions, whence do they derive competence to judge far more complex matters?

Further, the bishops are loathe to endorse higher defense spending because they do not want to shortchange "other urgent, unmet human needs,"[25] and they beg off the entire problem by disavowing any "notion of 'making the world safe for conventional war,' which introduces its own horrors."[26] Additionally, if they were realistic about the problems of military defense, they might change their minds about "outlawing the production and use of chemical and biological weapons."[27] Not expectedly, they are silent about Soviet chemical warfare in Afghanistan and Southeast Asia, and they fail to see that a NATO chemical capability could help raise the nuclear threshold, while its absence in the face of Soviet combined-arms doctrine perilously lowers that threshold. But the bishops are not realistic. They do earnestly want to avoid war of any kind, but they would be more persuasive if they faced the harsh choices; by ignoring these they forfeit an opportunity to contribute to policy discussion.

IV

I will not offer here a lengthy consideration of the bishops' proposals to promote peace. These range from a feckless endorsement of the United Nations as a step toward world government to a perverse recommendation to create a global political body that would maintain surveillance over the earth and have the power to prevent any nation from bellicose preparations. What a monstrous totalitarianism this would entail escapes the bishops, who blithely suggest that this might be accomplished without infringing on any nation's sovereignty.[28] Since the bishops pay homage to the UN as a vehicle of world political order, though, brief reflection on this proposition is worthwhile.

Although the United States has contributed some 25 percent of the UN's operating expenses, which total more than $1 billion annually, the bishops encourage the United States to "adopt a stronger supportive role with respect to the United Nations."[29] The bishops might be excused for understating America's unparalleled support of the UN since its inception, but their persistent illusion that the UN represents the hope for international political order and the advance of human rights, despite a generation's experience, exemplifies their lack of realism.

No clear-eyed observer of the UN's nearly 45-year track record can believe any longer in the early utopian expectation that it would peacefully resolve international conflicts. Rather, former Ambassador Jeane Kirkpatrick notes the UN actually serves to exacerbate conflicts. "I am," writes Kirkpatrick, "more bothered by far by the tendency of the United Nations to make conflict resolution *more difficult* than it would otherwise be, at least in a good many cases."[30] This happens, Kirkpatrick points out, because when a problem such as the Golan Heights issue becomes a UN issue, the number of parties involved greatly expands to include many who would never otherwise have been concerned. Also, the UN politicizes and publicizes issues such as Namibian independence, breeding polarization by forcing states to choose sides. Finally, the UN pattern of bloc politics fosters a spurious solidarity where the interests of nations are subordinated to the interests of a group hostile to the real welfare of those nations, for example, support for the PLO by conservative Arab states.

Given these realities and considering that the European nations sharing a common heritage have been unable to achieve political unity, how the bishops imagine that Western liberal democracies could fashion a global political order with Marxist totalitarian states and the anti-Western, tin-pot dictatorships of the Third World surpasses comprehension.

Taken together with their solicitude for human rights, the bishops' fantasy about the United Nations strikes one as extraordinary. This is the body, Kirkpatrick reminds us, that bullies South Africa, Israel, and noncommunist Latin American nations while blinking at the slaughter of three million Cambodians by Pol Pot, the murder of a quarter of a million Ugandans by Idi Amin, and the daily, systematic repression of Soviet citizens. And it is the body that has equated Zionism with Nazism. The moral hypocrisy and cynicism of the UN concerning human rights are matched only by its trivialization of this noble ideal, as when the Covenant on Economic, Social, and Cultural Rights proclaimed a paid vacation to be a human right. Walter Berns, who served as alternate U.S. representative to the UN Human Rights Commission in Geneva, describes his experience in this manner: "The UN is the only organization with which I have been associated where it is taken for granted that members do not necessarily speak the truth."[31] Berns recounts the placid reception given the explanation by the chief Soviet delegate to the commission that the Berlin Wall exists not to keep East Germans in but to keep West Germans out.

V

In the end, the bishops' failure is one of prudence. The prime virtue in political and moral affairs, prudence is the steady habit of choosing the appropriate means to a good end. The bishops' intention is laudable. They fervently hope for peace and wish to say no to war. But wishing will not make it so. The bishops can no more wish peace into existence than they can make the earth flat or the sun revolve around the earth by declaring it to be so. One cannot decry the horrors of unlimited nuclear war or deplore the misfortune of war altogether and then disregard every prudent means of averting those ends. The trouble with the bishops is that they want to have clean hands in politics, but as Peguy once said, to have clean hands in life means to have no hands at all. It is no small historical irony that the bishops' jejune observations about world politics come from representatives of a Church once so adroit at the manipulation of political power.

The pastoral letter contains a sober understanding of Soviet totalitarianism, which is inimical to the very freedom the bishops themselves enjoy. Yet it will probably take more than prayers to preserve the peace and freedom of the world. The bishops should emulate Lincoln's prudent expression of gratitude for the victorious Union Army: Thanks to God and credit to Grant!

No more than the bishops do other men want war, but sometimes men choose a course that may lead to war because they reject the alternatives as worse. Perhaps, finally, the bishops reflect that loss of civil courage in the West discerned by Solzhenitsyn, manifesting itself in a refusal to risk what is precious in the defense of common values.

NOTES

1. "Rome Consultation on Peace and Disarmament: A Vatican Synthesis," *Origins* (Washington: NC Documentary Service, 7 April 1983), p. 691.
2. "The Challenge of Peace: God's Promise and Our Response," *Origins* (Washington: NC Documentary Service, 19 May 1983), p. 26.
3. Abraham Lincoln, "Reply to Christians of Chicago, 1862," in *The Political Thought of Abraham Lincoln*, ed. Richard N. Current (Indianapolis: Bobbs-Merrill, 1967), pp. 216-17.
4. "The Challenge of Peace: God's Promise and Our Response," *Origins*, p. 7.
5. Ibid., p. 9.
6. "Rome Consultation on Peace and Disarmament: A Vatican Synthesis," *Origins*, p. 694.
7. "The Challenge of Peace: God's Promise and Our Response," *Origins*, p. 12.
8. John Courtney Murray, *We Hold These Truths: Catholic Reflections on the American Proposition* (New York: Sheed & Ward, 1960), p. 261.
9. "Rome Consultation on Peace and Disarmament: A Vatican Synthesis," *Origins*, p. 695.
10. "The Challenge of Peace: God's Promise and Our Response," *Origins*, p. 17.
11. Ibid., pp. 14-15.
12. "Rome Consultation on Peace and Disarmament: A Vatican Synthesis," *Origins*, p. 693.
13. Ibid., p. 694.
14. "The Challenge of Peace: God's Promise and Our Response," *Origins*, p. 15.
15. Ibid.
16. Ibid.
17. Ibid., p. 16.
18. Central Committee of German Catholics, "On the Current Peace Discussion," in *The Apocalyptic Premise: Nuclear Arms Debated*, ed. Ernest W. Lefever and E. Stephen Hunt (Washington: Ethics and Public Policy Center, 1982), p. 327.
19. "The Challenge of Peace: God's Promise and Our Response," *Origins*, p.18.
20. Ibid., p. 20.
21. Ibid., p. 18.
22. Ibid.
23. Karl Kaiser et al., "Nuclear Weapons and the Preservation of Peace." *Foreign Affairs* 60 (Summer 1982): 1157-70; see also McGeorge Bundy et al., "Nuclear Weapons and the Atlantic Alliance," *Foreign Affairs* 60 (Spring 1982): 753-68.
24. "The Challenge of Peace: God's Promise and Our Response," *Origins*, p. 21.
25. Ibid.
26. Ibid.
27. Ibid.
28. For an insightful discussion of this issue see Walter Berns, "The New Pacifism and World Government," *National Review*, 27 May 1983, pp. 613-20.
29. "The Challenge of Peace: God's Promise and Our Response," *Origins*, p. 25.
30. Jeane J. Kirkpatrick, *The Reagan Phenomenon—and Other Speeches on Foreign Policy* (Washington: American Enterprise Institute for Public Policy Research, 1983), p. 95.
31. Walter Berns, "Taking the United Nations Seriously," *Public Opinion* 6 (April-May 1983): 42.

This article originally appeared in the December 1983 issue of *Parameters*.

4

Is It Ever Moral to Push the Button?

By JAMES L. CARNEY

The White House, December 31, 1997: "Mr. President, Mr. President, wake up!"

The voice was low but urgent. Adam Cunningham, 42nd president of the United States, roused himself slowly, leaning on one elbow as he stared bleary-eyed at his digital clock. Its numbers reported dutifully: "3:30 a.m." A cold wintry morning in Washington on the last day of 1997. "What is it, Ben?" he asked his military aide, Colonel Ben Thomas.

"Sir, we've confirmed reports of a massive Soviet ICBM launching! We estimate about 1500 warheads are inbound right now. Our Space Defense System isn't fully operational yet. What's up there, though, should take out about 30 percent of their inbound missiles. An additional 600 missiles appear to be aimed at China. Sir, we expect initial detonations to generate a massive electromagnetic pulse in about 20 minutes, with the bulk of the attack coming five or ten minutes later. It looks like that main attack is aimed at our own missile silos and our air and submarine bases. Also, we got a message from Premier Lenintsov on the Hot Line. Our strategic forces are being alerted now, Mr. President, and await your counterattack order."

Cunningham leaped to his feet, struggling to think rationally in a storm of thoughts and emotions. Forty-five seconds later he was in the White House Situation Room reading the Hot Line Message from Moscow.

"Mr. President," it began. "We deeply regret that we have found it necessary to launch a preemptive strike against your country to protect our own nation against the preemptive strike which you planned to launch as soon as your strategic defenses were fully in place next year. However, we have targeted only your strategic military forces in this first strike. Washington will not be hit. Nor will New York or your other major urban centers. If you withhold any counterstrike, we will not launch follow-up attacks against these important targets. But if you do respond, then our reserve rockets and our sea-launched ballistic missiles will be launched against the entire political and economic infrastructure of the United States. As you know, more than 150,000,000

Americans could die in such an assault. We will be watching our radar screens for your response. I assure you that we will be magnanimous in victory and will provide all necessary assistance to enable your great country to recover from this misfortune and to take its place as a full partner with the socialist nations of the world."

The Hot Line stood silent. President Cunningham gazed at it with a numb mixture of fury and horror.

"Mr. President," Ben interrupted, "We must give the order to launch or it will be too late!"

Cunningham stared at him. He thought of the inbound missiles and the millions of deaths and incalculable damage that were bound to result even if Lenintsov was not lying about the initial targeting. He realized that deterrence had failed; the great colossal gamble that the world had been safely betting on for over fifty years had failed! The nightmare had come true! Now he, one human being with no chance for meaningful consultations with any of his principal advisors, had to decide whether to double the ante for a post-nuclear world. He thought of his grandchildren and the Soviet children he had met on his summit visit in 1994. He recalled the tenets of his deep Christian faith and its proscriptions against unnecessary killing. Killing, slaughter, massive annihilation—no words seemed nearly adequate to describe the Death which was on its way. But he also thought of the Soviet treachery. He remembered the Iron Curtain and the repressive puppet regimes which sprouted up everywhere the Soviets achieved power. He grimly contemplated a future stretching endlessly forward in which the dreams of democratic freedoms throughout the world would vanish inexorably in a stranglehold of gulags. Even the memory of the world's greatest experiment in democracy would fade as Soviet revisionist historians rewrote the events of the 20th century to exalt the achievements and innocence of the USSR and denounce the perfidy and aggression of the Western democracies. It also occurred to him that Lenintsov might be lying, that the major urban centers of the United States were indeed targeted in this first strike.

It was now 3:35 a.m. Colonel Thomas announced that the president's helicopter was ready and pressed him again for the decision to launch a retaliatory strike. President Cunningham paused for a silent prayer requesting guidance and turned to his aide with his decision. (To be continued.)

The Nuclear Dilemma and Just War

The foregoing scenario is fictional and perhaps highly improbable. But it could happen. It is possible that one human being will some day find himself confronting the failure of nuclear deterrence in one awful moment of decision. Could he morally elect to respond with a nuclear counterstrike? Although the policy of nuclear deterrence which has formed a military shield for the Western world (as well as the Eastern world) for the past forty years has rested upon the mutual belief that the retaliatory threat would be carried out, nearly all analysts of just war tradition would say that the president may not justly respond with a nuclear counterstrike against Soviet population centers under the circumstances presented above.[1] In their view, the policy of Mutual Assured Destruction is immoral.

But today's nuclear moralists, while quite correct in their conclusion that modern total war is incompatible with any reasonable philosophy of ethics and morality, can provide us with no key to escape this trap we have built. No sane person would hesitate to condemn modern total war, much less nuclear war, as an abomination against humanity. Yet this kind of war remains a very real possibility.

A fundamental premise underlies the just war tradition: the unchanging nature of mankind, a nature in which good and evil always coexist. All human beings commit immoral, wrong, unethical, sinful, or otherwise dubious acts during their lives here on earth. These acts include killing other human beings. Because of this unfortunate propensity, it has been necessary for man to defend himself from aggression if he would prolong his stay on this planet for any appreciable time. This requirement, in turn, has led to the development of rules of conduct—the principles of just war—for the management of such mortal conflicts so that the moral fabric of society would not be lost in the struggle.

Perhaps unfortunately, our technological skill has steadily advanced, despite the almost complete lack of corresponding moral progress in humanity as a whole. As a consequence, wars have become more and more brutal and destructive as man's tools of war have become more and more efficient. In 1945, human beings achieved the power to cause incomprehensible destruction and loss of life and perhaps severed for all time any rational connection between all-out war and international politics.[2] Yet the need for self-defense has not diminished and is not likely to do so in the future. After eons of bloodshed, there is no reason to hope that mankind will evolve in this life into a more benevolent creature who does not resort to aggression to obtain unjust ends.

The principles of just war are divided into two sections. The first, *jus ad bellum*, refers to the justice of deciding to participate in a war; the second, *jus in bello*, refers to the rules of morality which govern the way any war may be conducted.

Principles of Just War

***Jus Ad Bellum* (Just Recourse to War)**

Just Cause
Legitimate Authority
Just Intentions
Public Declaration (Of Causes and Intents)
Proportionality (More Good than Evil Results)
Last Resort
Reasonable Hope of Success

***Jus In Bello* (Just Conduct in War)**

Discrimination (Noncombatant Immunity)
Proportionality (Amount and Type of Force Used)

Each of these principles merits elaboration.

Just cause

Just cause means having right on your side. In general, just cause embraces four types of situations. First, and most important for this discussion, is self-defense against unjustified aggressive actions. Self-defense is the only just cause formally recognized in modern international law.[3] Three other types of just cause are the right to intervene to protect one's "neighbor," the right to punish wrongdoers, and the right of the state to protect its fundamental ideology.[4]

Legitimate authority

Legitimate authority refers to the lawfully constituted government of a sovereign state. Only the primary authority of the state has the power to commit its citizens to war.

In the nuclear age, the problem of legitimate authority has taken on a new dimension and may now be said to be more vitally concerned with the conduct of war than with the decision to participate at all. This is because the only slim hope mankind has for achieving some reasonable balance between the aims and consequences of a nuclear war is to keep it limited. But keeping it limited requires controlling it, which in turn requires effective command, control, communications, and intelligence systems on both sides of the conflict. This is incompatible with a decapitation targeting policy, which aims to remove a hostile nation's leadership at an early stage in hopes of curtailing its ability and willingness to continue the fight. Decapitation is not only of dubious validity in light of contemporary nuclear weapon control procedures but also gambles away any possibility of controlling escalation with a nuclear conflict.

Just intentions

This element of *jus ad bellum* in Western thought was first articulated at length by St. Thomas Aquinas, who based it upon natural laws.[5] It may also be said to derive from the Judeo-Christian "love thy neighbor" ethic. This obligation does not cease in wartime. We are not permitted to forget that our enemy is also our neighbor, even though most neighborly obligations are suspended for the duration of hostilities. Revenge is not a morally acceptable basis for conducting war. Although it is permissible to intervene to prevent your neighbor's cheek from being struck, the war must be prosecuted with reluctance, restraint, and a willingness to accept peace when the security objectives which justified the war in the first place have been achieved. Although classified under the *jus ad bellum* section of the principles, "just intentions" has even greater significance for the individual soldier in the conduct of war, philosophically underlying the rules of war which protect noncombatants and require acceptance of surrender and humane treatment of prisoners of war.[6]

Aqu[illegible] origin[illegible] aggre[illegible] unavo[illegible] Later[illegible] justif[illegible] colla[illegible] viola[illegible] safe[illegible] effo[illegible] nor[illegible] inc[illegible]

In terms [illegible] having a reasonable relationship [illegible] achieved and the war means being used to achieve them.

Last resort

This principle recognizes the destructive consequences of war and insists that it be avoided if at all possible, consistent with the legitimate interests of the state. It means that negotiations, compromise, economic sanctions, appeals to higher authority (the United Nations, for example), and the like must be pursued to redress grievances, if possible, before resort to war is justified.[11]

Reasonable hope of success

The state must not squander the lives and property of its citizens in a hopeless effort.

Nuclear weapons have had at least one positive effect in terms of just war tradition. Their existence causes nations to be much more cautious about initiating hostilities against any nation that might employ them. In other words, they raise the threshold for war. This has resulted in a period of almost unprecedented peace between the major powers since the end of World War II. That is not to say that there have been no wars. There have obviously been

wers have not been direct
ly the level of death and
scale of the two World Wars.
mplications for any reasonable
bello principles, discrimination (or
ionality, are both casualties when
the vicinity of large population centers.
over acceptable war modes has focused on

ld Davidson has written on this aspect:

> oral commentary on war since World War II, whether focused on the air
> combat, has discussed the problem of noncombatant immunity. The issue
> er noncombatants should be immune to attack; there has been general
> on this point since classical times. Rather, the problem is deciding "who" is a
> batant; that is, the problem of discrimination. The difficulty of differentiating
> en combatants and noncombatants has escalated with each stage in the development
> odern warfare; the advent of conscript armies and large standing armies in Napoleon's
> ra, new weaponry developed in the industrial revolution, the mobilization of whole
> societies in major wars, the large-scale employment of guerrilla or insurgency war and
> terrorism, and the invention of weapons of mass destruction.[12]

Davidson goes on to explain that noncombatants have traditionally been divided into two groups, based on class and function. The "class" of noncombatants refers to persons who have been defined as not acceptable as military targets, including medical personnel and clergy, whether in uniform or not, infants and small children (normally all children), the infirm, aged, wounded, or sick, and those otherwise helpless to protect themselves. Those who are noncombatants by "function" include farmers, merchants, and others not directly involved in the war effort. Davidson continues:

> Among civilians, those who make war decisions or produce war materials are generally considered as direct contributors to the war effort and, thus, are combatants. Those who perform services or produce goods necessary for living are noncombatants, even though their service or goods may be used by military personnel. This line of reasoning, for example, allows bombardment of munitions factories, but not canneries.[13]

Proportionality

Just as proportionality is one of the *jus ad bellum* principles, so does moral proportionality apply to the means by which war is waged. With respect to *jus in bello*, proportionality means that the amount and type of force used must be such that the unjust consequences do not exceed the legitimate objectives.

Compliance with this principle requires an affirmative answer to the question: "If I take this military action, will more good than harm result from it?" The problem, of course, is often in defining what is meant by "good" and what is meant by "harm." Are human lives to be regarded as equally valuable, for instance? How many villagers may be killed in an air strike to eliminate a sniper—or a machine gun emplacement? And is the policy to be evaluated by a single engagement or from the perspective of the whole war?

Just War Tradition in Modern Total War

The principles of noncombatant immunity, as historically defined, and proportionality, measured by political goals versus the cost in lives and destruction, no longer seem at all compatible with any conceivable war between the world's great powers.

In simpler times, wars were fought by monarchs almost as personal struggles, using small armies of professionals and mercenaries; noncombatants had almost nothing to do with combat. Killing them was not only murder without military justification but unwise as well since they were the source of the state's peacetime wealth. This state of affairs remained until the Napoleonic wars in the 18th century. With the French and industrial revolutions, however, the entire citizenry of a nation became involved in these struggles.[14] Soldiers were drawn from a conscript base consisting of all able-bodied young men. War material was produced nationwide. The war was propagandized and supported throughout the body politic. During World War I, the areas away from the fighting sectors became known as the "home front."[15] The distinction between combatant and noncombatant began to blur, especially in the face of arguments that the sources of support (psychological and material) for the enemy were legitimate targets to force him to terminate hostilities.

By the time World War II arrived, no one doubted that total war included attacks upon the economic and industrial capacity of the enemy. "Rosie the Riveter" was an acknowledged part of the war effort and proud of it. Bombing runs on munitions factories, transportation facilities, and industrial plants in Nazi Germany were generally acceptable military activities under the moral principle of double effect, which legitimized collateral damage to the civilian sector. Even the use of night time area bombing by the British Bomber Command against German cities produced no popular outcry against the obvious violation of noncombatant immunity.[16] Both sides perceived the struggle to be between the opposing states, not merely those in uniform.[17] The distinction between combatant and noncombatant was substantially dissolved, erased by the harsh realities of total war in the 20th century. The experience of World War II illustrates the difficulty of implementing a moral strategy based upon a distinction between those citizens holding the guns and those citizens stretching back through the chain of support all the way to the miners excavating the ore which will be fashioned into the bullets fired by those guns.

This does not mean just war principles should be abandoned. Clearly such principles should be preserved to the maximum extent possible. But the essential point remains that all the brilliant articulations of highly desirable moral principles in warfare are of no practical value unless they can be applied in the world of flesh and blood. If notions of noncombatant immunity and proportionality are to be accepted as requiring a nonstrategic or nonnuclear response to an overt nuclear attack by an aggressor nation, then proponents for this moral position must also bear the burden of resolving the paradox of allowing evil to triumph rather than permitting the only effective means of counterattack. Until a satisfactory solution to this most fundamental of just war issues is offered, the moralists' condemnation of the inevitable slaughter inherent in nuclear war places them ultimately in the camp of nuclear pacifism. If the equation Defense = Excessive Destruction is unassailable, we may all mourn the terrible fate that has placed such fearsome technical prowess in such morally infirm vessels as mankind, but there is no realistic choice except to play out the hand as best we can and strive in the meantime for a more effective means of control.

The two just war principles most jeopardized by the existence of nuclear weapons are discrimination (noncombatant immunity) and proportionality. Morally legitimate targets in modern total war include a nation's industrial sinews and military installations and facilities. But even if only these targets are attacked in a strategic nuclear assault, the death and destruction from fire, blast, radioactivity, and possible "nuclear-winter" effects would cause staggering losses for the entire nation and probably bystander nations as well.[18] Although millions of noncombatants would lose their lives as a result of these attacks, the principle of double effect would appear to excuse this as an unavoidable consequence of legitimate targeting.[19] If so, then the distinction between combatant and noncombatant becomes almost meaningless in such a strategic nuclear barrage. But double effect does not apply if the collateral damage is disproportionate to the permitted objective.

Would the nuclear attack described above be disproportionate? To answer this, one has to first decide, disproportionate to what? If one looks only at the physical consequences of the attack, then it seems clearly disproportionate. But if survival of the state is at stake, and no other means of effective defeat-avoiding warfare are available, then it seems the principle of proportionality would not be violated. In any case, it is not only nuclear weapons that are threats to proportionality. In World War II, the fire bombing of Tokyo in March 1945 caused between 80,000 and 120,000 deaths, with the latter figure more likely closer to the actual toll.[20] The bombing of Hamburg from 24 July to 3 August 1943, also with incendiaries, caused 50,000 deaths and 50,000 injuries, and left 800,000 homeless.[21] The firestorms caused by the Dresden bombings of February 1945 left approximately 70,000 dead in a city with almost no military value.[22] By contrast, the nuclear explosion over Nagasaki on 8 August 1945 caused around 40,000 deaths.[23] The world's first hostile nuclear explosion, at Hiroshima on 6 August 1945, destroyed 60 percent of the city and killed about 80,000.[24]

Even if conventional munitions can cause as many casualties and as much damage as nuclear weapons, however, they do have two comparative virtues: it takes longer to apply them, with less resulting chance of the atmospheric effects predicted by nuclear-winter theorists; and they do not leave behind a lingering curse of radioactivity. Is it therefore better not to use nuclear weapons? Yes. Are their effects always disproportionate? Not if their use is necessary to avoid losing the war and if the user has satisfied all the other just war principles, including just cause (which, one notes, is not available to an aggressor nation).[25]

Since the destruction and death in a modern total war between the great military powers are certain to be disproportionate to any political cause other than survival of the state—whether nuclear weapons are used or not—the only solution to the problem is to avoid total war between these powers.

The Logic of Armageddon

The present solution to avoiding war is called deterrence. Although nuclear deterrence has taken a beating from many moralists, no one has yet come up with a better solution. In actuality, the theory of deterrence is as old as armed conflict. It means nothing more than doing those things, whether constructing fortifications, raising armies, taking hostages, or building nuclear bombs, that will discourage attack by an enemy force. What moralists dislike about nuclear deterrence is its implicit threat to actually use the weapons.[26] This is quite the ultimate paradox, however, because only the threat of nuclear weapons can offset the threat of other nuclear weapons (in the present state of technology). There is no other defense available. It is difficult to see how this is immoral in any easily understood sense of the term, considering that the alternative is to leave one's nation defenseless.

The real problem with deterrence is not in having nuclear weapons to back up the threat, but in having the will to use them in appropriate circumstances. It should be clear that "appropriate circumstances" are only the direst of national emergencies, but they must include retaliation for a first-strike nuclear attack against the United States or its allies. Without at least the opponent's perception of one's willingness to make good on the deterrent threat, there can be no deterrent effect from those forces. This is merely stating the obvious. To resolve the dilemma of maintaining a deterrent effect—which is good because it preserves the peace—while at the same time avoiding the immorality of intending to use nuclear weapons in an immoral way (note that almost any strategic use of nuclear weapons is going to produce harm disproportionate to any reasonable sense of conducting war as a "continuation of politics"[27]), some moralists have suggested that we either bluff or simply not declare our actual intent.

There are three problems with this approach. First, bluffing involves lying in one form or another. Second, the people who will actually fire these weapons are scattered all over the globe and they are carefully selected to ensure that they will be willing to push their respective buttons when the time comes. Further, contingency plans must be made to respond to various war scenarios. If, in fact, the United States intended under no circumstances to launch a strategic nuclear attack, it would not be long before the secret would be out and the deterrence effect would be eliminated. Third, an unresolved intent does not resolve the moral dilemma for the decisionmakers—the president of the United States and those military officers who will be involved in launching a nuclear response. These officials are entitled to feel comfortable in their own minds with the awesome responsibility that the nuclear balance of terror imposes upon them. On the other hand, a secret intent not to fire raises the opposite problem. The president is charged by the Constitution of the United States to defend the country. He cannot do this by idle threats. Similarly, American military officers take an oath to uphold the defense of their nation. Consider, then, the following "logic tree":

- Defending the nation is a moral obligation of the highest order for soldiers.
- At present, nuclear deterrence is required for national defense.
- Deterrence requires credibility to be effective.
- There can be no lasting credibility without the will to implement a threat.
- Therefore, it is moral to respond to nuclear aggression with a nuclear attack that is as limited as circumstances permit to defend the United States.

Despite this argument, the consequences of the actual use of nuclear weapons would be so severe as to give any moral person great pause. What is the choice facing our President Cunningham? He can do nothing and accept the victory of the Soviet Union with all the dreadful consequences which might follow from that, including pogroms, gulags, suppression of individual freedoms, extermination of the great heritage of the United States, and world domination by an atheistic Communist party. Or, he can push his own button, in which case millions of Soviet citizens will die, the threshold for nuclear winter will be considerably lowered, and he will risk a second, more massive attack by the Soviet Union against the United States. What a choice! Is either one moral in any reasonable sense? Not in my opinion. So what should he do?

Three Possible Solutions

There appear to be only three ways out of this box we have created for ourselves. One is to find another means of defense. The Strategic Defense Initiative offers a glimmer of hope, but only a glimmer. Any effective defensive shield must be cheaper to maintain and expand than it would be to construct offensive systems to overcome it. It must be comprehensive enough to counter both ballistic systems and air-breathing systems, such as cruise missiles. It must be within the nation's fiscal capability to construct and operate. And it must be reliable. SDI is a long way from meeting any of these tests.

A second way out of our nuclear dilemma is arms control. But arms control has never resulted in major reductions from either power's strategic nuclear stockpiles, and not even the Intermediate-range Nuclear Forces agreement signed by President Reagan and Soviet leader Gorbachev in December 1987 alters this reality. All that such agreements have accomplished is to set limits on the expansion of each side's nuclear arsenal or reduce medium- and shorter-range nuclear missiles. Maintaining the status quo or improving it at the margins will not resolve our quandary. Unless there is a more substantial breakthrough in verification procedures, arms control offers little hope of ever eliminating the strategic nuclear threat completely even if START proves to have some success. Further, many thinkers have reservations about the risks of eliminating nuclear weapons, because that throws us back to reliance on conventional arms and armies. They fear that this will lower the threshold for war between the great powers. We got rid of Hitler, Tojo, and their henchmen in World War II, but beyond that not much good was accomplished for the fifty *million* deaths.[28] In any event, no one wants to pay such a price again, no matter what the weapon of choice. Therefore, arms control seems an unlikely cure for our total war fears.

Yet another problem with arms control is that it does not stop the technological race. Whenever any new weapon breakthrough occurs, it may be outside the scope of existing agreements, or it may induce the discoverer to renounce the restrictive agreement. Renunciation could be appealing to the discoverer because of the temptation to reap the fruits via a new strategic advantage or because it feared the other side would make the same discovery and secretly exploit it. SDI seems to fit both categories but is perhaps entitled to a more benevolent view because it is purely a defensive system.

A third way, the most radical but also the most promising as a long-term solution, is the establishment of some sort of world authority with enough power to enforce the renunciation-of-force doctrine in the United Nations Charter.[29] As the Catholic bishops noted in their pastoral letter, we have entered "an era of new, global interdependencies requiring global systems of governance to manage the resulting conflicts and ensure our common security."[30]

Whether we like it or not, the time is approaching when we must move on to a more effective, less dangerous governance than that embodied in the nation-state system that has served us since feudal times. We need not surrender all sovereignty. That is obviously unworkable. But we need to begin to explore ways to create an international body capable of at least enforcing the peace, an international sheriff's office complete with posse. Under this concept, military forces would no longer exist to implement state policy. Rather, their function would be to preserve international peace, much in the nature of a domestic police force.[31] To the extent that the impulse for war represents valid grievances, then an international enforcement authority must also include means of hearing and resolving such disputes. The political challenges inherent in linking disparate cultures, races, ideologies, and religions in a worldwide governing body, with merely a limited charter to prevent wars, are enormous. But we have made progress in that direction. Each of the World Wars of this century led to the creation of a world body intended to prevent future wars. The League of Nations was a dismal failure, perhaps primarily because the United States refused to participate. The United Nations is a significant improvement, but is impotent in the face of a Security Council veto. The potential tragedy facing us is that we may have to undergo one more worldwide trauma, one which will dwarf all those that have gone before, to make us realize we cannot have it both ways: we cannot have full independence and a world organization capable of enforcing the peace.

President Cunningham's Decision: . . . "All right, Ben," the president said. "God help us, and especially me when I face Him if I am wrong, but I don't think the Russians will launch their second attack if we respond against their forces only. In any event, I swore to uphold the Constitution, which lays responsibility for defending this country squarely on my shoulders. If we don't strike back, we've surrendered. I doubt the American people would forgive me for that. Hand me the 'football.' I am going to initiate Attack Option Amber—1000 missiles targeted only on Russian soil and only at their strategic nuclear weapon systems. No industrial centers and no major cities, especially Moscow, will be directly targeted. I want to make maximum use of our ICBMs and reserve our SLBMs, our nuke-capable aircraft in Europe, and our surviving strategic bomber force for any counterresponse that may yet be necessary. Get a message out to Lenintsov on the Hot Line five minutes before we launch, explaining what we are doing and warning the S.O.B. that if he launches his second wave he can kiss his country goodbye. And, Ben?"

"Yes, sir?" replied Colonel Thomas, caught in midstride.

"I won't be needing that helicopter. The Vice President should be airborne soon in his command center, and he can handle any subsequent actions if I've guessed wrong. If Lenintsov launches a second wave, it's only right that I should pay the price I will have charged to the entire nation."

NOTES

1. See, for example, James Turner Johnson, *Can Modern War Be Just?* (New Haven: Yale Univ. Press, 1984), p. 193; Michael Walzer, *Just and Unjust Wars* (New York: Basic Books, 1977), pp. 269, 282-83; National Conference of Catholic Bishops, *The Challenge of Peace: God's Promise and Our Response* (Washington: U.S. Catholic Conference, 1983), Art. 148, p. 47; Paul Ramsey, *The Just War* (New York: Scribner, 1968), p. 247; William V. O'Brien, "The Failure of Deterrence and the Conduct of War," in *The Nuclear Dilemma and the Just War Tradition*, ed. William V. O'Brien and John Langan (Lexington Mass.: Lexington Books, 1986), pp. 158, 176; Albert Carnesale et al., *Living with Nuclear Weapons* (New York: Bantam Books, 1983), p. 157.

2. Perhaps never was an utterance more perfectly attuned to its occasion than J. Robert Oppenheimer's quote from the Bhagavad Gita, 94:15, on 16 July 1945 at the explosion of the first atom bomb: "I am become death, the destroyer of worlds."
3. Compare the League of Nations Covenant, the Kellogg-Briand Pact (Pact of Paris, 1928), and Articles 2 and 51 of the United Nations Charter; Johnson, *Can Modern War Be Just?* p. 19; and James Turner Johnson, *Just War Tradition and the Restraint of War* (Princeton, N.J.: Princeton Univ. Press, 1981), p. 30.
4. Johnson *Can Modern War Be Just?* pp. 19, 176. See also Abbott A. Brayton and Stephana J. Landwehr, *The Politics of War and Peace: A Survey of Thought* (Washington: Univ. Press of America, 1981), pp. 64-66.
5. Donald L. Davidson, *Nuclear Weapons and the American Churches: Ethical Positions on Modern Warfare* (Boulder, Colo.: Westview Press, 1983), pp. 5-7.
6. Ibid., pp. 26-28; compare *The Challenge of Peace*, Art. 313, p. 94.
7. Davidson, pp. 6-7.
8. Walzer, pp. 151-59.
9. Davidson, p. 28; U.S. Department of the Army, *The Law of Land Warfare*, Field Manual 27-10 (Washington: GPO, 1956), pp. 15-16. Paragraphs 20-27 present the formal treaty rules for the commencement of hostilities.
10. Davidson, pp. 29-31.
11. Ibid., p. 29.
12. Ibid., p. 32.
13. Ibid.
14. Johnson, *Can Modern War Be Just?* pp. 129-30.
15. Ibid., p. 129.
16. See B. H. Liddell Hart, *History of the Second World War* (New York: Putnam, 1972), pp. 594-97. Hart openly characterizes this policy as "terrorisation" (pp. 596-97). Walzer, however, says it was a justified overriding of those restraints on the grounds of "supreme emergency," based upon reasonable perceptions of the British government at the time (Walzer, pp. 259-61).
17. Martin van Creveld, *Military Lessons of the Yom Kippur War: Historical Perspectives* (Beverly Hills, Calif.: Sage, 1975), p. 49: "It is one of the clichés of our time that, under modern conditions, warmaking capability and the other constituents of society—its demographic, economic, and political power—are inescapably linked together as never before; hence, that it is the totality of the state's forces and not its military instrument alone that wins or loses wars."
18. Philip J. Romero, *Nuclear Winter: Implications for U.S. and Soviet Nuclear Strategy* (Santa Monica, Calif.: Rand, 1984), pp. 1, 3, 8.
19. Davidson (p. 7) lists four conditions which are required before unjustifiable collateral effects may be permitted as a result of an otherwise lawful military action: (1) the effect must be unavoidable; (2) the actor's intention must be right—he does not intend to cause the collateral damage; (3) the unintended effect may not be a means to the intended effect; and (4) the unintended effect is not disproportionate to the intended effect.
20. Peter Young, ed., *World Almanac Book of World War II* (New York: World Almanac Publications, 1981), p. 330.
21. Ibid., p. 220.
22. Ibid., p. 324.
23. Ibid., pp. 352-53.
24. Ibid., p. 352.
25. Compare Walzer's "supreme emergency" theory, which he posits as a basic survival interest of the state which overrides normal application of just war principles (Walzer, pp. 252-68). For an excellent critique of Walzer's theory, see David Hollenbach, "Ethics in Distress: Can There Be Just Wars in the Nuclear Age?" in O'Brien and Langan, pp. 15-17.
26. "But the unavoidable truth is that all these policies rest ultimately on immoral threats. Unless we give up nuclear deterrence, we cannot give up such threats, and it is best if we straightforwardly acknowledge what it is we are doing" (Walzer, p. 282).
27. From Carl von Clausewitz's famous dictum: "We see, therefore, that war is not merely an act of policy but a true political instrument, a continuation of political intercourse, carried on with other means." Carl von Clausewitz, *On War*, ed. Michael Howard and Peter Paret

(Princeton, N.J.: Princeton Univ. Press, 1984), p. 87.

28. According to David Wood ("Conflict in the Twentieth Century," *Adelphi Papers*, No. 48, p. 26), 17 million military and 34,305,000 civilian personnel were killed or died of injuries in World War II. Demonstrating that a war without disproportionate civilian casualties and without the horrors of obliteration bombing can still be an affront to just war principles was the killing of 8½ million soldiers during World War I (Wood, p. 24), a conflict which accomplished nothing other than to set the stage for World War II's far worse carnage.
29. Article 2(4), UN Charter provides: "All members shall refrain in their international relations from the threat of use of force against the territorial integrity or political independence of any state, or in any other matter inconsistent with the Purposes of the United Nations." Note, also, Article 51: "Nothing in the present Charter shall impair the inherent right of individual or collective self-defense if an armed attack occurs against a Member of the United Nations, until the Security Council has taken measures necessary to maintain international peace and security."
30. National Conference of Catholic Bishops, *The Challenge of Peace*, p. 75.
31. See ibid., Art. 310, p. 94: "The purpose of defense policy is to defend the peace; military professionals should understand their vocation this way."

This article originally appeared in the March 1988 issue of *Parameters*.

5

Morality and the Nuclear Peril

By WILLIAM BARRETT

For some time a fragment of an imaginary conversation has been running through my mind; it goes something like this: My grandson asks me, "Grandfather, what were you doing before we capitulated to the Russians?" And I answer, "Grandson, I was debating the logical niceties of war and morality among my philosopher colleagues." With the way things are now going, the speed with which the balance of power is tilting against us, I may not have to wait for my grandson to ask the question.

All philosophical and moral questions are carried in the context of our actual situation. When the actuality is benign, we tend to forget it, and we seem free for a while to spin our hypothetical and contra-factual cases in the thin air of abstraction. But even in such cases of ease and relaxation we proceed at our peril if we forget this fact of actuality; the actual situation must always be part of our human context. The options we face in life—the big ones—as William James reminded us, are usually forced options, ones we wouldn't face at all if we didn't have to. In the present case, in the situation of the world as it now stands, this actuality is so urgent and threatening that we could not forget it if we wanted to, though I must admit that a good deal of philosophical discussion often seems to take place as if that actuality never existed.

Two predominant conditions define our present situation in the world today. First is the fact that the United States is confronted by an implacable enemy in the form of the Soviet Union. This enemy, moreover, is not a nation-state in any traditional sense and is not to be dealt with wholly within the framework of traditional diplomacy, despite the naivete of some of our officials. How can you enter into reliable agreements with a state that for the more than 68 years of its existence has not dealt even minimal justice to its own citizens? Further, as a communist state, it is the spearhead and leading power of international communism.

The American people and most of their politicians still do not understand the nature of communism. Perhaps only ex-Marxists or those dissidents who have lived under Marxist rule grasp it. But this brief article is not the occasion to dwell on that fact. Since our subject here is morality, or touches on morality, suffice it to say that the communist state is an evil, an oppressive blight on the human spirit, organized with all the apparatus and weapons of the modern age. This evil thing, furthermore, is committed to our destruction. That ultimate hostility is both a part of communist doctrine and a necessity for it in practice. The communist state cannot stand long beside the capitalist world in peaceful coexistence and competition. The discrepancy becomes too glaring. "West Berlin," Khrushchev remarked, "sticks like a bone in my throat." Why? It was not a military threat. Quite simply, the contrast between East and West at that focal point was too uncomfortable and shocking. In the same sense, the United States sticks like a bone in the throat of the whole communist world. So far as the communists are concerned, the bone has to be eliminated.

The second overriding fact in our actual situation is the presence of nuclear weapons. It might have been well if such weapons had never been invented, or invented only after humanity had become morally mature and the planet was at peace. (But there one begins to drift off into hypotheticals—which, alas, is so easy to do.) The facts are that these weapons exist, we have them, and the other side has them. In this situation any option we elect is bound to be a forced option. What to do then? As moral individuals pursuing the moral aspect of the matter, we naturally think of these weapons and the awful havoc they will wreak if ever used, and we recoil. Why not renounce them altogether? That would seem to be the clearcut way to moral purity, perhaps even sanctity (though we might remember there have been saints among the warriors as well as the peacemakers).

The answer to the foregoing question, obviously, is that the other side would not follow suit and our unilateral disarmament would, in fact, be capitulation. Of course, as has been suggested by some, we could follow the path of passive resistance in the manner of Gandhi in India; in due time, and without the destruction of nuclear war, liberty might slowly and painfully reappear upon this earth. Such was the rationale, when any was offered, behind the slogan "Better red than dead" when it first gained currency in the 1950s. The example of Gandhi's passive resistance, however, would not be altogether relevant to that future situation of capitulation. Gandhi was dealing with British rulers bound by their own traditional moral compunctions and sense of fair play; he was not dealing with an implacable communist regime. Furthermore, the British rule was already there when Gandhi began his crusade; he did not invite the British in by capitulation in order then to practice passive resistance against them.

If not capitulation, then, the only other choice open to us is resistance. Indeed, if we are concerned with the morality of the matter, there should be no doubt of the propriety of this option. In the face of so grim an evil, so distorting of the human mind and spirit, our duty would plainly be to resist with all the energy and powers we command. But—and this point must be emphasized—a token or half-hearted resistance would be equivalent to capitulation. We are brought up abruptly at this point by the unpleasant reality of nuclear weapons. If we are not to capitulate, it follows that we do not renounce these weapons. What then? Do we sit on the stockpiles of nuclear weapons as our deterrent? The other side is not proceeding so passively. Those in the Soviet high command pursue a strategy other than mere deterrence. Their war plans envisage a nuclear war as a war that they can successfully wage and win. Because of the greater dispersion of their cities and population, and because the communist leaders are willing to accept a rate of civilian casualties far in excess of what we would find tolerable, they calculate that nuclear war could provide them a significant comparative advantage.

We can thus expect that some day the following scenario might be enacted: During a certain crisis in our relations with the Soviet Union—say, something like the Cuban missile crisis in 1962—their leader approaches our president and declares, "We are ready for atomic war, are you?" At this point the American president backs down, and the first step in our surrender has been taken. Here, terrorism seems to have become a principle of statecraft. Perhaps in this period of ubiquitous and random terrorism—the age of assassins prophesied so amazingly by the French poet Rimbaud in the 1890s—it is only proper, after all, that the terrorist philosophy should find its official embodiment and codification in a nation-state.

Yet this terrorist aspect of the situation should not weaken, but in fact should strengthen, the force of the moral imperative that claims us, or that ought to claim us: the imperative, namely, that we resist the evil all the more when it shows its most violent side. But, just here, alas, tactical complexities of a moral as well as a military nature tend to becloud our sense of the basic imperative. There is a wise remark by Kant, one of his most profound, though philosophers in the hunt for more subtle matters tend to overlook it; Kant remarked that the honest citizen, the decent citizen, knows what his duty is—he does not have to learn it through the dialectic of philosophers. If this were not so, the moral life of mankind could not be carried on and the race would have long since foundered. I know that it is wrong to lie, without being required antecedently to settle all the tactical complications and circumstances in detail that lying or telling the truth in any given situation may bring with them. It would be regrettable, though I am sorry to say that it seems to have happened among some intellectuals, if those casuistical complexities were allowed to weaken the force of the original imperative; we would begin then, because we hadn't settled all the dialectical details, to question whether it was really wrong, after all, to lie. Now it is even more difficult to settle the intricate questions of what might constitute a just or unjust act of war in given situations. But does one have to resolve these questions in advance to know that tyranny and terror ought to be opposed?

In any actual situation the distinction between a first strike and a completely justified preemptive strike could be a very academic and formalistic question to settle. A terrorist appears in a plane brandishing a bomb, and holds the passengers captive. At a certain moment he turns away carelessly and I, happening to have a pocketknife handy, stab him in the back and kill him. Afterward, one of the passengers, a young pedantic squirt, protests that the terrorist's back was turned and I really didn't have to kill him. In fact, we found out later that the bomb wasn't activated. But I doubt whether the young man's protests would win the sympathy of the other passengers. Now, in retrospect, I wonder—and I say "wonder," for I am just entertaining this question—whether the argument for a preventive war advanced in the late 1940s when the Soviets did not yet have the bomb—and advanced by, surprisingly enough, Bertrand Russell among others—I wonder whether the argument would appear so shocking to some of us now as we look back on it from this particular point in time. Of course, the whole occasion has vanished, but it makes an interesting topic for moral conjecture.

But, such conjecture aside, my main point comes back to that of Kant: we can know our moral duty in a certain situation without having resolved antecedently all the difficulties or complexities that may attend it, and we cannot let the deliberation upon these latter weaken our primary resolves. Details, of course, have to be attended to and if possible planned for. But he who enters any situation with a firm purpose is more likely to find that the details fall in place, and above all the opponent will know when he encounters that strength of purpose and will perforce respect it.

It is the morality of calculation that is more likely to find itself at sea in the details of the actual situation and in consequence become irresolute and infirm of purpose. The responsibility of the individual here and now, whether we call the present situation war or not, is to maintain this resoluteness and not to succumb to the spirit of appeasement that in so many subtle forms is now adrift throughout the land.

"So, dear Grandson, I come back to you at the end. It is my duty to do all in my power to make sure that the imaginary conversation spoken of at the beginning can never take place. In any case, if anything like it should, I could not be a party to it, for it would have to take place over my dead body!"

This article originally appeared under the title "Morality and the Present Peril" in the March 1981 issue of *Parameters*.

6

Military Intervention in Civil Wars: Do Law and Morality Conflict?

By TELFORD TAYLOR

Despite frequently heard statements to the contrary, nations today do not live in a Hobbesian world—that is, in a pure state of nature. Unlike the beasts of the jungle, mankind is forever talking about, and even doing something about, the extension of law to govern quarrels and disagreements among nations. The effective rule of international law is still a remote prospect, but the talk and the deeds—in modern times focused in international organizations such as the League of Nations and the United Nations—are part of the contemporary scene, and they considerably influence the play of both force and morals among the nations.

Neither the duty nor the wisdom of abiding by the relevant provisions of international law is unanimously acknowledged. There are those who argue that there is a morality that transcends law, and that a nation's acts may be moral even though illegal. Specifically with regard to the question of intervening in civil wars, the question can be framed thus: Are situations ever likely to arise where we as a nation should flout international law on the ground that intervention, rather than nonintervention, is the moral course of action? The answer, I believe, is no. I do not believe that law and morality can be so casually thrown into separate compartments, or that the supposed conflict is a necessary one. Analysis will reveal, as I hope to show, that our national interests—which sometimes may mandate intervention—can be served by a proper regard for both law and morality.

I am well aware that the validity, including the consistency, of my position is by no means self-evident, and that I must give it some foundation before decorating the superstructure. Are legal prohibitions as flexible as I have implied? Is there any logic or policy in a system under which those affected by the law are entitled to weigh its importance and interpret it in their favor when considerations of morals or policy so dictate? And if we look either at the classic texts on international law or at the Charter of the United Nations, do we not find, in the former, explicit injunctions against aid to either side in civil strife once the insurgents are recognized as belligerents, and, in the latter, prohibition of intervention in matters of domestic jurisdiction and of forceful violation of the territory or independency of any state?

There is distinguished support for the point of view that we can extract only a very rigorous set of prohibitions against intervention in civil strife from either the UN Charter or the classic texts.[1] But I believe that this absolutist position is based on unsound premises. Furthermore, I believe it can be shown that the gulf between law and morals or policy in this context is not so wide or unbridgeable as is often supposed.

Looking first at such classic writings as those of Lassa F. L. Oppenheim, Sir Hersh Lauterpacht, Donald C. Hodges, and many others, one does find,in varying forms, the general position that civil war, as long as its course threatens no other nation, is an internal or "domestic" matter from which other nations must, in law, stand aloof. But these pronouncements must be read in the context of other passages in which exceptions to the rule—including self-preservation, maintenance of the balance of power, and the prevention of atrocities—are sometimes discussed with approval. The views of these writers of past generations are by no means unanimous or unqualified, and, great as is the respect in which some of them are held, theirs are mere learned opinions, not treaties or collective declarations of an official nature.

Much more important, however, is the fact that these writings are the product of a period when war was regarded as a lawful means of achieving national objectives. Our own Army's famous General Order No. 100, drafted by Dr. Francis Lieber, then of Columbia University, and promulgated in 1863, speaks of war not as something unlawful, but as "the means to obtain great ends of state, or . . . defenses against wrong"; and this remained the accepted view at least until after World War I and, in some quarters, much longer. Oppenheim himself described intervention as "*de facto* a matter of policy just like war."[2] Thus an intervention could always be "legalized" by a declaration of war, a device actually resorted to by Great Britain and Germany during the Venezuela dispute in 1901. The point has been cogently made by the late Professor Brierly:

> The extremist form of intervention is war, and until recently modern international law . . . has not attemped to distinguish between legal and illegal occasions for making war. . . . There was a certain unreality in attempting to formulate a law of intervention and at the same time admitting, as until recently it was necessary to admit, that a state might go to war for any cause or for no cause at all without any breach of law.[3]

Viewed closely, therefore, these pre-1945 condemnations of intervention do not really label it as intrinsically *unlawful*, but as *unneutral*. If a nation wished to preserve a state of neutrality with both the incumbent government and the insurgent belligerent, it had to stay out of the quarrel. Thus, prior to 1945, the law of intervention is really part of the law of neutrality rather than the law of war.[4]

The benchmark year is 1945, which witnessed the international adoption of the London Agreement under which the Nuremberg trials were held and the UN Charter. Both of these documents condemn and purport to render unlawful the initiation of aggressive wars, and both recognize, explicitly or implicitly, the right to use force in self-defense. The charter embodies an international agreement that disputes be peacefully settled and that breaches of the charter be dealt with by collective action through the UN organization, and it likewise prohibits interference in matters within a state's domestic jurisdiction. I think it is beyond argument that these documents worked a fundamental change in the legal structure of international society, that the provisions I have mentioned constitute binding international law to the full extent that any international agreement constitutes law, and that the U.S. government is fully committed to observance of these limitations on the use of force.

But the foregoing statement of the problem is incomplete; indeed, it is only a beginning. The framers of the charter saw clearly enough that the organization might disintegrate should the Security Council embark on collective forcible action over the objection of one or more of its Great Power members, and the so-called "veto" provision (Article 27) was adopted as a guard against that hazard. However, the result is that there may be, as there have been, situations in which collective enforcement through the United Nations is, in effect, embargoed. And the "uniting for peace" resolutions of the General Assembly, adopted during the Korean War, go only a very little way toward coping with that difficulty.

Well aware of these probable consequences, the charter framers recognized the "inherent right of individual or collective self-defense" against "armed attack" (Article 51), as well as "regional arrangements" for dealing with "matters relating to the maintenance of international peace and security" which are "appropriate for regional action" (Article 52). The charter thus explicitly envisages the legitimacy of individual or group resort to force outside the charter's enforcement provisions.

But "outside" the charter does not mean "in conflict with" it. Nothing in Articles 51 and 52 or elsewhere absolves states acting outside the charter from respecting the purposes on which the charter is based and its prohibitions against acts of aggression and other breaches of peace. From a legal standpoint, the question is whether these limiting provisions stand in the way of American interventions of the type which many—including myself—would regard as pragmatically and morally justified. In my opinion, they do not.

There are, of course, problems in construing the general language of the charter. "Self-defense" and "aggression" are words denoting abstractions, the application of which in particular instances will forever arouse disagreement. But that is a failing which afflicts many specifications of prohibited or protected conduct, as every lawyer knows. "Aggression" and "self-defense" are not meaningless concepts, and they are no less precise in contour than "negligence," "reasonable care," "due process of law," "equal protection," or "obscenity," to name only a few of the phrases that courts constantly wrestle with.

The primary difficulty is not with the wording of these provisions, but with the lack of any interpretive and enforcing authority which law-abiding nations will respect and other nations fear. It is idle to expect the emergence of such an authority in the foreseeable future; therefore, in the present turbulent state of international relations, and considering that the United Nations' actions are now generally restricted to investigative and conciliatory steps, we must expect continuing use of armed force. Those using it will seek to justify it under Article 51, and those opposing it will condemn it under paragraphs 4 and 7 of Article 2. Some of these justifications will be transparent, some debatable, and perhaps some well-founded. The judgments passed on these episodes by both the countries involved and the onlookers will be subjective and heavily influenced by ideological and bloc viewpoints.

In looking for objective factors to bring to bear on the interpretation and application of problematic Charter terms such as "domestic jurisdiction," "threat to peace," and "act of aggression," there are two factors I would like to stress. The first is that official spokesmen for the Soviet government, including General Alexsei Yepishev (Chief of the Political Department of the Soviet armed forces) and Stepan Chervonenko (Ambassador to France), in 1979 proclaimed extension of the so-called "Brezhnev Doctrine" not only to the forcible maintenance of friendly communist regimes anywhere in the world, but also to the use of armed force to overthrow "bourgeois" governments.[5] This is flagrantly contrary to the charter stipulations and, threatening as it does that the march of communism backed by force will always be an advance and never a retreat, greatly increases the risk to the security of other nations and the degree of danger to peace inherent in any Soviet intervention, such as Afghanistan.

The second factor is that, despite the mention of "armed attack" in Article 51 of the charter, the right of self-defense should not be regarded as triggered only by such action.[6] The world is much more tightly knit economically than it was when the charter was adopted, and action involving no armed force may sometimes be more lethal than an armed attack. A good example would be the intentional blockage of the Strait of Hormuz by means of sunken ships, assuming such is technically feasible. That, or stopping the flow of Mideast oil by other means, might not only be economically disastrous to other nations, but also soon render them virtually defenseless, and would, I believe, furnish a basis for collective counteraction under Article 51.

In summary, I think it possible and indeed probable that the United States in shaping its policies will not have to face a conflict between morality and legality. The UN Charter is more like a constitution than a municipal ordinance; many of its provisions are like those in our Constitution which have been called "magnificent generalities," the intent of which is to provide a basis in the future, with changing circumstances, to do what needs to be done to preserve the essential structure intact.

In presenting this point of view, by no means do I suggest that our country should throw its military weight around except in circumstances of clear necessity. I would not countenance the cynical notion that because the charter provisions are general they can be bent to any desired purpose. Use of the word "intervention" does not obscure the fact that intervention by force of arms, unless the victim is both friendless and too weak to offer resistance, means war. Geopolitics is an even less exact science than domestic politics, and even unopposed interventions may entail ultimate consequences adverse to the intervenor.

For 68 years, nations have been in search of a more stable international order through international organization. The very fact that these efforts persist, despite the often discouraging course of events, bears witness to the depth of feeling which animates the aspiring architects. Why else do men of intelligence, with wide and varying opportunities to invest their energies, carry on the work of shaping declarations and norms for the governance of international relations? Despite the ambiguities in the General Assembly Declarations of 1965 and 1970,[7] the general thrust of these unanimously adopted resolutions is unmistakably anti-interventionist.

I would like at this point to return for a moment to the matter of the "Brezhnev Doctrine," which I broached earlier, and the continued aggressive march of communism across the world's stage. The threat to world order posed by this communist march is sometimes facilely equated to that posed by the Nazis, but in my opinion the importance of the question does not lie in trying to strike a balance of evil, but in noting differences between German Nazism and Soviet Communism which are, I think, pertinent to our present subject.

If one looks back at the situation in 1933 when Hitler took power and compares it with the situation in 1917 when the communist regime in Russia took power, the differences are extraordinary. Hitler came into power in a country that was heavily industrialized and possessed a large, well-educated middle class, extensive professional and technological resources, an extraordinarily impressive military history, and an officer corps of acknowledged competence. The communist authorities in Russia came to power in a country that had a thin layer of artists, intellectuals, engineers, scientists, and others, but it was very thin indeed. Russia was underdeveloped and had a low level of general education and scant technological resources.

What did the two countries do with what they had? The Germans, of course, created a military striking force of extraordinary strength, but with short staying power. Why was it that Britain, with far less resources than Germany, was able in 1940 to pass Germany in the production of aircraft? Why was it that when Albert Speer took charge of the German war economy in 1943 he was able to pick things up so much? It was because there was so much slack in the system owing to the superficial economic organization for war under the Nazis, typified by the lack of reliance on the industrial power of women, and many other things that could be mentioned.

In contrast, despite all their disadvantages, the Soviet Union has built up an enormous, well-equipped, and technologically developed military machine. More important than that, they have a decision-making procedure far better than anything the impulsive, now-brilliant, now-blind, sort of direction that the personality of Adolf Hitler produced.

Therefore, in terms of the degree of threat, it seems to me that there is no comparison between the two. The threat from communism, organized the way it is, is far the greater. Even more important than that is the fact that there was very little of Nazism that had appeal much beyond Germany's borders, while there are proclaimed values in communism that have a deep and wide appeal. Why did we have the proliferation of those who were called, at the time, "fellow travelers" in the 30s? Because there were many who had no interest in violent revolution, but regarded the Communist party as offering the only road to stable race relations, unionization, and other social goals. Many of these values are still proclaimed by communism. It has a wide intrinsic appeal. And, coming now to the present day, the Soviet Union has, at least until recently, been much shrewder than we in its sensitivity to and ability to exploit the worldwide move toward national self-determination and nationalism in general. Thus we have been repeatedly cast in the position of seeming to back the incumbent against the insurgent, and the "reactionary" values against the revolutionary nationalist aspirations of others.

This is obviously a factor which we haven't yet overcome, a factor which we must take account of in assessing not only the prospect of success in our military initiatives, but also the probable reaction in the rest of the world. Part of the opinion of the rest of the world is embodied in the United Nations and the prohibitions the charter embodies. I suggest therefore that the value of due regard for the purposes and spirit of the charter is not only legally and morally valid, but also is eminently practical as a matter of enlightened self-interest.

NOTES

1. See e.g. Derek W. Bowett, "The Interrelation of Theories of Intervention and Self-Defense," in *Law and Civil War in the Modern World*, ed. J. N. Moore (Baltimore: Johns Hopkins Press, 1974), pp. 38-50.
2. Lauterpacht, as editor, struck this passage from the 5th edition of Oppenheim's *International Law* (London: Longman's, Green, 1937) on the ground that he thought it inconsistent with other passages. See the 5th edition, vol. I, p. 265, note 3.
3. J. L. Brierly, *The Law of Nations*, 5th ed. (Oxford: Clarendon Press, 1955), pp. 308-09.
4. See Lassa F. L. Oppenheim, *International Law*, ed. H. Lauterpacht, 7th ed. (London: Longman's, Green, 1960), vol. II, pp. 659-60, for an implicit acceptance of the analysis above.
5. See "Soviet General Says Entire Bloc is Ready to Fight in Afghanistan," *The New York Times*, 12 April 1980, p. A6; and "Kremlin's European Policy," *The New York Times*, 22 April 1980, p. A14.

6. See the discussion of this point by Sir Humphrey Waldock in Brierly, *The Law of Nations*, 6th ed. (Oxford: Clarendon Press, 1963), pp. 417-18, the thrust of which appears to be unanswerable.
7. General Assembly Resolution 2151 (21 December 1965) and 2625 (24 October 1970).

This article originally appeared in the June 1981 issue of *Parameters*.

II. THE ETHICAL DIMENSION OF MILITARY PROFESSIONALISM

7

Two Kinds of Military Responsibility

By MICHAEL WALZER

It is one of the purposes of any institutional hierarchy, and most especially of the bureaucratic or military chain of command, to resolve questions of responsibility. Who is responsible to whom, and for what? That is what the organizational chart is supposed to show. Once an official or a soldier locates himself on the chart, or in the chain of command, he ought to know exactly who his superiors are and who his subordinates are and what they rightly can expect of him.

Let us consider now the hierarchical position of a middle-level officer in time of war, a field commander responsible for making tactical decisions. He has a twofold responsibility that can be described in simple directional terms. First, he is responsible *upward*—to his military commanders and then through the highest of them, the commander-in-chief, to the sovereign people, whose "officer" he properly is and to whose collective safety and protection he is pledged. His obligation is to win the battles that he fights, or rather, to do his best to win, obeying the legal orders of his immediate superiors, fitting his own decisions into the larger strategic plan, accepting onerous but necessary tasks, seeking collective success rather than individual glory. He is responsible for assignments unperformed or badly performed and for all avoidable defeats. And he is responsible up the chain to each of his superiors in turn and ultimately to the ordinary citizens of his country who are likely to suffer for his failures.

But there are other people likely to suffer for his failures and, often enough, for his successes too—namely, the soldiers that he commands. And so he is also responsible *downward*—to each and every one of them. His soldiers are in one sense the instruments with which he is supposed to win victories, but they are also men and women whose lives, because they are his to use, are also in his care. He is bound to minimize the risks his soldiers must face, to fight carefully and prudently, and to avoid wasting their lives, that is, to persist in battles that cannot be won, to not seek victories whose costs overwhelm their military value, and so on. And his soldiers have every right to expect all this of him and to blame him for every sort of omission, evasion, carelessness, and recklessness that endangers their lives.

Now these two sets of responsibilities, up and down the chain of command, together constitute what I shall call the hierarchical responsibilities of the officer. I assume that there can be tensions between the two, and that these tensions are commonly experienced in the field. They have to do with the regret that officers must feel that the primary instruments with which they fight are human beings, to whom they are morally connected. But I don't think that there can be direct conflicts and contradictions between upward and downward responsibility. For there is only one hierarchy; a single chain of command; in principle, at least, a singular conception of victory; and finally a commitment up and down the chain to win that victory. It cannot be the case, then, that a commander who sacrifices his soldiers, so long as he does the best he can to minimize the extent of the sacrifice, does anything that he does not have a right to do. Whenever I read about trench warfare in World War I, I can hardly avoid the sense that the officers who sent so many soldiers to their deaths for so little gain in one attack after another were literally mad. But if that is so, the madness was reiterated at every level of the hierarchy—up to the level where political leaders stubbornly refused every compromise that might have ended the war. And so officers further down, at least those who carefully prepared for each successive attack and called off the attacks when it was clear that they had failed, did not act unjustly, while officers who were neither careful in advance nor willing later on to admit failure can readily be condemned for violating their hierarchical responsibilities. And all this is true even if the war as a whole, or the continuation of the war, was unjustified, and even if this way of fighting it was insane. I do not think it can ever be impermissible for an officer to send his soldiers into battle: that is what he is for and that is what they are for.

But the case is very different, I think, when we come to consider the officer's responsibilities for the civilian casualties of the battles he fights. As a moral agent, he is also responsible *outward*—to all those people whose lives his activities affect. This is a responsibility that we all have, since we are all moral agents, and it is, at least in the first instance, non-hierarchical in character. No organizational chart can possibly determine our duties or obligations to other people generally. What we ought to do when we face outward is determined by divine or natural law, or by a conception of human rights, or by a utilitarian calculation in which everyone's interest, and not only those up and down the hierarchy, must be counted. However that determination works out in particular cases, it is clear that the duties or obligations of moral agents may well conflict with the demands of the organizations they serve. In the case of a state or army at war, the conflict is often dramatic and painful. The civilians whose lives are put at risk are commonly neither superiors nor subordinates; they have no place in the hierarchy. The injuries done to them can be and often are wrongful, and, what is most important, they can be wrongful (so I want to argue) even if they are done in the course of military operations carried out in strict accordance with the precepts of hierarchical responsibility.

The distinction that I have drawn between the two kinds of military responsibility—the hierarchical and non-hierarchical—is, of course, too sharp and neat. There has been an effort of long-standing to incorporate the second of these into the first, that is, to make soldiers answerable to their officers for crimes committed against the civilian population and to make officers answerable to their superiors (and even to their enemies) for the crimes committed by their soldiers. This is a commendable effort, and I don't want to underestimate its value. But I think it is fair to say that it has not been very successful. It works best with regard to those crimes against civilians that are, so to speak, superfluous to the war effort as a whole—and best of all when the superfluousness is a matter of indiscipline. The ordinary desire of a commander to retain command of his soldiers will lead him to repress indiscipline as best he can and to hold his soldiers to a high and consistent standard of conduct. At least, it should do that: for the best soldiers, the best fighting men, do not loot and rape. Similarly, the best soldiers do not wantonly kill civilians. Massacres of the My Lai sort are most often the result of fear and rage, and neither of these emotions makes for the maximum efficiency of the "war-machine" that soldiers sometimes ought to be. Like looting and rape, massacre is militarily as well as morally reprehensible, for it represents a loss of control as well as a criminal act, and so it is more or less easily dealt with in hierarchical terms.

I say "more or less easily" because even superfluous injury often takes place within a context of command and obedience: My Lai is again an example. What we require of soldiers in that situation is that they refuse the orders—the illegal or immoral orders—of their immediate superior. That refusal does not constitute a denial of or a rebellion against the military hierarchy. It is best understood as an appeal up the chain of command over a superior officer to the superiors of that superior officer. Given the structure of the chain and its purposes, any such appeal is problematic and difficult, a matter of considerable strain for the individual who undertakes it. He is still operating, however, within the conventions of hierarchical responsibility.

But when the killing of civilians is plausibly connected to some military purpose, those conventions seem to provide no recourse at all. Neither in the case of direct and intended killing, as in siege warfare or terror bombing, nor in the case of incidental and unintended killing, as in the bombardment of a military target that results in a disproportionate number of civilian deaths, is there any effective responsibility up or down the hierarchy. I don't mean that individuals are not responsible for such killings, only that there is no hierarchical way of holding them responsible or at least no *effective* hierarchical way of so holding them. Nor is there any way of pointing to the organizational chart and explaining to whom responsibility can be attributed. For in these cases, the hierarchy seems to be working very much as it was meant to work. Here are victories, let's assume, victories won at a wonderfully low cost to the soldiers who win them. Their commanding officer can look up and down the hierarchy and feel good about what he is doing.

I should make that last point more strongly: the officer can look up and down the hierarchy and feel that he is doing what he ought to be doing. He is pursuing victory with all the means at his disposal, which is what his superiors want him to do, and what we, as members of the sovereign people, want him to do. And he is pursuing victory at the least possible cost to his own soldiers, which is no doubt what they want him to do. And so he meets the moral requirements of his hierarchical position. It is worth noticing that these are exactly the moral requirements that President Truman claimed to be meeting when he approved the use of the atomic bomb on Hiroshima. He made his decision, so he told us in his radio broadcast of 9 August 1945, in order to end the war and to save American lives. Those two purposes, he seemed to assume, exhausted his responsibilities. And that is not an implausible assumption if we think of him only as a commander-in-chief of a nation and an army at war.

We can say, I think, that Truman's argument does address the full range of his hierarchial, but not the full range of his moral, responsibilities. But he might have gone on to argue—though it is important to say that he did not go on to argue—that he knew himself to be responsible as a human being and a moral agent for all the civilian deaths caused by his decision. But, he might still have said, his responsibility to the American people as a whole and to individual American soldiers took precedence over his responsibility for Japanese civilians because of his hierarchical position. And any officer further down the hierarchy could make the same argument: that his oath of office and his immediate bond to his soldiers determine what he ought to do, whatever other considerations he might acknowledge.

Now, if this argument encompassed the whole truth, then the killing of civilians, so long as it was connected to some military purpose, could no more conflict with hierarchical responsibilities than the different sorts of hierarchical responsibilities could conflict with one another. Civilians would be subordinated, exactly as soldiers are, to military purposiveness, and then further subordinated to the safety and preservation of our own soldiers (and the other side would subordinate civilians in exactly the same way). In effect, they would be incorporated into the hierarchy at its lowest point and recognized within the system of hierarchical responsibility only when they were needlessly and superfluously attacked. But this incorporation is nothing more than an act of conquest and tyranny. For the civilians whose lives are at stake are citizens of other countries who have no place in *this* hierarchy. The middle-level officer that I am considering is not their agent; no legal or bureaucratic procedures make him answerable to them. Nor are they his agents, subject to his command, submitted to his care and protection. Indeed, he sees them only when he looks outward, away from his hierarchical responsibilities. And if he is to recognize them, to attend to their interests and rights, he may well have to turn away from his hierarchical responsibilities and diminish the care and protection he affords to his own soldiers—that is, he may have to impose added risks on the soldiers for the sake of the civilians. The conflict, then, is a real one.

Because the conflict is real, it is vitally important that it be mediated in some institutional form. But I don't know of any easy or obvious way of specifying, let alone of establishing, the appropriate form. Ideally, an army ought to be watched and checked by something like a civilian board of review. But if we think of the place that such boards occupy alongside police departments in some of our major cities, we can immediately see the problems that would arise in the case of an army. For while the board of review represents civilians as potential victims of policy neglect or brutality, those same civilians are also the ultimate employers of the police. They elect the mayor who appoints the police chief, and so on. They have a place in the urban chain of command, perhaps a double place, at the top and bottom of the chain. But citizens of other countries have, as I have just argued, no place at all in the chain and no power over the political leaders who appoint army generals. They are potential victims, and that is all they are, and we cannot imagine them effectively represented by any civilian board of review.

They might be represented internationally, by a court like the Nuremberg tribunal after World War II. But it is an interesting feature of the decisions made at Nuremberg and by the associated courts that they did not go very far toward enforcing the non-hierarchical responsibilities of soldiers. Mostly, they worked at the margins of the moral space that I have meant to mark out with that term, condemning individual officers for the killing of hostages, of sailors helpless in the water, and of prisoners of war. But they convicted no one for siege warfare or terror bombing or any form of disregard for civilian lives. In part, this was because these kinds of warfare were by no means peculiar to the Germans. In part, it was because the legal status of these kinds of warfare is at best uncertain. Traditionally, in the laws of war, hierarchical responsibilities have dominated non-hierarchical responsibilities. Recent revisions of the law, at Geneva in 1949 and again in 1978, have not produced any radical challenge to that domination.

I must conclude, therefore, that the non-hierarchical responsibilities of officers have, at this moment, no satisfactory institutional form. Nor are they likely to have until we include them systematically in our understanding of what military office requires. Conceivably, this might be easier to do in an era when so many wars are political wars, fought as much for the loyalty of the civilian population as for control of land and resources. In such a time, one would think, responsibilities outward and upward will often coincide or at least overlap more extensively than in a time of conventional warfare. And then purposive crimes as well as crimes of indiscipline might come under hierarchical scrutiny. But in all times, and in conventional as well as political wars, we ought to require of officers that they attend to the value of civilian lives, and we should refuse to honor officers who fail to do that, even if they win great victories thereby.

"The soldier," wrote General Douglas MacArthur at the time of the Yamashita trial, "is charged with the protection of the weak and unarmed. It is the very essence and reason of his being . . . [a] sacred trust." Now, I suppose that is overstated. The "reason" of soldiering is victory, and the "reason" of victory is the protection of one's own people, not of other people. But the others are there—the ordinary citizens of enemy and of neutral states—and we are not superior beings who can reduce our risks by slaughtering them: certainly soldiers cannot do that. The lives of the others may or may not be a sacred trust, but they are an ordinary responsibility whenever we act in ways that endanger them. And we must make a place for that responsibility within the more specialized and more easily institutionalized "reasons" of war. Since the most immediate and problematic moral tension is the conflict between outward and downward responsibility, between responsibilities for enemy civilians and one's own soldiers, this means first of all that we have to insist upon the risks that soldiers must accept and that their officers must require. I cannot detail these risks here with any hope of precision. What is necessary is a certain sensitivity that the chain of command does not ordinarily elicit or impose. No doubt, that sensitivity would make soldiering even harder than it is, and it is already a hard calling. But given the suffering it often produces, it cannot be the purpose of moral philosophy to make it easier.

This article originally appeared in the March 1981 issue of *Parameters*.

8

Ethical Issues of Military Leadership

By KERMIT D. JOHNSON

Several years ago, I awoke at 0500 hours thinking about an ethics talk I was scheduled to give at the U.S. Army War College Memorial Chapel. As I allowed my mind to wander in free association, I got more than I bargained for. I started out with a flashback of Vice President Nixon's visit to the heavy mortar company I commanded on Okinawa in 1954.

It was pleasant to recall that my company had been selected for the vice president's visit because we consistently had the best mess on the island. However, this triggered a thought about my mess sergeant. For some unknown reason, he would come up with juicy steaks whenever they were needed, whether they were on the menu or not. I recalled that he had some contacts with the Air Force and apparently was involved in trading, but I never bothered to look into it.

My next thought was that trading in steaks wasn't much different from trading in bullet-proof vests. This brought to mind the supply sergeant of another company I commanded during the Korean War. He had no administrative ability whatever, but he always had a good supply of bullet-proof vests. The only thing that helped me out of Korea without supply shortages was those bullet-proof vests—valuable trading materials.

These uncomfortable thoughts, dredged from the semi-subconscious at five in the morning, formed the starting point for my thinking about the ethics of military leadership. But still another question forced itself upon me: "Is this the sort of thing which forms the substance of Watergate and mini-Watergates?"

With this as background, I can't pose as a flaming prophet or crusader in the ethical area. Maybe this is just as well. Perhaps in order to have an ethical consciousness we should be aware of our personal fallibility. In recent reading, I've noticed this awareness in Abraham Lincoln's life. He was constantly at odds with puritanical moralists and idealists whom he could never please. Yet Lincoln knew very intimately what we are like as human beings. It came out in a comment he made about our judicial system as he quoted Thomas Jefferson, with approval: "Our judges are as honest as other men, and not more so. They have, with others, the same passions for party, for power, and the privilege of their corps."[1]

At the outset, I must admit that I am probably as silent, as tactful, as self-protective, and as non-risk-taking and gutless as anyone else. Yes, I have been forced to take some clear-cut goal-line stands—those Martin Luther deals where you say, "Here I stand. I can do no other," whether it's to the detriment of efficiency report, career, or whatever. However, this is exceptional.

On a day-to-day basis, the tightrope is a better metaphor. I believe that we walk a tightrope, constantly oscillating between the extremes of crusader and chameleon: both roles are difficult and we burn up a lot of energy attempting to walk the tightrope between these two positions. The crusader, to use a phrase of J. D. Salinger, seems to "give off the stink of piousness" or self-righteousness.[2] On the other hand, the chameleon is so non-principled that if you told him "A" was right one week and then that "non-A" was right the next week, he'd dutifully and loyally click his heels together and say, "Yes, sir."

My own self-understanding, then, in discussing this matter of ethics is that of a tightrope walker caught alternately between the positions of crusader and chameleon—in one instance donning the uniform of a pure knight in shining armor and, at the other times, crawling into my chameleon skin of comfort and compromise. To the extent that readers have felt this ethical tension, I hope this article will encourage fellow crusader-chameleons to surface those ethical issues with which we all struggle from day to day.

In the December 1973 issue of *Worldview*, Josiah Bunting, a former Army officer and a crusader type who wrote *The Lionheads*, refers to "the tyranny of the dull mind," which, he says, "one so often encounters in the military." But he's objective enough to speak also of "the tyranny of the gifted mind" and he says these types are more dangerous because they withhold their true judgments lest they jeopardize the hopes for success which their ambitions have carved out for them.

He quotes B. H. Liddell Hart, discussing British officers, at this point:

> A different habit, with worse effect, was the way that ambitious officers, when they came in sight of promotion to the general's list, would decide that they would bottle up their thoughts and ideas, as a safety precaution, until they reached the top and could put these ideas into practice. Unfortunately, the usual result, after years of such self-repression for the sake of their ambition, was that when the bottle was eventually uncorked the contents had evaporated.[3]

What Hart is saying should not be limited to promotion to general. The process starts much earlier. I would have to agree that if we don't *now* expose the relevant ethical issues that affect our daily lives, when we become Chief of Staff or Chief of Chaplains and open up the bottle, we're going to find that there isn't any carbonation left, no zip. It will be gone. It simply can't be saved that long.

I would like to emphasize four pressing ethical issues for leaders in the military establishment to consider. The first is the danger posed by the acceptance of various forms of *ethical relativism*, or the blurring of right from wrong. It appears obvious that the erosion of a sense of right and wrong in favor of a "no-fault" society poses a threat to sound ethical judgments.

A brilliant young major, now out of the Army, once told me that we can never say anything is right or wrong. He said very blatantly, "Everything is relative. There is no right or wrong." I then asked him if the killing of six million Jews in World War II was wrong and whether the actions of an Adolph Eichmann were wrong. He said, "Well, it depends on what was going on in Eichmann's mind." What basis does this man have for making ethical judgments with his belief that all is relative?

Less blatant but equally devastating to ethical judgments is a subtle and disguised form of ethical relativism practiced frequently in the military setting. It comes out of the tendency to have a functional or pragmatic attitude. I've heard Army officers say impatiently, "Hell, don't give me all that theory. I just want to know what works."[4] This, of course, *is* a theory—"what works is right." Such a hazardous ethical position is made worse by emphasis on getting the job done, no matter what. Performance of the mission is everything; therefore, the question of what is right often gets lost in the shuffle of practicality and necessity, if indeed ethical questions are even raised.

A second ethical issue every military leader should face is what I call the *loyalty syndrome*. This is the practice wherein questions of right or wrong are subordinated to the overriding value of loyalty to the boss. Loyalty, an admirable and necessary quality within limits, can become all-consuming. It also becomes dangerous when a genuine, wholesome loyalty to the boss degenerates into covering up for him, hiding things from him, or not differing with him when he is wrong.

General Shoup, a former Marine Corps commandant, once said something like this: "I don't want a 'yes' man on my staff, because all he can give back to me is what I believe already." Now for a leader to honestly say this and to attempt to carry it out, I would think he would have to be very secure. To turn it around, the less secure a leader is, the greater his need for psuedo-loyalty, that is, for fewer ideas that threaten his position. The simplest and quickest way he can get this type of loyalty is through fear. There is little doubt in my mind that fear is often a motivational factor in Army leadership, and also a major trouble spot in terms of ethical practice. This is confirmed in a study titled *The United States Army's Philosophy of Management*, done by eight officers in the Army Comptrollership Program at Syracuse University. With reference to a survey of officers and civilians on managerial practices in the Army, the report said:

> From the statements concerning fear, one can conclude that the use of fear is perceived by a majority of respondents, especially the lower-ranking respondents, to deeply pervade the Army's organization structure. Lower-ranking respondents generally believe that managers are unwilling to admit errors and are encouraged to stretch the truth because of how fear operates within the system. They believe that fear itself and the life-and-death power of efficiency reports are the primary means used by their superiors to motivate

> subordinates' performance. When lower-ranking officers are afraid to tell superiors about errors, embarrassing situations for the individual, the manager, and the organization can arise when the errors are finally disclosed. The persistence of fear as a stimulator of performance can have repercussions.[5]

This report says that "when lower-ranking officers are afraid to tell superiors about errors" it is an "embarrassing situation." More than this, the use of fear to guarantee a sterile form of loyalty contributes to an environment where suppression of truth is guaranteed.

Concern about what might turn out to be an "embarrassing situation" leads into a third ethical trap on which we've been particularly hung-up for years in the Army, namely, the anxious worry over *image*. We frequently run scared; instead of acting upon what is right, we often hear: "You know, if we do this, it'll be embarrassing to the Army's image."

Whereas with the loyalty syndrome people are reluctant to tell the truth, with the image syndrome they aren't even interested in it. What becomes important is how things are perceived rather than how things really are. Thus, a dream world of image is created which is often different from the world of reality.

Let's look at some quick examples:

- The old recruiting poster: not "Join the U.S. Army" but "The Army wants to join you." How true is it?
- A general at his new duty station who tells his information officer: "You're going to make me my next star."
- A unit commander who says: "This is the best unit in the U.S. Army," and then refuses to seriously consider negative input.
- And what about our craze for "innovation?" How much of it is based on a desire for good publicity or catching our rater's eye with "dash and flash," and how much of it is based on the desire for quality and solid achievement in the unglamorous "bread and butter" items of our daily job?

As you read this, add examples from your own experience and you will probably arrive fairly close to my conclusion: at times, the obsession with image in the U.S. Army borders on institutional paranoia.

A fourth ethical trouble spot in our military experience involves *the drive for success*. This is the masochistic whip by which, sometimes, we punish ourselves and by which we sometimes are beaten sadistically by others.

In Vietnam, I escorted a speaker who was sponsored by the Department of Defense. I took him to see some of the best and the brightest of our leadership. On one occasion, I heard a high-ranking officer tell our visitor about a field grade officer who objected to the body count and to the wisdom of some current operations. The general to whom we were talking repeated gruffly what he told this field grade officer's superior: "Give 'em some candy and send 'em back up." In other words you can buy off his ethical sensitivity—give him some medals and ribbons and send him back to his unit.

Compare this with a comment by one of the respondents in the section on

"Integrity" from the *Study on Military Professionalism* done by the U.S. Army War College in 1970: "One of the most violent reactions we got was from the body count, particularly from the young combat arms officers recently back from Vietnam . . . basically being given quotas, or if not given quotas, being told that their count wasn't adequate—go back and do it again."[6] "Give 'em some candy and send 'em back up." But at what price success or even survival?

The internally generated drive for success that we all possess is compounded by the externally demanded results which signal success. In one word this adds up to *pressure*. We have this in common with other professions. While reading a study of 1,700 executive leaders entitled "How Ethical Are Businessmen?" conducted by *Harvard Business Review*, I found the following comments under the title "Pressure":

> A controller resents "repeatedly having to act contrary to [his] sense of justice in order to 'please.' In upper middle management, apparently, one's own ethical will must be subordinated to that of interests 'at the top'—not only to advance, but even to be retained."
>
> The sales manager of a very large corporation phrases his views most bluntly: "The constant everyday pressure from top management to obtain profitable business; unwritten, but well understood, is the phrase, 'at any cost.' To do this requires every conceivable dirty trick."
>
> A young engineer testifies that he was "asked to present 'edited' results of a reliability study [he] refused, and nearly got fired. [He] refused to defraud the customer, so they had others do it."[7]

It may be small comfort to realize that business leaders also experience pressures to buy off ethical sensitivity, through jeopardy of career advancement or retention. Yet one would hope for better standards in the military services where profit motive demands are absent, and where its members are dedicated to a lifetime of service to their country.

Interestingly enough, the *Harvard Business Review* study also indicated that there were pressures from bosses which helped employees to act ethically. The study concluded: *if you want to act ethically, find an ethical boss.*[8]

Fortunately, there are a great many leaders in the Army who, by personal example, offer this ethical encouragement to others. However, while the Army neither compels its personnel to compromise their ethical principles nor condones their unethical behavior, the importance of an institutional drive to push ethical leaders to the fore becomes significant since individuals cannot always choose their commanders. It also means building into the institutional structure and leadership training process such emphasis on ethics that leaders who use unethical methods will be exposed.

The task of building an ethical environment where leaders and all personnel are instructed, encouraged, and rewarded for ethical behavior is a matter of first importance. All decisions, practices, goals, and values of the entire institutional structure which make ethical behavior difficult should be examined, beginning with the following:

First, blatant or subtle forms of ethical relativism which blur the issue of what is right or wrong, or which bury it as a subject of little or no importance.
Second, the exaggerated loyalty syndrome, where people are afraid to tell the truth and are discouraged from it.
Third, the obsession with image, where people are not even interested in the truth.
And last, the drive for success, in which ethical sensitivity is bought off or sold because of the personal need to achieve.

Before being sentenced for his Watergate role, Jeb Stuart Magruder testified: "Somewhere between my ambition and my ideals I lost my ethical compass. I found myself on a path that had not been intended for me by my parents or my principles or by my own ethical instincts."[9] In the Army, we must ensure that the ambition of the professional soldier can move him along the path of career advancement only as he makes frequent azimuth checks with his ethical compass.

NOTES

1. Elton Trueblood, *Abraham Lincoln, Theologian of American Anguish* (New York: Harper and Row, 1973), p. 123.
2. J. D. Salinger, *Franny and Zooey* (Boston: Little Brown, 1955), p. 158.
3. Josiah Bunting, "The Conscience of a Soldier," *Worldview* (December 1973), p. 7.
4. Scientific research by James W. Tyler in *A Study of The Personal Value Systems of U.S. Army Officers and a Comparison with American Managers*, an unpublished University of Minnesota thesis, August 1969, has shown "first-order" values to be pragmatic ones such as high productivity, organizational efficiency, one's boss, and achievement. "Second-order" values are ethical and moral values such as trust, honor, dignity, equality, etc. See U.S. Army War College, *Study on Military Professionalism*, Carlisle Barracks, Pa., 30 June 1970, pp. B-6, B-7.
5. Management Research Center Report, *The United States Army's Philosophy of Management*, Syracuse University, August 1972, p. 77.
6. *Study on Military Professionalism* pp. B-1 to B-10.
7. George A. Smith, Jr., *Business, Society, and the Individual* (Homewood, Ill.: Richard D. Irwin, 1962), pp. 59-60.
8. Ibid., p. 52.
9. *New York Times*, 22 May 1974, p. 37.

This article originally appeared in a 1974 issue of *Parameters* (vol. IV, no. 2).

9

Values and the Professional Soldier

By JAMES L. NAREL

"I believe in UFOs."
"No you don't."
"What?"
"No you don't."
"What are you saying?"
"I'm saying that you don't believe in UFOs."
"But I've just told you that I do."
"And I'm telling you that you do not."

What could be more exasperating than to have someone claim to know, better than we, what we believe? After all, our beliefs are the most personal things about us. Another person might claim to know that the subject of our belief is incorrect—for example, that UFOs do not exist—but it does not seem comprehensible that he or she could claim to know, better than we know ourselves, *what* we believe. Yet, at least in a sense, that is what this essay does. It is not an argument about UFOs, but about values, and it makes the claim, which may seem preposterous at first, that some people do not believe what they sincerely profess to believe concerning values. More particularly, it makes the claim that some people in the military do not believe what they profess about some ethical concepts relevant to their profession and, furthermore, that this confusion has importance negative consequences.

Consider the following two assertions:

"I don't believe there is any ethical view that is more true, more accurate, or more valid than any other ethical view. Morality is dependent upon culture; what is right in one culture may be wrong in another, and vice versa. We usually end up professing the values of our particular society because we have been taught to see these as 'right.' Had we been raised in a substantially different environment, our ideas about morality might bear little resemblance to the ones we now have. Therefore, who is to say which ethical system is best? One view is as good as another."

A second assertion: "All ethical claims are either meaningless or hypocritical because, in the final analysis, everyone does what is in his or her own best interest. However much we claim to be interested in the welfare of others, we always put ourselves first. We serve others only after our own needs have been satisfied, and then our 'unselfish' acts are really motivated by the desire to increase our own prestige or self-satisfaction or perhaps to alleviate feelings of guilt or indebtedness. Since this is a fact of human nature, any moral claim that urges us to act out of concern for others is a sham."

These two opinions are voiced frequently in discussions about values. The arguments have gained in popularity even though—or perhaps because—they reject traditional moral norms. The person who expresses one or the other view seems to imply that he has advanced beyond a blind acceptance of his society's customs and codes and is able to think about these concepts in a more objective way. Furthermore, the two views enjoy added prestige because they are "realistic." Their adherents seem courageously to have abandoned the quaint and comfortable tenets of tradition and to have faced the world as it really is.

There is a sad irony in all of this. It has nothing to do with the value (or lack of value) of either view or with the increasing popularity of both. It is possible that one or the other is an accurate assessment of the true nature of morality, and the arguments do demonstrate a willingness to confront questions of value objectively. But many who voice the arguments have not examined them thoroughly. A precise and comprehensive investigation of the issues could uncover inconsistencies—not necessarily in the ethical views themselves (though that, too, is possible), but in the network of personal beliefs that includes these views. In other words, a person may conclude that, since one or the other argument sounds rational and acceptable, it must constitute his or her belief about the subject (we do tend to accept as true those propositions that appeal to our reason and involve no obvious flaw in logic). Yet that person may simultaneously hold other beliefs that contradict this one. For example, an individual who on one occasion maintains that one value system is as good as another may, at some other time, express the opinion that there is something inherently unjust about slavery. Obviously, both these beliefs cannot be consistently maintained since it is certainly possible to imagine a value system that finds slavery morally acceptable. Such a person, then, probably does not really believe that all value systems are of equal worth, even though he may sometimes think he does.

While it may be difficult to identify people who are willing to articulate a serious defense of slavery, many people in the military *are* ready to defend one of the two ethical views expressed above. Yet, in several ways, both these positions are inconsistent with the concept of the professional soldier. A person cannot consistently maintain either view and simultaneously be committed to the goals of the military profession. This is not quite as serious a problem as it may first appear because many of those people in uniform who find the views rational will, after study and reflection, find that the views are not *actually* part of their beliefs. The issue does have important ramifications, however, since continued confusion about the beliefs can lead to serious misunderstandings of, or misjudgments about, the profession.

The view that all moral systems are ultimately subjective is called relativism. The cliche "It's all relative," when used thoughtfully in a discussion of values, means that the speaker rejects the notion that there is some objective "ground" for morality. He recognizes that most people conduct their lives in accordance with some framework of values, but he maintains that the framework is itself the product of their environment and social conditioning. As a result, when other people claim a certain action is "right," the relativist argues that they really mean that their particular culture approves of, and encourages, such behavior. If some other social group collectively disapproved, owing to its cultural experience, the action would, in the relativist's view, be *wrong* in that setting.

There is nothing logically inconsistent about such a view of morality. It does create the possibility of a particular act's being both right and wrong at the same time, but this is not a contradiction. For a relativist the word "wrong" does not mean "violating an objectively true principle of morality"; it means, simply, "not acceptable within a particular social grouping." But a person who claims to be a relativist, if he is to avoid inconsistency, must accept all the consequences that logically derive from this normative system. This means he must be willing to admit that no action can be held to be *objectively* wrong. Cruelly abusing helpless children, for example, cannot be judged as inherently wrong; it must be viewed simply as socially unacceptable in most cultures. Furthermore, if a culture were discovered in which child abuse was routinely practiced, the consistent relativist could make no adverse judgment. He would have to maintain that there is nothing objectively wrong with the attendant human suffering; it is merely a matter of cultural preference.

Now this is not what is believed by most people who entertain the notion that morality may be relative. More likely they believe that it is not right for one person or culture to impose its value system on another. "People should be allowed to do anything they choose as long as it doesn't hurt someone else. Live and let live!" This may be a comparatively liberal viewpoint but *it is not relativism*. Such a view does not claim that *all* values are subjective. It contends that some, perhaps many, are situation- or culture-dependent, but it accepts other values as universal. The live-and-let-live doctrine implies the right of individuals and cultures to be free of unwanted interference. It urges tolerance of diverse views. It assumes that human beings have inalienable rights and that their liberty ought not arbitrarily to be curtailed.

But it might be asked whether this is not simply a semantic distinction. One may not be a relativist in the sense that it has been defined here, but if one is content to accept the values of others as being fine for them, aren't the practical consequences the same?

The distinction is real. If a person were a true relativist, he would have to admit that the values of his native culture are objectively no better and no worse than those of any other. Hence, his commitment to those values, if he felt any, could only be a matter of convenience or custom. On the other hand, the person who is committed to tolerance and respect for human rights sees these values as having objective validity. One can expect that such beliefs will influence his attitudes and behavior in a more profound way. He might be willing, for example, to accept inconvenience or even to endure danger or suffering in order to support his values.

It is difficult to imagine a thoroughgoing relativist as a dedicated military professional. A relativist might choose to engage in soldiering; indeed, he might find that the military environment is more consistent with his tastes or preferences than is the civilian world. For example, he may enjoy engaging in adventurous, dangerous, or violent acts or may feel more secure operating in a rigidly structured social hierarchy. But are these the characteristics that define the military professional? While these attitudes might partially describe him, they might also characterize a mercenary or a uniformed bureaucrat. The concept of a professional typically involves something more, namely, binding oneself to particular *principles*. This is particularly true in America, where it is not to a person that the professional soldier swears his allegiance, nor is it a geographical area that he promises to protect when he takes his public oath. Support and defense of the Constitution require fealty to the principles, to the values, proclaimed by that document. Would it be reasonable for the person who truly believes that one declaration of values is as good as another to promise to engage in brutal combat simply because one of these allegedly arbitrary value systems is threatened or endangered? A genuine relativist would have to forgo such action.

And what about the egoist? Egoism is the claim that self-interest is the focus of all human action and that a moral system, if it is to have objective validity, must take this truth into account. Like relativism, the egoistic argument may be, but is not necessarily, a correct statement about the nature of morality. But some persons who see its claims as rational and compelling may not have made a careful study of egoism and may hold other moral views inconsistent with the egoist position. This would be true of the professional soldier who *thinks* he accepts egoism but who has not reconciled it with his commitment to military values.

Because so much of what any person routinely does is motivated by self-interest, it is easy to slide into an almost unquestioned acceptance of egoism. Choosing to put on one's shoes in the morning is a "selfish" act in the sense that the decision is made with little or no consideration of others. The same is true of one's decisions to bathe, eat, exercise, and so on. What about holding the door for someone, or picking up another person's dropped parcel? Behavior that is seemingly other-directed can also be interpreted as having a selfish motive: following rules of social etiquette, for example, will likely secure similar treatment in return and will enhance the prestige of the polite person in the eyes of others. The argument can be extended to even the most dramatic actions, and persons who give up their lives for their comrades can be seen as doing so primarily in pursuit of an eternal reward or in a subconscious effort to alleviate personal guilt. It is man's nature to act in his own interest, the egoist claims; the dictum is universal and inexorable.

Now, this claim is not self-contradictory, and it cannot be disproven. It is not surprising, then, that many people who encounter the argument erroneously conclude that it is *necessarily* true. But an assertion that alien beings are observing mankind from another dimension is also irrefutable, since no evidence can be produced to show that it is false. One is not thereby compelled to accept the claim as true. Similarly, egoism constitutes one way of interpreting human behavior and, as a theory, it contains no absurdities or inherent contradictions. But the same can be said for many conflicting theories. Indeed, when measured against competing views, egoism is burdened in that its central tenet seems counterintuitive to most people. The egoistic argument hinges on the assertion that *all* (not simply "most") human actions are motivated by self-interest. If so much as a single event in all human history was characterized by true selflessness, egoism would have to be considered invalid: observing that men are frequently selfish is far different from claiming they are always totally selfish, and that their nature requires them to be so. And, when one thinks about it, the argument for selfishness is not all that persuasive. It depends upon one's willingness to believe that even the most innocent act of human kindness is really determined by self-interest. Does one assist a passerby by retrieving his dropped parcel *in order* to feel good, or does one do it out of genuine consideration for the other person and then feel good after the fact? The egoist seems to be arguing that one can never know one's own mind in matters like these; if one thinks his concern for others is genuine, he must allow this opinion to be overruled by an outside observer who claims to know more about the samaritan's motives than the samaritan does.

Though the egoist's claim is not necessarily false, neither is his theory nearly so compelling as it may initially appear. It may be that many people have been maintaining two contradictory views: that all actions must be selfish (because the egoist argument cannot be refuted), but that some actions are genuinely unselfish (because they clearly seem to be motivated by concern for others). The military professional who is convinced by the egoist has probably fallen into just this predicament. His professional commitment and many of the values he supports as a member of the military, however, are inconsistent with egoism.

Why couldn't an egoist logically be a career soldier? After all, the service does have its attractive features. Moved by personal desires for a secure job, a guaranteed income, early retirement, leadership opportunities, travel, and excitement, couldn't a person decide on a military career because it satisfied his own needs? Certainly. Without doubt, satisfying one's needs and otherwise serving one's self-interest are motives for virtually everyone choosing the service life. There is no denying that everyone is partially, and perhaps inescapably, motivated by self-interest. But could a person who is motivated *only* by self-interest pursue a military career? It is unlikely, although possible, that he could. Would such a person be a military professional? Decidedly not.

Once again one encounters the distinction between the professional and the person who soldiers only for pay. It is neither merely a semantic distinction nor a wholly arbitrary or subjective one. As the very name of the vocation implies, those who select the military *service* as a profession are placing themselves at the disposal of others. They are pledging to direct their efforts toward the national, not their personal, welfare. They will routinely be expected to subordinate their own interests to those designated by someone else as being the interests of the unit or of the nation. Without doubt those broader interests will sometimes conflict with pure self-interest. In such circumstances one could hardly expect the egoist in uniform to act like a professional. Would it be reasonable to think that a person motivated solely by self-interest would unhesitatingly obey an order that places his life in extreme danger? Or that he would be the source of such an order himself? Or, in less dramatic circumstances, that he would render a report that reflected badly on his own performance? The motivation that characterizes professional behavior in the military is frequently antithetical to egoism.

This conclusion does not imply that there are numerous egoists in uniform who ought to change careers or, at least, admit that they are unprofessional. On the contrary, there are probably very few egoists in military ranks; but those ranks may contain many dedicated, self-sacrificing professionals who pay unwitting homage to an egoist perspective that does not accurately reflect their true values.

Are there any practical consequences to these conclusions or are the implications trivial? Although military officers may not recognize the contradiction between ethical relativism or egoism and the nature of the military profession, the consequences of holding inconsistent convictions are anything but trivial. Like so many other social institutions, the military profession suffers at times from a spiritual malaise that undercuts our collective confidence, saps our energy, and produces a cynicism that seems to feed on itself. The problems may be due in no small part to confusion about values.

Several of the important values traditionally espoused in the military profession have already been identified in this essay. They include commitments to uphold national principles, subordination of personal interests, obedience, courage, and loyalty. But each of these is in conflict with either relativism or egoism or both. What happens, then, when a person who thinks he is persuaded by the relativist or egoist argument attempts to commit himself to a profession that maintains the importance of values inconsistent with those theories? At best the confusion causes only a minor diminution of moral certainty. But all too likely the consequences will be more profound. For example, the profession urges us to be prepared to make the ultimate sacrifice in defense of the values articulated by Washington, Jefferson, and others. Yet relativism tells us that, from an objective standpoint, these cannot be shown to have any greater moral merit than the values held by King George III, Mussolini, or Joseph Stalin. And while our oath of office commits us to endure danger in order to protect others, egoism claims that human nature absolutely prohibits acts of genuine self-sacrifice. If we are confident that, put to the test, we could be counted upon to act in consonance with our professional values, we are probably implying that our belief in the relativist or egoist propositions is less enduring than our patriotic or professional devotion.

Beliefs to which we cling tightly in times of crisis, we often squander foolishly when faced with subtler challenges. How do we respond, for example, to a proffered assignment that probably will not promote our career? We may acknowledge that the position needs a competent individual, but we may also prefer and suggest that it be some *other* competent individual. At moments like these, how are we likely to regard the argument that, as professionals, we ought to subordinate our personal interests to the greater common good? As we deal with the problem, our confusion about egoism or relativism can have insidious consequences. Since we do not see our colleagues rushing to sacrifice themselves, we may conclude that the egoists have it right: people do not willfully act against their self-interest. Having arrived at such a conviction, we become less ready than ever to accept the task simply because it needs to be done, and we confront a genuine gathering conflict of beliefs. We continue to pay lip service to the profession's espoused values—in this case, call it self-sacrifice—but we are anything but convinced that self-sacrifice is actually practiced or even possible. The apparent norm—and thus the right action according to the relativist—tells us that we should not take the assignment. We convince ourselves that we cannot really be expected to acquire the virtue of self-sacrifice, and we become cynical as the virtue is preached by the hypocrites. The egoist prophecy of selfish behavior thus becomes self-fulfilled, and the most blatant forms of careerism can be rationalized as prudent and proper.

A clearer understanding of egoism and relativism will not, of course, cause careerism or other professional maladies to disappear. Such understanding can, however, reassure us that the values of the profession, the ones that may well have attracted us to service in the first place, are not illogical or unrealistic after all. We may come to doubt the opinion that all value systems are of equal merit. We may decide that a particular system may indeed be of superior worth. The result can be a renewed and heightened appreciation of the values contained in the Constitution we are pledged to defend. We may conclude as well that the egoist does not have the only explanation of human nature and that all people are not necessarily always selfish. The result can be a new willingness to see, in ourselves and others, at least the *possibility* of genuinely unselfish action. Acknowledging that such behavior is possible constitutes a first step toward agreeing that it can rightly be expected of a military professional. In both cases the process begins with the recognition that neither relativists nor egoists have a corner on the truth and that competing views have much to recommend them.

While each of us is undoubtedly aware of lapses in professional behavior, by ourselves and others, we should celebrate the daily observation of performance that reflects genuine commitment to traditional values. If there is confusion in speaking about values, the actions of many people in uniform speak louder than words. People do, at least on occasion, give evidence that they discriminate among value systems and that they can act in the interest of others even at some personal cost (while yet mistakenly claiming to agree with relativists and egoists who argue that this is not so). Clearing up the confusion can have important beneficial effects. It can reduce the temptation, when we are frustrated or disillusioned, to lower our personal standards and our expectations. It can also heighten our professional sense of self-worth by permitting us to take full credit for our dedication and self-sacrifice. We can respond with confidence to cynics and naysayers and can come to regard the profession's espousal of traditional values as noble yet realistic, demanding yet attainable.

This article originally appeared in the December 1981 issue of *Parameters*.

10

Ethics and the Senior Officer

By CLAY T. BUCKINGHAM

Army officers are devoting a lot of thoughtful consideration to the subject of ethics. The purpose of this chapter is to present a firsthand appreciation of various ethical tensions that confront senior Army officers. To accomplish this I will briefly explore the foundations of our ethical system, offer some thoughts about how this ethical system should apply specifically to the military profession, and finally take an empirical look at the tensions in the military society that provide fertile grounds for ethical abuses.

The term "ethics" is used to mean the study of human actions in respect to their being right or wrong. Whether we like it or not, ethical reflection has seldom been carried out in isolation from theology. Ethical values generally reflect our view of human life as it is embodied in the teachings of the prevailing religion, because all human conduct, essentially, takes place in relationship to other human beings. Therefore, if I believe that human life, that is, *all* of human life without exception, has equal and infinite value, then my concept of right and wrong conduct will reflect this conviction. If I believe that human life has limited value, let's say limited by what it can contribute to the common good, then my concept of right or wrong conduct will reflect this conviction. If I believe that some forms of human life have more worth than others—that, say, males are more valuable than females, or whites are more valuable than blacks, or Americans are more valuable than Cambodians, or the rich are more valuable than the poor, or Jews are more valuable than Arabs—then my concept of right and wrong conduct will reflect whichever of these convictions I hold.

Our Western value system of right and wrong is based primarily on what Jesus taught concerning the origin and value of human life, augmented by the Old Testament lawgivers and prophets. This is what we commonly call the Judeo-Christian tradition. Although these teachings have been eroded and in some cases prostituted radically through the centuries, they still strongly influence the attitudes of Americans and other Westerners and form the core of our ethical concepts. In the Judeo-Christian view, man was created by God in

His image; that is, with awareness, with purpose, with personality, and with inherent worth. All forms of human life was equally endowed by God with worth and dignity. There is no distinction between male and female, between black or white, rich or poor, aristocrat or peasant, Americans or Cambodians, Jews or Arabs, old or young, born or unborn, smart or dumb, with regard to inherent worth and dignity. All are created with equal worth, with equal dignity, with equal status, and with equal rights within the human race.

From this basic belief has come the thesis that whatever protects or enhances human life is good, and whatever destroys or degrades human life is evil. Thus, our whole moral and ethical concept of right and wrong stems from this thesis-antithesis of good and evil, and I believe that we cannot consider right and wrong within the military profession outside of this framework; that whatever protects and enhances life is good, and whatever destroys and degrades life is evil. The great concepts of justice, mercy, compassion, service, and freedom are immediate derivatives of this central distinction between good and evil as received from our Judeo-Christian heritage.

Before addressing ethics within the military profession, I will deal briefly with the ethical basis for our profession. The moral justification for our profession is embedded in the Constitution—"to provide for the Common Defense." We are that segment of the American society which is set apart to provide for the defense of the remainder of that society. The word "defense" is key. We are to defend our territory, because that is where our people live, but in an expanded sense, we are defending our value systems, our way of life, our standard of life, our essential institutions, and whatever our government declares to be our national interest. Our Founding Fathers were realists. They knew that most of the rest of the world did not share our view of the value and worth of human life. They recognized that we lived in and would continue to live in a dangerous world, one in which only the strong, or those allied to the strong, can remain free. Only the strong can influence whether peace will be preserved or broken, because strength deters aggression and discourages conflict, and weakness invites aggression and encourages conflict.

Those who provide for the common defense, who protect the lives of our citizens, can best do so by creating a strong, effective deterrence to would-be aggressors. As military people our objective is "not to promote war, but to preserve peace" and to protect life. Even if deterrence fails and we go to war, our final objective is peace. Ours is an honorable profession with an ethical purpose entirely consistent with our basic view that whatever protects and enhances life is good.

I will now turn to ethics as they specifically apply to the military profession. In essence, professional ethics is that body of written or unwritten standards of conduct by which that profession disciplines itself. One writer said, "Professional ethics are designed to assure high standards of competence in a given field." In the general case, then, that conduct which contributes to the attainment of the purpose of that profession is good. The conduct which detracts from the attainment of the purpose of that profession is bad. Various professionals have adopted either written or unwritten codes. Doctors, nurses, engineers, journalists, lawyers, businessmen—all have established standards of right and wrong for their respective professions. For instance, the written code of Hippocrates states that the medical profession is dedicated to the preservation of life and should be of service to mankind. Certain practices inimical to that goal are forbidden in the Hippocratic code.

In the military profession we do not have an all-inclusive code of ethics, although we do have documents which contain broad and compelling standards of professional conduct. Some would say that the West Point motto of "duty, honor, country" is all that we really need. But those values, as good as they are, do not give a conceptual basis for their implementation. What is duty? What is honor? What do we mean by country? Lieutenant Calley probably considered that he was doing his duty at My Lai. Our code of conduct for POWs sets forth right and wrong conduct under those limited but extremely trying conditions. Have you ever thought of our Oath of Allegiance as a document of ethics? It is—of sorts. "I will support and defend the Constitution of the United States against all enemies foreign and domestic." That sounds great. But whose interpretation of the Constitution? The latest Supreme Court decision? And who are these domestic enemies? Anyone who disagrees with our interpretation of the Constitution? And what is the role of the Department of Defense in fighting domestic enemies? I thought that was the role of the FBI. And further, the Oath states, "I will obey the orders of the officers appointed over me." Well, yes, assuming they're legal, assuming they're consistent with my moral standards.

But back to my earlier statement: If that conduct which contributes to the attainment of the purpose of the profession is good, and that which detracts from the attainment of the purpose of the profession is bad, then for the military profession, whatever enhances the common defense essentially is good, and whatever diminishes the common defense is essentially bad. But this must be tempered by the larger issue, that whatever protects and enhances human life is good and whatever destroys life or diminishes the quality of life is bad.

This consideration leads, of necessity, to a brief discussion of means and ends. I think it should be an absolute rule among military people that ends do not justify means. Nor that means justify ends. Both ends and means must be consistent with our fundamental values. Honorable ends cannot be achieved by dishonorable means, nor do honorable means justify dishonorable or unethical ends. Although the general welfare of our nation is an honorable and ethical purpose, the selective elimination of nonproductive members of society, although it would contribute to the general welfare, cannot be tolerated. Domestic tranquility, although an honorable purpose, cannot justify police brutality or unlawful detention. Common defense is an honorable purpose, but misrepresentation of an enemy threat before a congressional committee cannot be justified by the belief that it is necessary in order to acquire funding for an important weapon system.

So can we make any general rules for ethical conduct within the military profession? I think so. Essentially, what is right is that which enhances the accomplishment of our basic purpose, the common defense, provided that it is consistent with our overall view of the value and dignity of all human life and that the means to accomplish it are acceptable. Or, ask these questions: Does the action we are about to take or the policy under consideration contribute to the national defense? Is it consistent with the protection and enhancement of life? Are both ends and means consistent with our national values?

Given these thoughts, I will now turn to the empirical aspects of the subject, the tensions within the Army which provide fertile grounds for ethical abuse. All military officers have experienced these tensions, and they will continue to characterize the environment in which senior officers will serve. The higher the position, the more complex and less precise are the issues. The last job I really understood was being a tank platoon leader in combat. As I progressed upward, the ethical environment became more murky, less clear, less subject to specific rules and simple solutions. However, an officer's usefulness to the nation and overall credibility will be fundamentally affected by his ability to enter an environment where absolutes are hard to find, and still make wise and ethical decisions. These tensions will require of you a bedrock of ethical values.

The one tension that will be most consistently with you involves the ethical use of authority. The authoritarian structure of our profession, even though essential, is the natural breeding ground for the unethical use of authority. The power and influence of a colonel are greater than that of a lieutenant colonel. The influence of a general officer is truly awesome. This fact requires a clear understanding, first, of the meaning of rank.

Within our hierarchical, authoritarian structure, there are various levels of responsibility. Each level of responsibility is assigned a commensurate degree of authority. Rank is simply a badge of the authority vested in a person to carry out a specific level of responsibility. Company-level responsibility requires company-level authority, and the rank of captain is associated with that level of authority. So lieutenant colonel rank represents the authority necessary to carry out battalion-level responsibilities; colonel, brigade-level responsibilities; major general, division-level responsibilities. When authority is used in the fulfilling of responsibility, it is used legitimately and ethically. When authority is used for purposes not directly associated with carrying out assigned responsibilities, it is being used illegitimately and unethically. Conversely, if I fail to use my authority to carry out my responsibilities, my negligence is itself unethical, and someone who will use that authority should be given my job. The question is: Am I using my authority, my rank, fully but solely for the purpose of carrying out my responsibilities?

As you go up in rank, those of lower grade tend more readily to assume that you are using your authority legitimately and ethically, because of the high regard with which juniors hold very senior officers. Thus, the general who directs his pilot to arrange a flight plan on an authorized TDY visit so as to remain overnight at a city not specifically on the most direct route, so that the general can visit his mother who is in a nursing home, will be assumed by the pilot to be fully authorized to do so. The Pentagon colonel who calls an action officer in from leave because the colonel thinks his general might ask a question which the action officer is best qualified to answer will be assumed to be using his authority ethically. Think about that.

This gets to the guts of the use of authority. In my opinion, one of the most widespread and patently unethical uses of authority is the exploitation and degradation of subordinates, which is a generally accepted institutional practice. It is an encouraged institutional practice, and it is wrong. We have fostered the image of the successful leader as the one who doesn't get ulcers, but gives ulcers; as the one who is hard, unfeeling, even vicious.

Some may disagree, but I think that is true. Whom do we admire? We admire the man with "guts." What do we really mean by this? We mean the man who drives his people hard, who has the reputation for firing subordinates, who goes for the jugular, who works his people 14 hours a day, and who takes his objective in spite of heavy and possibly unnecessary casualties. We set these people up and idolize them. Even in industry. We like the kind of guy who moves in as the CEO and fires three-fourths of the vice presidents the first week. He gets things done! He's got guts! But what about the perceptive, cool-headed leader who takes a group of misfits and molds them into an effective, highly-spirited team? Or the colonel who can see the great potential of a young commander who is performing only marginally and through coaching and encouraging, turns him into a first-rate performer? Or the leader in combat who takes his objective with no casualties? Or the brigade commander who has the guts to resist the arbitrary, capricious order of a division commander to fire a faltering battalion commander because the colonel believes that with the proper leadership that battalion commander can be made into a successful one? Or the Pentagon division chief who defies the norm and refuses to arrive in his office before 0730, or to require his action officers to do so, and who manages the workload of his division so that every man gets a reasonable amount of leave, seldom has to work on weekends, and gets home every evening at a reasonable hour?

We seldom hear about these people. We don't hold them up as examples as we should. The higher we go, the more important it is to be careful that our impact on the lives and careers and families of our subordinates is positive and not negative. I can think of a division artillery commander in Germany who ruled by fear, who was hated by his subordinates, and who was the proximate cause of a number of serious domestic crises. I can think of a lieutenant general in the Pentagon who purposely intimidated his subordinates and associates in order to get his own way. I can think of a colonel, the executive to a former Chief of Staff, who blossomed like a rose to his superiors, but who was vicious, demeaning, and bullying to his subordinates. I can think of a colonel in the Pentagon who never showed appreciation and voiced only criticism and whose subordinates gradually became discouraged and frustrated and unproductive.

In contrast, I can think of an Army lieutenant general whose modus operandi was to make his subordinates successful in their jobs. He said, "I'll have no problem with my job if I can make all of my subordinates successful." I think of a division commander in Germany with whom I was closely associated, who spent countless hours talking with subordinates at every level, coaching them, encouraging them, teaching them. I think of a Pentagon division chief who looked for opportunities to push his action officers into the limelight, who volunteered them for prestigious positions as secretarial-level "horse-holders," who worked in the background to cross-train his people so that no one would ever have to be called back from leave, who personally took the rap when things went wrong, and who, in my opinion, ran the best division in the Pentagon. It all gets back to how they looked at people, their value, their dignity, their fundamental worth, their potential.

The higher you go, the easier it is to misuse authority. The checks that we were subject to as junior officers become less evident and less compelling. We gradually begin to believe that we really don't need to seek the counsel of others. We are at first surprised by and then pleased by the freedom of action accorded us.

For instance: "I really have to visit Germany, but should I do so this winter? No, I'll wait until the weather's better. Let's see, where can I go this winter? I really need to visit Panama and Hawaii. Let's visit Panama or Hawaii this winter."

We begin to rationalize small personal indiscretions that we would never accept in a subordinate, like having our personal car worked on by a division mechanic during duty hours, or allowing our wife to bully the post engineer into refurbishing the kitchen of our quarters out of cycle. Sometimes we begin to believe that we are somehow above the law—they really didn't have a person of our status and responsibility in mind when they wrote it, did they?—and we divert funds, appropriated for barracks maintenance, to refurbish the interior of a rod and gun club, or piece several segments of minor construction money together to accomplish some major construction projects that were disallowed in the last appropriation cycle. These examples are taken from my personal knowledge. As a rule, and this is very important I think, general officers do not get relieved for incompetence. They do get fired for indiscretions, which is simply another way of saying that they've used their authority unethically.

A former inspector general of the Army for whom I have great regard and who was, in a sense, the conscience of the Army for the four years that he was the IG, told me that at any one time about ten percent of the general officers in the Army were under investigation of some kind or another. Most of those charges turn out to be either false or simply a matter of perception, i.e. where the general did something which others perceived to be unethical but really was not. As General Creighton W. Abrams, Jr., once said, "The higher you go on the flag pole, the more your rear-end shows."

The second great tension involves the ethical use of military force. The higher you go the more you'll be called on to exercise judgment in this arena, although some with relatively moderate rank in key positions have great influence on such matters. For instance, a U.S. Marine Corps major on the National Security Council staff wrote the point paper that convinced the president to send Marines into Lebanon. The Weinberger-Shultz debates often fell into the category of this tension regarding the ethical use of military force. When should it be used? Under what circumstances? In what strength? In defense of U.S. territory only? Or in defense of U.S. interests? Or in defense of our allies? What are our interests? Grenada? Lebanon? The Straits of Hormuz? How about Vietnam?

Our involvement in Vietnam was purely ethical in the sense that the United States had no really compelling self-interest. We simply wanted to prevent 16 million South Vietnamese from becoming slaves to a totalitarian neighbor. But what about the level of force used? Was it ethical *not* to saturate-bomb Hanoi in an effort to force the North Vietnamese government to call off the invasion of South Vietnam? How about Czechoslovakia, Hungary, Afghanistan, the Iranian rescue operation? Should force be used only if there is a reasonable chance of effecting a desirable outcome? General Matthew Ridgway, then Chief of Staff, went to President Eisenhower in the summer of 1953 and personally talked him out of sending American ground troops to Vietnam after the French defeat at Dien Bien Phu at the hands of the Viet Minh. Was he more ethical or less ethical than the Chairman of the Joint Chiefs of Staff who failed to intercede ten years later to prevent combat troops from being sent into South Vietnam? Could *failure* to use military force in the defense of freedom be unethical? That's a good question. And what of the Bay of Pigs? Was it moral for the President to call off the air strikes at the last minute, thus practically insuring failure? Was it moral for the chairman of the Joint Chiefs of Staff to agree to the calling off of those air strikes? Did the operation in and of itself have an ethical purpose?

And now today, what of the use of military power to accomplish our purposes in Central America? What are our purposes in Central America? Is the use of military force the only way to accomplish these purposes? If so, how much force? In what form?

In addition to these two prime ethical tensions, there are others that every senior officer will confront, although the forms might vary. I will briefly cite several. One ethical tension is that what is just and fair to an individual may conflict with a policy that attempts to correct long-standing injustice. One of the major problems here is that an open and frank discussion is not only discouraged but virtually impossible due to the emotionally explosive nature of the issue. I'm speaking of course about establishing quotas or their look-alikes for minorities and women in various selective processes like promotions, schooling, command, and other visible assignments.

Another ethical tension is loyalty to the organizational position or policy versus adherence to personal conviction when the two are in conflict. In testimony before a congressional staff, how can you present the OSD or Army position if you personally disagree with it? The same ethical dilemma confronts a Chief of Staff who personally disagrees with the President's chosen strategy. Another ethical tension involves the conflict between ambition and selflessness. What is legitimate ambition? We preach selflessness as a sterling quality of character and then we tend to reward ambition. It is ironic that one Chief of Staff who talked a lot about selflessness was, in his rise to that position, one of the most openly ambitious officers I know.

Another ethical tension is between people and mission. Does the goal of having combat-ready units justify neglect of families? Conversely, does the proper care and nurture of families excuse having noncombat-ready units? Can we achieve both? Should dependents accompany their sponsors overseas? Does it detract from readiness, or contribute to it? Is it ethical to separate families from their sponsors in peacetime under any circumstances? What are the effects of separating families? We've muddled through this one, perhaps not very successfully.

A final ethical tension involves the difference between honesty and deception. Decisions at every echelon in our structure are made based upon the information available to the decision-makers. If that information is inaccurate or incomplete, the decision may well be faulty. The decision may be faulty even if the information is accurate and complete, but it is more likely to be faulty if the information is inaccurate and incomplete. Therefore, it is essential that information provided to our superiors, to our subordinates, and to our peers be accurate and complete. The oath of a witness in a trial to tell "the truth, the whole truth, and nothing but the truth" should be the oath of a professional officer.

This was brought home to me as a tank platoon leader in the Korean War. It was nighttime. The tank battalion of which I was a part had been heavily engaged during the day in support of an infantry regiment in a river-crossing operation. Now we were defending against a flank attack by a Chinese force on the near side of the river. There were a lot of mortar and artillery fire, including illumination and white phosphorus; many casualties; and general confusion. The friendly force was withdrawing and I ended up with my tank platoon fighting sort of a rear-guard action in pitch dark along a road. About the time I got my platoon past a certain checkpoint, I got a radio call from my battalion commander asking if I was the last friendly force to cross the checkpoint. Since we were in close contact with the advancing Chinese force, I said yes, we were the last. Shortly thereafter a long and intense American artillery barrage was laid down in the area I had just vacated. The next morning my battalion commander came to me in our assembly area. He told me he had called the artillery into that area because of my statement that I was the last unit out. In fact, I was not. A friendly infantry unit somehow had been intermingled with the Chinese force and had sustained casualties in the artillery barrage. Gently, but clearly, the battalion commander said, "Buck, you made me tell a lie."

I've never forgotten that. I had told him what I perceived to be true, but was not. I should have qualified my answer, explaining that in the dark and confusion I could report only that my tanks had crossed the checkpoint. That was the only thing I knew for sure. The rest was speculation. Many times since then I've been tempted to speculate beyond what I knew and was certain to be true and I have sometimes yielded to that temptation.

As DCSOPS of USAREUR during the Turkish invasion of Cyprus, I was reporting to CINCUSAREUR on the situation so far as we knew it. The actual invasion was of less importance to us than the threat to our nuclear weapons in both Greece and Turkey, stemming from intense animosity by both sides toward Americans for failing to take a clear stand with either country on the invasion. I was discussing the threat to our nuclear weapons with CINCUSAREUR and unconsciously began to drift away from the known facts into speculation about what might be true. The CINC looked squarely at me and said, "General, stop bugling. I can't make decisions on speculation. You're intermingling facts with possibilities."

In many situations at high levels of command, the issues of honesty and deception are not recognized as such. One of the most common deceptions is the exaggeration of need in order to get what is really needed, knowing that the initial request is certainly going to be reduced. Money is usually the object, at least in the Pentagon environment. In fact, the whole program budget procedure, in my view, is essentially deceptive and unethical. The annual requests for operations and maintenance funds come in from the major commands over four-star signatures claiming that the request is the bare minimum they can live with. The DA action officers in the planning and budgeting arena don't believe a word of it. They look at what the command got the previous year, do some puts and takes, and come up with their own figures. The whole process at the major command level was a waste of time, energy, and money. Commanders' statements are given about as much credence as a Dan Rather commentary on the objectivity of the news media. Then the Programming and Budgeting System, in crunching together the Program Objective Memorandum, inflates those requests which are the "pet rocks" of influential Pentagon pachyderms, and submits them to OSD knowing full well that OSD will cut some of these programs back, knowing they have been inflated by the Army. Of course, OSD may take the money thus "saved" and add it to other programs based on what some assistant secretary of defense perceives to be important, or what the current wind of opinion is regarding what will sell on the Hill and what won't.

Another blatantly unethical practice in the programming and budgeting arena is what I call the "multiple stampede effect." Newly assigned Lieutenant General A or Assistant Secretary A comes along with Project A which has been his obsession for years. It requires major multi-year funding. He forces it into the program, stampeding the appropriation directors to get on the team, and so the program is funded at the expense of other ongoing programs. Lieutenant General A is then promoted and made a MACOM commander where his influence in the central programming and budgeting procedure fades considerably. Now Lieutenant General B arrives on the scene with Project B, his personal "pet rock," and he is able to push his project through the Program Budget Committee and into the next year's Program Objective Memorandum. And where does the money come from? From Program A. So Program A and all the other Program A's are cut back to make way for Program B and all the other Program B's sponsored by the powerful new Lieutenant General B's who will be replaced the next year by Lieutenant General C's with their projects.

Thus we have programs by the dozens originally spawned by the stampede effect of strong-willed, powerful proponents, which are distorted from their original purpose and deflated by inadequate funding, and flop around from year to year due to changes of emphasis and priority at DA level. The people assigned to manage these programs in the field never know from year to year what they can expect in the way of support. Over the course of my last 12 years on active duty, I was involved in the programming and budgeting procedure for ten of those years, eight of them at the DA level and two at the MACOM level. I used to leave Program Budget Committee meetings in the Pentagon feeling unclean, polluted, like I needed to go to confession. The whole system is wasteful of the money our citizens have entrusted to us for their common defense. And most of the senior programming and budgeting participants recognize this. Almost every year that I was in the Pentagon, the Director of PA&E or the Director of the Army Staff or the DCSOPS or the Vice Chief of Staff vowed to implement reform and instituted new and different procedures—none of which, as of 30 June 1982, when I retired, had fundamentally improved the system in my opinion.

Another aspect of the honesty/deception tension involves readiness reports. First of all, even the most accurate unit readiness report is a deception unless it is considered in the context of the Army's capability to sustain that unit in combat. The tooth-to-tail, combat-support ratio debate is a case in point. Combat divisions in Europe with C-1 ratings give our national leaders a false sense of confidence if these divisions cannot be sustained in combat past the first few weeks. The readiness of the whole force is what is important. If you are in the force structure business you are contributing to massive deception if you fail to provide adequate combat support and combat service support to our combat divisions. If you are in the programming and budgeting business you are contributing to a massive deception if you fail to program sufficient ammunition or repair parts to sustain our divisions in combat. The readiness reporting system is not and cannot be purely objective. Subjective judgment always enters in, but the intent, the motive, is what is important.

Consider a new division commander in Europe who has been in command about a month. His predecessor, a young, ambitious major general, is the new USAREUR Chief of Staff. The new division commander makes his assessment and gives his division a C-3 in training, a drop from C-2. As USAREUR DCSOPS, I review the reports. All the other divisions report C-2. I discuss the reports with the Chief of Staff. He takes strong exception to the C-3 rating of his old division, recognizing that if the report is accurate, his own leadership, judgment, and candor are in question. The Chief of Staff challenges the judgment of the new division commander, indicating to him that he's using an unrealistic standard to measure the training status of the division. The new division CG holds his ground. The Chief of Staff then questions the motive of the division commander, saying that he obviously wants to show a lower rating on his first report so he can show improvement later on. The division commander holds his ground. The Chief of Staff then begins a subtle campaign to discredit the division commander in the eyes of the CINC. Time passes. The Chief of Staff moves rapidly on to a three-star job and is promoted to lieutenant general. The division commander, who is highly respected both by his peers and by his subordinates, completes his tour and transfers to a job in the Pentagon, and eventually retires as a two-star with 35 years of service. In retrospect, the division commander's subjective judgment on the training status of his division may have been too severe, although I do not in any way question his motive. As DCSOPS, I would have judged all divisions essentially the same in training. Maybe they all should have been C-3. Who was right?

The officer efficiency report system is even more complex. Here the ethical principle of fairness conflicts directly with the ethical principle of honesty. Am I being fair to my people to rate them honestly in accordance with the intent of the OER regulation when I know that across the Army my contemporaries are inflating the reports of their people? Am I justified in waging a one-man campaign for strict honesty when it comes at the expense of my people?

Another aspect of honesty involves what you show your boss when he comes to visit. Conversely, what you should be looking for when you visit your subordinates may be inferred.

The scene is Fort Hood. I am Chief of Staff of the 2nd Armored Division. The Army Chief of Staff is coming to visit the post and wants to see tank gunnery training in progress. Recently the division has received a large number of infantry rotating back from Vietnam combat duty. Department of the Army has selected us to convert these infantrymen quickly into tankers, and to integrate them into our tank battalions. Most of these Vietnam veterans have only a few months to go before leaving the Army. They are not at all interested in becoming tankers, and as a matter of fact, they're not really interested in anything but getting out of the Army. We have developed a strenuous, four-week TBT (to be tankers) program, which includes familiarization firing on ranges 1 through 5 of the tank gunnery course. The TBTs will be firing Table 4 main gun when the Chief of Staff visits. All indications are that they will be doing poorly considering the extreme brevity of their preliminary gunnery training, their record on the subcaliber ranges, their general lack of technical aptitude, and their negative attitude.

A senior adviser suggests to the division commander that we should take our best NCO gunners and have them firing when the Army Chief of Staff visits the range. The point is made that an Army Chief of Staff usually visits any given division only once during the tenure in command of a division commander. Our division is a fine division. It has a good reputation. We have some great battalions. Field training has been going well. Maintenance is up. To show the Chief of Staff what we know would be subpar marksmanship will give him a distorted view of the overall standards of the division and will be a disservice to the Chief of Staff. An alternative is put forth. Why not simply change and reprint the training schedule with attendant back-dating, bringing one of our better-trained tank battalions off of maintenance cycle and putting them on the range on the day the Chief visits.

As division chief of staff, I opposed these proposals, stating that the Army Chief of Staff needs to know the trauma we are undergoing resulting from a DA decision to convert short-term Vietnam infantrymen into qualified tankers in four weeks. After all, I argued, the Chief of Staff is an experienced commander with a reputation for fairness and will understand our situation, and anyway, it would be deceptive to alter the training schedule and substitute training in which he might be more pleased. We owe it to him to tell it like it is, to show him what he needs to see, not just what he may want to see.

The division commander sides with me, and we make no special arrangements to change the schedule. The Chief of Staff visits the range. The outward appearance of the range—that is, the police, the ammunition stacks, the communications, the flags, the condition of the tanks, the saluting, the uniforms—is superb. But the gunnery is atrocious. Few rounds hit the targets. Although the CG had carefully briefed him on the whole situation enroute to the range, the Army Chief of Staff is incensed. He calls the firing to a halt, dismounts the TBTs, the NCOs, the officers, and gathers everyone around him. He berates everyone for such a rotten example of gunnery, for the waste of ammo, for the poor NCO instruction, for inadequate officer supervision. Then he takes the CG aside, mercifully out of hearing of the troops, but in their full view, and proceeds to tear the division commander apart; he thereafter leaves the range without a single word of appreciation for anyone. The division commander is philosophical. "The Chief of Staff is in a foul mood today," he says. "Nothing would have pleased him. He is exhausted from a killing schedule. He has been under severe attack by the press in recent weeks. He will calm down and the whole episode will pass away."

The Army Chief of Staff never visited the division again during the CG's tenure of duty. And the CG, until then considered to be a rising star, eventually moved on to another major general's position, well out of the mainstream of the Army, from which he retired.

Before I left the division, the CG gave me a superb efficiency report, and I was selected for brigadier general just a year later. Was I right or wrong in recommending that we not change the schedule or substitute experienced gunners for the TBTs? Did my decision contribute to the common defense? Was it consistent with our basic value systems? It certainly ruined a great division commander's career, and the influence of his character and competence was lost to the Army. On the other hand, I got away unscathed, except for a deep sense of continuing sadness at which I had done to my boss.

In conclusion, I can give no easy answers regarding these ethical tensions. I can, however, from my experience, conclude that an officer's ethical framework for addressing each of them needs to address the three fundamental questions: Does the action contribute to the national defense? Is it consistent with the protection and enhancement of life? Are the means to accomplish it acceptable? Standing firm ethically can exact a cost, perhaps a steep one. As professionals we must be willing to pay it.

This article originally appeared under the title "Ethics and the Senior Officer: Institutional Tensions" in the autumn 1985 issue of *Parameters*.

III. TOWARD A MILITARY PROFESSIONAL CODE

11

Ethical Bases of the Military Profession

By ARTHUR J. DYCK

Ever since the publication of his book *The Soldier and the State* in 1957, Samuel Huntington has been much referred to as an authority on the nature of military service as a profession.[1] However, there are new voices in the lively discussions of military professionalism which raise some excellent questions not adequately addressed by Huntington and others with similar concerns. This essay seeks to: (1) delineate a concept of the professions that suggests a basis for consensus; (2) characterize the military profession in both its distinctiveness from and its similarity to other professions; and (3) indicate the importance of professional ethics.

Professions: A Definitional Framework

After examining a whole range of proposals defining the word "profession," Morris Cogan finds a definite consensus on one point: the word "profession" is an honorific word. Based on what he finds to be fairly common among a variety of views, Cogan suggests four characteristics signifying why it is an honor to be a professional: (1) A professional is engaged in a "vocation whose practice is founded upon an understanding of the theoretical structure of some department of learning or science, and upon the abilities accompanying such understanding"; (2) The professional applies this understanding and these abilities to vital and practical human activities; (3) The practices of the professional are modified "by knowledge of a generalized nature and by the accumulated wisdom and experience of mankind, which serve to correct the errors of specialism"; and (4) The professional, serving the vital needs of human beings, has as a first ethical imperative altruistic service to clients.[2]

Cogan's inclusive understanding of that which confers the honorific status of profession on some kinds of work has been criticized by those who seek to distinguish more sharply the professions from other forms of remunerative activity. Eliot Freidson claims that a profession is founded not only on learning, but on science.[3] For Freidson, this means that ministers are not professionals, and that lawyers, in contrast to medical doctors, inadequately possess the ideal character of the professional. Presumably the uninitiated can grasp the law and apply it in ways that are not analogous to medicine. Freidson's view, however, represents a deviation from the major bulk of scholarly thought on these matters.

A. M. Carr-Saunders and P. A. Wilson choose to exclude some commonly recognized professions on the grounds that they are not involved in the vital practical human affairs of which Cogan speaks. Astonishingly, they exclude the army "because the service which soldiers are trained to render is one it is hoped they will never be called upon to perform."[4] The ethicist James Luther Adams finds it unbelievable that the army is omitted from such a broadly conceived study, given "the increasing role of military bureaucracy in our world and also the military man as diplomat and as government executive."[5] I would certainly agree with Adams.

Even the criterion of altruism has come under attack by the relentless Freidson. After all, he argues, anyone can be altruistic or egoistic; how can altruism, then, be seen as a distinctive feature of a professional? Freidson correctly points out that some of the ethical concerns of professionals do come from moral standards that everyone shares, but what he overlooks is the importance of appropriate ethical standards for professional conduct as shared by the community, and how these shared standards apply uniquely to ethical issues and problems of a given profession. Therefore, a demand for professional altruism, though necessary, is not a sufficient moral demand to make of any specific profession or its activities. The military profession is no exception in this respect.

Professions: Universal Characteristics

The traits Cogan singled out as typifying a true professional thus bring us close to a complete and widely held view regarding the nature of professions. We would add the further conditions that professions possess standards of competence defined by a comprehensive and self-governing organization of practitioners, a high degree of autonomy for individual practitioners and the professional group, and some specific code of ethics or ethical standards by which members of a profession are guided in the performance of their services. To all of this, some would add that service to the larger community rather than economic gain is the dominant motive.

Every profession involves a client-professional relation demanding professional adherence to some set of ethical standards. Decisions involving the conduct of war, the acceptance and handling of divorce cases, or the advisability of surgery are scarcely to be seen as morally neutral. To be sure, each of them involves an assessment based on particular knowledge, skills, and experience. But at the same time each involves an assessment of whether one is ultimately increasing or decreasing benefits and injuries to those served by the professional activities in question. Decisions regarding the development and application of technology used by professionals are similarly never totally neutral. When to activate or deactivate a respirator, when to declare an issue within or outside the province of the courts, when to consider a weapon appropriate for development and use—all these require ethical reflection. With respect to weapons, there are critical problems currently before us. To what extent can we morally justify the proliferation of weapons that predictably destroy the lives of noncombatants? Difficult questions regarding the protection of innocent lives arise at a number of points in the entire weapons decisionmaking process.

On the basis of the foregoing considerations, we may now establish the three broad characteristics of all professions: (1) special or unique competence in the performance of special tasks and services; (2) general or social competence in the performance of professional and community-related tasks and services; and (3) a professional-client relationship. These characteristics are further elaborated in the accompanying table.

The Military Profession

With these professional characteristics in mind, we can see why Huntington's account of the military as a profession has been and continues to be useful. He has delineated the specialized military expertise imparted to officers through their military training. Furthermore he finds a commitment to general social competence, based in large part on appropriate education at the college and graduate level. This education includes much more than the specialized learning that distinguishes military officers from physicians, lawyers, and other professionals. Indeed, there is considerable stress in the military upon disciplines concerned with human relations and the understanding of societies. As with all professions, military service, in Huntington's view, is an essential social service.

Going further, Huntington specifically identifies the sense in which we can speak of a professional-client relation between officers and those they serve. In essence, he defines the client of the military professional to be society and the special responsibility of the military professional toward the client as that of providing military security. The most immediate expression of this responsibility is in the subordination of the military professional to the state or government that represents the wishes of the client, that is, the wishes of society. Huntington locates the ethical aspect of this professional responsibility in the officer's love for perfecting his skills, but, beyond that, in his social obligation to use those skills solely for the benefit of society (the client). It should be noted also that the military has the earmarks of a typical professional organization in the rules and regulations governing the conduct of its members and in the moral conscientiousness demanded of its members in adhering to those regulations.

THE THREE CHARACTERISTICS OF PROFESSIONS

I. Special or Unique Competence in Special Tasks and Services

- Specialized training and education (e.g. medical school).
- Autonomy based on unique skills (e.g. setting a broken limb).
- Performs unique social service (e.g. practice of individual medicine).
- Skills subject to rational analysis and judgment by standards of competence.
- Membership in professional associations (e.g. American Medical Association).

II. General or Social Competence in Professional and Community Tasks and Services

- General training and education (e.g. liberal arts, counseling, behavioral sciences).
- Broad social service (e.g. community health endeavors).
- Membership in community associations (e.g. civic, religious, social).

III. Professional-Client Relationship

- Consultation and service.
- Based on special trust, confidence, understanding, and confidentiality.
- Based on conformity to ethical principle.
- Primary motive is service, not financial gain.

Huntington also gives a plausible account of the unique expertise of the military. It is the management of violence. The claim of uniqueness is not totally correct, of course, since police forces are also managers of violence in subordination to the state. However, police do not manage violence from the perspective of national security, although they are part of achieving national security.

In a general way, therefore, Huntington has covered the major characteristics that are normally regarded as distinctive of professionalism. Yet, there are some additional and serious questions that should be raised about Huntington's account of the specific nature of the military profession. Indeed, Zeb Bradford and James R. Murphy specifically point to the insufficiency and narrowness of seeing the unique expertise of the military as the management of violence.[6] They argue correctly that the military is also involved in certain aspects of peacekeeping and deterrence. James L. Adams and Donald F. Bletz both refer to military officers as diplomats, possessing what Bletz calls "politico-military" expertise.[7] Surely it would be unrealistic to overlook the vital role that military officers have played in the restoration and maintenance of order following a number of major military conflicts in which this country has been involved. There is no reason to negate or downplay this role. It will surely continue to be important.

Bradford and Murphy also point out that much of the expertise that officers require and many of the tasks of the military are not directly related to anything we could call the management of violence. But we should not stress this insight unduly, because the military would lose its special reason for being if management by military officers could not be construed as management of personnel and techniques designed either to engage in violence or to deter others from it. In this sense, Huntington is on target.

However, even if we include these refinements of Huntington, none of the writers yet referred to deals explicitly with the way in which ethics relates to military professionalism. That military officers are supposed to be ethical is clear. That the military has an ethically responsible task is also clear. However, what military people need to know about ethics and how ethics relates to the management of violence is not adequately discussed by the literature I have seen on this subject.

For example, there is no consensus as to whether a military ethic should or should not be based upon some kind of code. In fact, the value of a code is disputed. Compare this situation with that prevailing in medicine and law. Both of these professions have codes and are engaged in discussions, not to eliminate codes, but to improve the existing ones. We see an exciting and growing debate within law and medicine regarding the extent to which knowledge of ethics as a field will help in this process and, beyond that, will be helpful in shaping professional responsibility and reducing abuses of clients. Increasingly, medicine and law are not only thinking about how to assure that professionals are morally sensitive, but also how to educate professionals in identifying and resolving ethical issues raised in the professional-client relationship itself.

In sum, some of the oldest professions are currently reassessing their formal ethical standards and the means by which these standards are set. The military has always sought to inculcate high moral standards in training its officers. It is not surprising, therefore, that many of the questions being raised by medical and legal professionals are being asked seriously and intelligently by military professionals of every rank. This concern for ethics in the military is only partly the result of serious instances of questionable professional conduct in recent years and the publicity attending honor scandals at the military academies. For it has been a long-standing and admirable tradition of the military to ask how best to achieve exemplary moral behavior on the part of its professionals. In keeping with this fine tradition, I wish to consider some of the ways in which the military profession has conceived of itself ethically, and to suggest how these conceptions may be extended and refined. I do this not in the spirit of giving final answers, but rather in the spirit of urging an agenda worthy of further discussion and debate.

A Tentative Outline

A traditional approach to professional responsibilities in the military consists of emphasizing the three central concepts: duty, country, and honor. Some have maintained that these concepts are no longer adequate for thinking about ethics in the military, but we shall discover why they are still cogent and rich in meaning.

Duty

Duty implies not only the obligation to do one's job conscientiously, but also to do so within ethically acceptable norms. The ethical aspect of duty for military professionals has at least two major facets. First, military professionals, like all other professionals, need a knowledge of basic moral principles and some facility in applying them; professionals also require some understanding of why these moral principles are essential to our daily life together as human beings. Second, professions have their own particular moral responsibilities and ethical guidelines that specify how best to recognize and maintain their specific obligations to clients. In its broadest dimensions, probably the most basic set of guidelines for military professionals is found within the criteria evolved by the various theories of the just war.

In this short essay, it is not possible to discuss every relevant moral principle, but we can at least illustrate the value of being explicit about moral principles and the reasons for adhering to them.[8] Take truth-telling, which is surely one of the most fundamental moral principles, not only for military life but for every human community. Consider for a moment why this is so. Would I enter into any agreement with you or be willing to engage in any joint venture, never mind the dangerous venture characteristic of combat, if I thought that you did not recognize lying as morally wrong? All communication depends on trust in the reliability with which information and instructions are given.

Of course, it can be argued that the foregoing is just the kind of simple notion of duty that is unrealistic for guiding behavior. Surely all of us recognize that if in lying we can save a life, we would, other things being equal, tell a lie. This is generally the case. However, such an example only underlines the necessity to be very clear about our most basic moral affirmations, because in a wide variety of circumstances life is valued more than truth. But there is also a wide variety of circumstances in which lives and important practical affairs hinge on absolute fidelity to the truth. Since this is so, it is important to understand cases in which people are convinced that they should forgo their adherence to truth. It is understandable, for example, that General Lavelle in the war in Vietnam could reason that, by instructing his pilots to fire before taking the risk of being fired upon, he would be potentially or actually saving the lives of many of his men.[9] However, at the same time, Mr. Kissinger, relying on the truthfulness of American officers, was publicly claiming that no such actions were being taken by American pilots. The potential failure of negotiations to end the war in Vietnam occasioned by such ignorance on the part of America's chief negotiator could have involved many more lives than those being contemplated by General Lavelle.

I know the Lavelle case is not a simple one. I wish only to claim that actions such as General Lavelle's deserve questioning. It may be true that he was asked to perform an action which he should not have been asked to perform. Yet, if that is granted, there were reasonable alternatives to lying which he might have chosen. Suffice it to say that part of educating a professional is precisely to increase the extent to which the morally appropriate options in difficult contexts are identified and understood. Sometimes actions are proposed, implicitly or explicitly, which are morally intolerable and must be seen as such. Every military person who is properly instructed knows that orders may be unlawful or immoral, and that it is not always one's duty to obey them.

The essential imperative of truth-telling is no less clear in the duty to report combat readiness. Falsifying a combat readiness report is potentially destructive of lives; further, it handicaps national leaders in making decisions concerning whether to engage in an otherwise justifiable war. A pattern of inaccurate readiness reports can lead to mistakes both moral and strategic.

As mentioned earlier, one of the most important sources of guidance for those who are slated to manage and deter violence is just war theory. Such theory has persisted in Western thought precisely because of the recognition that, although resort to violence and killing should generally be regarded as evil, we would occasion even greater evils if we desisted from violence and killing in all cases. Augustine, who is one of the first in the West to discuss just-war criteria, speaks about how he is to fulfill his love for his neighbor in situations where someone is about to kill a friend. Should he, Augustine, stand idly by and permit this to happen? Surely not. He should intervene and do whatever is necessary to prevent this unjust and unprovoked attack which threatens to lead to the death of his friend.

In a few simple statements, we have now reached the very heart of the service we expect from our military professionals—protection of the innocent against aggression in the form of violence. This means, however, that those of us who are not professional managers of violence are giving our approval to the use of violence. Under what circumstances should we give that approval? In giving it, we do not want to breed violent persons, nor do we wish to give away our usual high regard for refraining from violence; hence, we resort to just-war theory, which is designed to help guide us in this deliberation.

Space does not permit an extended explanation here of just war theory. I refer the reader to Ralph Potter's admirable bibliographical essay and the work of LeRoy Walters.[10] For our purposes, it is sufficient merely to list the acknowledge just war criteria.

In most accounts of just war criteria, it is agreed that war or other military actions that would involve killing or the risk of killing can be justified only if the following attributes characterize the action being contemplated:

- Just cause.
- Just intentions.
- Sanction by the highest lawful authority.
- Public declaration of what is contemplated.
- Due proportion, that is, less evil following from acting rather than not acting in the manner contemplated.
- Reasonable hope for success.
- Last resort after all reasonable pacific alternatives have been tried.
- Employment of just means to minimize risks to innocent noncombatants, avoiding also terrorism and torture.

As military professionals are well aware, a number of these criteria, particularly those pertaining to just means, form the basis for the current understanding of the laws of land warfare. All of us are becoming painfully aware, however, that the laws of land warfare, admirable though they may be, need to be thoughtfully and carefully updated to include the new dimension of nuclear weaponry. Military professionals as well as civilian leaders have a profound obligation to develop nuclear weapon employment policies and procedures that maximize national security, while at the same time minimizing injury and loss of life among noncombatants. This is no easy task, but it is essential to the future survival not only of morality, but of civilization. Helping all of us think through the necessity and character of just means in contemporary defense systems could well be one of the most important contributions that military professionals make to the peace, welfare, and moral quality of humanity.

One word about the insistence that using force should come as a last resort. Although it is clear that the civilian government has a strong obligation to encourage and create conditions for negotiating with actual and potential enemies, the military has always had a vital role in encouraging and carrying out diplomacy. This is the time to strengthen rather than weaken that time-honored military tradition.

Country

The military professional's clients are the people of his country. Strictly speaking, faithfulness to one's fellow citizens is expressed appropriately as a vow to uphold the Constitution. This means that effort on the part of any group, even the government itself, to advocate or use violence in an unconstitutional manner is subject to challenge by the highest authorities within the military profession. Every civilian leader and every military leader is sworn faithfully to follow the Constitution as the foundation of the law of the land.

But the ethics of military professionals must go beyond fidelity to law and its legal underpinnings. No constitution or law is obeyed and understood without the cultivation of moral conscientiousness and moral sensitivity. That is why every professional ethic, including the military's, also includes concern for honor.

Honor

It was possible to create a constitution that would found and undergird a community such as ours only because there were leaders who clearly discerned the most basic rights and freedoms that belong to human beings. A commitment to freedom, to the value of human life, and to equality of opportunity characterized those who drew up the Constitution and must equally characterize those who profess fidelity to it. Such concerns are quintessentially ethical in their import. They presuppose an education that sees ethics as an area of knowledge equal in importance to other disciplines and areas of technical know-how. To treat morality and ethics as purely subjective or personal concerns—and thus outside the pale of disciplined thought—is quite out of character with the findings of moral philosophy and religious ethics.[11]

In any discussion of honor, it is important to cite the necessity for courage, fairness, and complete trustworthiness on the part of military professionals. These are admirably stressed by General Maxwell Taylor in his provocative and thoughtful essay advocating a code of ethics for the military.[12] He is careful to emphasize the necessity for moral development alongside the necessity for acquiring physical, intellectual, and other forms of professional competence.

It is unfortunate when discussions of military ethics devolve to debate as to whether the military should have a code or should instead stress ethical awareness as products of educational and developmental processes. The distinction seems based on a false dichotomy. Evolving and contemplating a code are themselves ethically educational and developmental processes of importance. General Taylor unfortunately does not say anything about just war criteria in his suggested code. This seems to me a serious omission that should call for broad and open discussion among military professionals. At the same time, many professional schools are recognizing that it has been an error to drop formal instruction in ethics from curricula. Whatever the limitations of such formal instruction, the very fact that it is not seen as sufficiently important is in itself a failure to give proper stress to reflection on the moral life and what it means to live one's life with honor.

I have tried in this essay to suggest something about our general understanding of professions, something of the unique qualities of the military professional, and something about the military ethic. I would like to close with a moving plea for education in ethics, as formulated in 1906 by Colonel Charles W. Larned while a professor at West Point:

> [Modern secular education] subordinates the ethical to every other idea . . ., renounces disciplinary control . . ., generally neglects the training of the sensory faculties and activities . . ., fails to enforce systematic physical training . . ., fails to inculcate the principles of good citizenship. . . . First, last, and always our civilization is irrevocably committed to morality and high principles as the heart's core of its life; and no education that does not base itself upon ethical actions as its prime motor can have any part or lot in civilization's higher development. Its first and its continuing function should be to guide the perceptions toward moral truth; to teach the discipline of passion; to cultivate the power of right perception and action, and the idea of the common brotherhood of man.[13]

NOTES

1. Samuel Huntington, *The Soldier and the State* (Cambridge, Mass.: Harvard Univ. Press, 1957), pp. 7-18.
2. Morris Cogan, "Toward a Definition of Profession," *Harvard Educational Review* 23 (Winter 1953): 48-49.
3. Eliot Freidson, *Profession of Medicine* (New York: Dodd, Mead, 1970), pp. 3-22, 77-84.
4. A. M. Carr-Saunders and P. A. Wilson, *The Professions* (Oxford: Clarendon Press, 1933), p. 3.
5. James Luther Adams, "The Social Import of the Professions," *Bulletin of the American Association of Theological Schools* no. 23 (June 1958): 152-68.
6. Zeb Bradford Jr. and James R. Murphy, "A New Look at the Military Profession," *Army* 19 (February 1969): 58-64.
7. Adams, pp. 152-68. Donald F. Bletz, "Military Professionalism: A Conceptual Approach," *Military Review* 51 (May 1971): 9-17.
8. For discussions of moral principles, see for example Arthur J. Dyck, *On Human Care: An Introduction to Ethics* (Nashville: Abingdon Press, 1977); and William K. Frankena, *Ethics*, 2nd ed. (Englewood Cliffs, N.J.: Prentice-Hall, 1973).
9. Gordon A. Ginsburg, *The Lavelle Case: Crisis in Integrity*, Air War College Professional Study No. 5255 (Maxwell AFB, Ala., 1974).
10. Ralph B. Potter, *War and Moral Discourse* (Richmond, Va.: John Knox Press, 1969), pp. 87-123; LeRoy Walters, "Historical Applications of the Just War Theory: Four Case Studies in Normative Ethics," *Love and Society: Essays in the Ethics of Paul Ramsey*, ed. James Johnson and David Smith (Missoula, Mont.: Scholar Press, 1974), pp. 115-38.
11. Dyck, *op. cit.*; Frankena, *op. cit.*
12. Maxwell D. Taylor, "A Professional Ethic for the Military?" *Army* 28 (May 1978): 18-21.
13. Charles W. Larned, "West Point and Higher Education," *Army and Navy Life* 8 (June 1906): 9-22.

This article originally appeared in the March 1980 issue of *Parameters*.

12

The Moral Dimension of War and the Military Ethic

By DONALD ATWELL ZOLL

The history of the military art is, from one perspective, a narrative of an important aspect of social ethics. This is obvious enough: warfare has been a major social activity of man, and all social events are bound up with questions of value, with human choices regarding beliefs about "right" and "wrong" conduct. In contemporary terms, however, the moral or ethical component in the postulation of military theory is generally ignored, primarily because we live in an age in which moral restraint on warfare has been minimal, to say the least, and, perhaps ironically, because full-scale nuclear conflict appears so appalling that it is difficult to conceive of any exchange of present military power that would obey any moral restraint. Thus warfare itself has become a "moral" issue.

Historically, however, the conduct of war has generally reflected prevailing moral attitudes in a number of ways. The most apparent of these has certainly been a self-conscious limitation upon forms of combat and even upon specific types of weaponry. It may well be that eventually the lure of victory, real or imagined, will prompt mankind to jettison previous moral limitations, but, from a historical perspective, the march of rampant technology has not been all that uninterrupted. Much has been made of the "conservatism" of military establishments in the adoption of otherwise attractive weapons and techniques. No doubt tunnel-visioned habit may account for much of this, but, on the other hand, some of this disinclination to employ military novelties has had a social and possibly a moral base.

A brief review of the motivations behind the limitation of various forms of warfare may be instructive. Consider, for illustration, the vivid example provided by 13th-century Europe where a still "universal" church imposed a "Peace of God" as well as other strictures on the conduct of war by means of the still potent threat of excommunication. Here, the regulation of conflict rested principally on the assumption that certain forms of behavior and certain tools of war were reprehensible for Christians to employ (at least on each other—the crossbow was so prohibited, but allowed against "infidels"). This theologically grounded form of restraint might be labeled as prohibitions against the violation of *a universal moral order*. Such interdicts were operating as long as the bulk of those determining the policy of states had any regard for the existence of a "universal moral order." In historical terms, the Reformation wrote *finis* to this—and the result was the Thirty Years War, notorious for barbarous excess. It is interesting to note, too, that this was hardly an exclusively Christian phenomenon. Certain Moslems, perhaps of a fundamentalist persuasion, long clung to the view that the sword was the only morally sanctioned instrument approved of by Mahomet and thus rejected the advent of artillery (to their grave misfortune in the wars with their coreligionists, the Ottoman Turks, who were less puristic in this matter).

Not all restraints were encased in religious legalism by any means. From the traditions of chivalry arose a "class mystique" that distinctly shaped moral attitudes toward warfare. It may be remembered that although the chivalric code per se hardly survived the 14th century in full array, most of the existing European aristocracies were still permeated by its spirit, tangible or otherwise, well into the period of the Industrial Revolution, and it was from such aristocracies that the officer cadres of the world's armies came. The code survived not as some quasi-Christian devotion to disembodied virtue, but rather as a *personal* standard of conduct rooted in self-esteem, in pride, both social and professional. It is well to remember that the "sportive" element in warfare, war as a gentlemen's game conducted by rules of deportment, was long-lived in Western tradition, still evident in those first bitter conflicts of the Industrial Age, the American Civil War and the Franco-Prussian War. Thus, one can speak quite literally about *class attitudes* being a limiting factor in the conduct of war.

The 18th century—the "Age of Reason," so called—illustrates another limiting phenomenon: *a philosophically derived social ethic*. Warfare, overall, in the 18th century was reflective of a pervasive revivification of humanitarian concerns, the limiting of conflict to avoid massive loss of life and despoilage of property. The dynastic and colonial struggles of this age were in part shaped by the impact of theories of "natural law" propounded especially by the French *philosophes*. It is provocative to point out that the greatest military engineer of that age, Vauban, was an intimate of the Parisian philosophers and defended his preoccupation with fortification on the grounds that defensive warfare was less costly and more humane.

Another limiting factor has been a *concern for the maintenance of professional self-interest*. I cite as the prime example of this the reactions among professional European soldiers to the post-Revolution *levée-en-masse* in France. The arguments against a "nation in arms" that called forth the mass of the populace for universal service were then couched in distinctly moralistic terms. The armies rallied by the embattled French Republic, brought to full development by Napoleon, were castigated as "armed hordes" and "undisciplined mobs" capable of savage pillage and disregard for the "rules" of warfare. No doubt, much of this protest may be taken with a grain of salt, but the "democratization" of military establishments meant the final withering away of the monopoly upon military control by the traditional aristocracies. Yet in fairness, too, it is reasonable to suggest that mass "patriot" armies have generally been less inclined to limit the scope of conflict. In post-World War I Germany, von Seeckt sought to re-arm the *Wehrmacht* beyond the limits of the Versailles Treaty, but to avoid, as well, a "popular" army of mass proportions.

The final abrogation of restraints of a moral character upon the conduct of warfare has been variously diagnosed. In the second half of the current century the only functional limitation on the scope of warfare has been a concept of *reciprocal advantage*, and yet this pragmatic dictum (as if lifted from Machiavelli's *The Prince*) is not wholly explainable in terms of the physical power of retaliation. Political factors obviously intrude, and politics is a realm in which action, if not instigated by moral concerns, is circumscribed by them very frequently.

It is not my purpose here to discuss the full-blown issue of inhibitions on the conduct of war that do or might arise from ostensibly moral sources. I wish, initially, only to make the point that a more or less formal concern for the impact of ethical considerations on military activity is hardly a vacuous academic pursuit. In this connection, one need only recall the strident and unhappy controversies that were spawned by the late war in Indo-China, issues that brought into question, among other things, the conduct of our troops there and the nature of what might loosely be referred to as the "professional ethics" of our career soldiery. Indeed, the discussion I am about to embark on must be undertaken with the realization that the American military establishment is still undergoing a "post-Vietnam" metamorphosis. I contended some years ago that many aspects of that conflict had done serious damage indeed to the internal élan of the professional officer class, but that much of this lamentable disarray was the result of a lack of *professional* indoctrination and self-awareness. Put another way, our soldiers in the field were often thrust into moral dilemmas that were, in substance, unnecessary (or wrongly resolved), because of the atrophy of a professional ethic. It is to this question, then, that I should like now to turn.

What must a professional military ethic be? Conceived of at its most rudimentary level, a professional military ethic must be built upon two basic considerations: first, the maximum attainment of objectives for which the profession itself exists and, second, a reconciliation with the precepts of humane values that have been manifested in the course of human history.

These otherwise simple premises raise problems at once. Are the two always compatible? Would not the survival of the society, in extremis, justify any and all means, including those not condoned by the second premise? I do not think that this is quite the problem it might appear, since a professional ethic is, fundamentally, a code for individual behavior, and the choice of saving the society by ostensibly immoral means is rarely a dilemma for the field commander. It is, rather, a political decision. That this is so suggests that, for the soldier, the suspension of rudimentary morality is hardly ever justifiable (questions of obedience momentarily aside). I raise this point for one reason only: a crucial feature of a professional ethic is the recognition of the *ethical status of the individual*; it is a code that is concerned with the moral validity of individual acts, even as a form of protection for the moral actor. The purpose, then, of a professional military ethic is not only the "maximum attainment of objectives," and the collective moral well-being of the occupation, but the enhancement of the moral status of the person who embraces it. It *should* have the effect of quelling the necessity for the entertainment of moral dilemmas.

More specifically, I believe there are five principal elements that form the base for a contemporary military ethic: personal honor; obedience and limits of moral freedom; relationships to the society as a whole; relationships to existing political institutions and forces; and the moral implications of command responsibility. Allow me to consider each of these in turn.

Personal Honor

One might think the term "personal honor" quaint in these times, but I remain convinced that it lies at the heart of the military ethic (conceiving such an ethic as being a specialized body of moral canons). Honor is, of course, a generally well-esteemed quality in all persons, not just those who pursue the military profession. I think, therefore, that it is necessary to talk rather precisely about honor in a military context, quite beyond its vaguely laudatory connotations.

The concept of "honor" is, I think, chivalric in express usage, although the groundwork for such a conception is Greco-Roman, especially the latter.[1] The cult of honor, in medieval times, was bound up with the idea of a hierarchy of fidelities, rather approximating the social structure of feudalism. Feudalism was, among other things, a series of reciprocal obligations; and honor, in its original context, implies this exchange of fidelities. In exchange for one fidelity (to God, to one's fellow man, to one's king and liege-lord), another fidelity was extended: the proferring of liberty, of esteem, of social status, even of mundane privileges. Thus, we today use the word to reflect this dichotomy. We receive "honors," we "honor" obligations, and so on. Honor is thereby a condition voluntarily assumed and, if maintained, productive of personal benefits, not the least of which is the extension of considerable personal freedom from mandatory regulation—"I give you my word of honor" is the equivalent of claiming exemption from actual inspection or verification. By subordinating oneself to a "code of honor," one is granted a considerable range of action, and one's motives are beyond question.

Of course, in earlier eras honor was closely associated with those who undertook military obligations (itself a feudal obligation).[2] But the chivalry of the *chansons des gestes* did not survive the 15th century. With the rise of professional armies, in contrast to feudal hosts, the preexisting devotion to honor was widely absorbed into the concept of the royally commissioned officer, fidelity to the nation-state replacing feudal vows. There was an increasingly autonomous character to this idea of honor as its theological ties weakened, especially in the Renaissance, and the elements of individual pride, dignity, and self-esteem became prominent. The concept of honor (related to fidelity) became wedded to the obligation of self-cultivation, of personal excellence. There is a vivid difference between this concept of pride, however, and egocentrism as conceived in voluntaristic philosophies or even Freudian ego-psychology. The pride that follows from self-cultivation and self-discipline is in accord with the acknowledged obligation of the person to fulfill his own nature (the idea is basically that of Aristotle), in contrast to self-gratification. The distinction is an important one, because excellence, the impulse toward the pursuit of self-generated standards, is vital to all significant human endeavors, the military arts among them. The soldier does not subsist on self-abnegation (glory is the legitimate compensation for his sacrifices, as most commentators from Plato on have conceded). Nor is his pride, derivable from his fidelity to honor, or even his professional excellence, which flows from the same source, an exercise in the "maximization of self-interest." Rather, they are rewards of freedom and self-identity.

The most important feature of this dedication to honor by military professionals, in more functional terms, has been to invest the officer with a necessary independence of mind. It is the presupposition of a dedication to a code of honor that allows for vital intellectual freedom in the military community. So long as an omnibus fidelity to a basic commitment to personal honor exists, then a notable freedom can proceed: the freedom to express unpopular theories, offer criticism, explore alternative methods, and even exhibit a sometimes invigorating professional eccentricity. This situation is the opposite of that which prevails in most civilian bureaucracies (except those embracing a stoically disciplined ethic themselves) where, minus a rigorous devotion to personal honor, the atmosphere is one of self-protection, conformity, pragmatic compromise, intellectual caution, and even, at times, mutual suspicion.

In general, with the decline of the significance of personal honor has come a corresponding diminishment of intellectual vitality in the military profession worldwide. Officers now tend to follow a political ethic rather than a military one, are far more cautious about marching to the beat of a different drummer, and are more concerned with protective adaptations that contemporary bureaucracy inspires. I am not contending that innovators, eccentrics, and intellectual Jeremiahs have invariably fared well personally in armies—although their presences have undoubtedly been significantly stimulating—only that as a regard for honor fades, the presumption of fidelity and the extension of personal liberty for the officer contract, and with them the opportunities for respectable dissent, career enhancements aside.

Obedience and Limits of Moral Freedom

The obligation to obey is never total, but with the soldier the *presumption* must always be of the legitimacy of command. I do not think this is true of the civilian at all. Quite the contrary, if I am given a command, a summary order, my first impulse and act is to question its validity and legitimacy. It is generally desirable that nonmilitary persons *not* be disposed toward unqualified forms of obedience. Why do people in general, then, obey at all, if they are inclined to do otherwise? In extension, how is the social ethic enforced? At risk of being accused of a certain cynicism, I conclude that obedience to social rules generally arises from some form of punitive sanction. This need not be the threat of jail or other drastic penalties, but can more commonly be a fear of a loss of social approbation or, more severely, social ostracism. No doubt many people obey the prime social injunctions out of a rational and voluntary understanding of their efficacy, but in the case of law—specific statutory prohibitions—I suspect that wholly voluntary compliance would be quite small.

No army can function on the basis of compliance to commands (or "statutory prohibitions") that is the result of punitive threat, certainly not under the stress of battle. I do not entirely discount, of course, the need for such punitive arrangements (armies, too, need policemen, courts, and jails), and I believe that many men enter combat convinced that the penalties for failure to do so may be harsher than the machinations of the enemy. But among military professionals, those who both accept and issue commands, the obligation to obey—to the point of self-immolation—is a *voluntary* commitment that presumes the legitimacy of command. This compliance is unique in human institutions, I believe, and yet it is an essential part of a military ethic.

It is possible, certainly, to conceive of commands that are either patently insane or morally reprehensible. I think that instances of their occurrence are relatively infrequent, but I concede that such instances would require a rational response. The *presumption* of command legitimacy is not a curtailment of essential moral freedom. *If* a reciprocal trust exists in mutual honor between commander and subordinate, then the subordinate is fully able to express his professional reservations about the prudence and rectitude of a command, and procedures should exist to facilitate this. The acceptance of an order is, in part, an abrogation of moral responsibility, *if* the person fulfilling the order has been free to declare his concerns about its contents, preferrably in a formal mode. This presumed infringement on moral accountability is justified by two factors: the recognition of the rational need to assign moral responsibility in a hierarchical pattern, and the ultimate freedom of the individual to accept the consequences of his final unwillingness to obey. Refusing an order is invariably accompanied by forms of risk, but, at times, officers have felt impelled to do so, motivated by professional concerns and accepting the consequences of their action.[3]

Relationships to the Society as a Whole

No military establishment exists exclusively for its own internal benefit, even in instances of rulership of states by explicit warrior societies. War, for sport or conquest, has frequently been a prime preoccupation of a society, but warfare has never been the sole *raison d'etre* of a culture. Thus, a military organization is ancillary to the social whole, at least in its rudimentary role as protector of the physical safety of the society. But that this is true does not necessarily imply that the social ethos totally defines the military participation in the social order.

What are then the principal determinants that undergird the professional ethic of this apparatus of protection? The most fundamental one may be the preservation of the society—but from what? In the first place, there is a shadowy distinction between the *society* and the *state*. I shall not here digress into a discussion of the problems of defining "state," but it is clear enough that some difference exists between a society (thought of as being an aggregate of the citizenry) and a formal institution or, perhaps, a symbolic construct, that embodies it as a state. Is there, then, a conflict between social loyalty and loyalty to the state? Does "preservation" of the society refer only to external aggressions or also to domestic insurrections? If both, then insurrections against whom or what? These conflicts of loyalties have been real enough; historically, they are simple to document. Interesting, too, is the fact that this broad issue has sharpened in recent times due to the "force monopoly" of the contemporary state, its possession of decisive weaponry generally unavailable to its citizens.

Moreover, the current age is one beset with a bewildering range of quarreling ideologies, a sizable proportion of them freely advocating the most violent means of securing social hegemony. To a large extent the contesting factions of religion have been replaced in modern industrial states by contesting claims of social preferment.

The contemporary military professional is harrassed on two fronts. Whom does he finally serve? What are the moral implications of this social turmoil that seethes around him?

Theological disputes in the past have less affected the homogeneity of officer corps than have these ideological conflicts (granting certain notable instances of bigotry in many armies). Does religious toleration (to the extent of the private worship of individuals) suggest, now, a comparable toleration of ideological dogma? It would be naive to assume that military officers are not exposed to and affected by ideological blandishments, and, indeed, the military occupation does not preclude the nominal options of the citizen in all particulars. But as religion is not overtly an ingredient in a professional military ethic, ideological premises cannot be so embraced either, regardless of how moralistic may be their motivations or, I might add, how generally they might be cherished in contemporary America. This would seem a more straightforward prohibition than it in fact is. In other terminology, the military ethic is not a body of patriotic sentiments, least of all a collection of social principles reflecting cultural preferences about arrangements substantially ungermane to the responsibilities of military professionals.

The military ethic is, rather, a code whose only recourse is to serve the physical embodiment of the state. Where is that "state" to be found? All other argumentative considerations aside, one virtue of the monarchical system is that it provides a visible, personal symbolization of the sovereignty of the state. In a monarchy, there is not much question of who is, *pro forma*, the "commander-in-chief," if you will. That personal connection with the embodiment of the state is far more difficult in a republic and, in some respects, even more awkward in the case of a despotic dictatorship (where power may be centralized but also unstable). Moreover, it is somewhat more aloof to venerate a written constitution in a glass box or, in the American instance, separate the role of chief of state from that of leader of the government, avowedly a political role. Generally, however, it is to the head of state, monarchical or republican, that the loyalty of the military is extended, not, of course, as a person, but as the emblem of national sovereignty, irrespective of the convolutions of political activity.

I think that this is an unavoidable commitment, to be tampered with only in the direst of extremities. Such extremities have arisen, of course. But it is not the function of a military establishment to evaluate the efficacy or even the legitimacy (in the broadly constitutional sense) of those who exercise sovereignty. The presumption of obedience to the state is rooted in a presumption that the state exists to advance the commonweal. The agents of the state—governments—have on occasion forsaken this primary obligation, to be sure, and I think the litmus test of this condition may be what amounts to the waging of war upon the citizenry by those operating under the aegis of state authority. Such occurrences have been rarer, historically, than might be supposed, however. It is one thing to conclude that a nation is either ill-governed or even ruled oppressively, by one's own standards, but quite another to presume that a government has embarked upon a policy of deliberate internecine pillage. I am not saying that all revolutions, all insurgencies, against existing regimes are unjustified, only that the judgment of the military professional of rival claims to social power must be confined by a prior fidelity to act on behest of the existing machinery of the state—except in the infrequent cases of intrasocietal depredation.[4] To do otherwise is to make military establishments either the pawns of contending social forces or to have them assume the loathesome role of a Praetorian Guard.

Relationships to Existing Political Institutions and Forces

It would be simpler, I grant, if military professionals restricted themselves to military matters and politicians attended solely to political ones. Needless to say, these areas, military and political, overlap (most apparently, of course, in "grand strategy," an amalgam of the two); but even if they did not, there are generals and admirals who yearn to penetrate the "affairs of state" and politicians who wish to direct armies.

Despite what might seem an evident division of labor, the increasing preoccupation of the professional military officer with political affairs arose, in part, from understandable and even commendable motives prompted by the mounting complexity of world affairs. Greater understanding of political matters appeared a wholesome attribute for the post-World War II officer, especially in view of the advent of military situations in which operations were overlaid with often complex political considerations (which is true, in a certain sense, of all warfare involved with counterinsurgency). But despite the apparent logic of this new orientation, the effort was excessive and resulted in three regrettable consequences: a neglect of pure military art, which, I believe it is fair to say, inhibited the success of American efforts in Indo-China; a further obfuscation of a military ethic and a professional appreciation of the vocation, and a growing tendency to replace a military perspective with a political one; and an increasing interest on the part of military professionals in wider governmental assignment.

Let me deal with the last of these points first. The history to date of political performance by former professional military officers is woeful, by and large, and remains so in truth despite the claims of their often zealous apologists. While ex-generals have made quite unsatisfactory presidents, former officers have also hardly done well as secretaries of state, directors of intelligence, ambassadors, or program chiefs. The reasons for this are worth examining. If those outside the military often tend to deprecate the intellectual demands of the profession of arms, soldiers very frequently have a simple-minded appreciation of the political arts and, furthermore, are rarely prepared, either educationally or psychologically, for the trials of careers essentially alien to them. Further, the best minds in the military generally are more than content to grapple with the intellectual challenges inherent in their own calling and have little enthusiasm for becoming politico-military hybrids.

It is necessary to rethink the relationship of military officers with the political realm, if only to revive an ethical foundation for the profession that is not transfused with political dicta. Politics obeys an ethic of its own—more intricate and no less noble in its composition than that of the military—but such a moral outlook is not appropriate to military circumstances. It is not merely a question of repulsing the enticements of political power; it is a matter of not adulterating military competency by an excessively political orientation, a world view, I might add, usually only dimly understood by most career officers.

The sharp line must be reestablished between the political and the military, and the reconstituted professional military ethic must include a strict prohibition against the incursion of professional officers into political governmental service and a reconcentration of talents and energies on the development of the military arts. This change of posture must also include the termination of the sub rosa participation of officers in partisan political affairs and the refusal of senior officers to become expressly identified with specific governmental administrations.

Such prohibitions enhance rather than restrict the freedom of officers to engage, quite publicly, in their ongoing *professional* life, indeed, to express military opinions that do not at all times echo the views of the current political administration. Military ethics should permit the free participation of officers in public discussion and even in disputes regarding matters *within their professional competence.* Too frequently, for illustration, the Joint Chiefs of Staff appear, justly or not, as a monolithic body devoted to the advocacy of whatever defense policies have been espoused by the civilian component of government, the administration in power. Defense policies, needless to say, involve considerations that go beyond explicitly military concerns, but for too long a sophisticated discussion of military affairs has been stifled by the application of politically motivated restraints upon such exposure of views, restraints imposed both from outside and inside the Department of Defense. I know of no other crucial area of public affairs in the United States about which the public at large is so ill-informed as national security policies. This is in part attributable to the relative silence of professional officers on these issues. Indeed, in another sense, the professional soldier has a claim on "academic freedom" as substantial as that of any other professional. Just as military rank cannot be the arbiter of the merit of ideas, neither can political interests dictate the professional ideas of conscientious officers.

The Moral Implications of Command Responsibility

Independent command responsibility (and I refer here to the command of major military forces of the size of field armies or their equivalents, and above) presents, I believe, some especial ethical considerations since, for all practical purposes, persons in such situations are confronted by the moral implications of having to determine the number of casualties that are acceptable in pursuit of a given objective. It is probably a universal expectation that success in war ought to be obtained with the fewest possible casualties and that skill in leadership is reflected by such accomplishment. But there are serious pertinent qualifications to this proposition. Indeed, numerous celebrated commanders have been accused by critics of causing exorbitant casualties (Frederick the Great, Grant, and Haig, just to choose three rather prominent examples among many). Study of the historical record suggests some conclusions in this regard. First, there are shifting levels of acceptable casualties, levels that are in part reflective of prevailing social attitudes and in part the result of differentials in resources, human and material. But the principal conclusion to be drawn, in brief—beyond some flamboyant examples of utter military stupidity—is that the relative sizes of casualty totals (beyond the sheer sizes of forces involved) cannot be judged on the basis of isolated conflicts, but must be appraised in terms of the overall consequences of a protracted campaign. Frederick, for illustration, was habitually short of manpower and generally sought to hoard it when possible. He managed his startling victory at Rossbach with extraordinarily few casualties, while at Torgau he was willing to expend his last grenadier to gain a decision. The explanation lies in the realization of a strategic purpose, of course. Grant's Wilderness campaign, at first appalling in its expenditures of manpower, is quite defendable in terms of its having effectively shortened the ability of the Army of Northern Virginia to resist.

I have made, here, what may seem to be an odd digression into the field of strategy, but I do so in order to focus on the moral dimension of independent command. Surely the commander must seek to conserve the lives of those he leads, but he must be prepared—have the moral resolve—to use his troops in ways most propitious to the culmination of his projected strategy, bringing it to a successful termination. Such a balancing of concerns is one feature of the art of generalship.

Further, the professional soldier must subscribe—indeed, as a postulate of his occupational ethic—to the thesis that military leadership *is* an activity in which skill and intellectual acumen are critical. That might appear truistic—except for the fact that I am convinced that some military professionals no longer believe it. The reasons for their skepticism arise, I gather, from three main assumptions: that technology has superseded intellectuality in the conduct of war, that conflicts are finally decided by intangible moral and psychological factors over which high-level commanders exercise little discretion other than deploying their forces before the enemy,[5] and that battles are won or lost by small-unit effectiveness and *not* by the personal skill of commanders. These assumptions are not borne out by historical evidence (even that of the current era), and the retention of these specious ideas is reflective of the rather widespread antihistorical bias that has until recently characterized American military education.

A vital part of any military ethic is the *moral obligation* of commanders to revere and cultivate the skills of command. The men they lead have every right to expect that this will be the case. Yet it is not always so. A thorough analysis, for example, of World War II will reveal in all the major armies numerous instances, regrettably, of incompetency that arose not only from ignorance and ineptitude but from a failure of military leaders to subordinate various forms of personal aggrandizement and hubris to the ends of recognizing skill in command as the prime criterion for high command.

What, then, is the corpus of a military ethic? It should contain a series of essential precepts: the recognition of the primacy of personal honor; a voluntary presumption of the legitimacy of command, subordinating personal conceptions of self-interest; loyalty to the state as the embodiment of social survival; a prohibition against active participation in political affairs; and the obligation to cultivate professional skill.

But this is merely a beginning, a bare skeleton that invites substantial amplification. Much is left to resolve, but I have tried to dwell on the most basic considerations as a means of illustrating how contentious the subject is. None of the above premises would be universally accepted, I would surmise, in or out of the military services. But I am thoroughly convinced, too, that the volatility of the present situation, both in terms of the national culture and the military profession itself, now demands what would be, in effect, an articulated professional ethic. The role of the military establishment in a society as irrepressibly pluralistic as the American makes the creation of that ethic even more crucial. No longer is it possible to assume that the social or academic conditioning of career officers is an adequate introduction to military ethics; I strongly suspect that even the service academies have somewhat cautiously downplayed the character of an independent professional ethic. But the fact of the matter is that those who serve the nation in a military capacity no longer can assume any dominant moral consensus in the United States. Such a lack of ethical homogeneity may be tolerable in the nation as a whole, but ethical incongruities are simply not feasible in a military establishment. That organism must be knit by a relatively tight ethical code—and perhaps one that must now be formally postulated in contrast to a looser and less juristic tradition. It is time to consider such a commitment to professional rectitude.

NOTES

1. Perhaps the most outstanding treatise on those virtues that befit a military commander is the *Meditations* of Marcus Aurelius—much of it written in a tent in the field by a most reluctant soldier. I should think it might well lie on the bedside table of all military professionals.
2. The basic education of gentlemen included training in arms until the late Renaissance (see Castiglione's *Libro del Cortegiano*—the "Book of the Courtier"—as a useful reference), and familiarity with weapons continued long after that. Officers with little or no formal military education (beyond, again, attendance at public schools or their Continental equivalents) persisted in Britain, along with the sanctioning of commissions by direct purchase, until the debacles of the Crimean War of 1854. The appearance of state-sponsored military schools took place in the late 18th century in Europe as a product of the increased need for technical competence in engineering and artillery, and these institutions were largely peopled, initially, by the sons of the emerging commercial classes, but their élan was clearly an outgrowth of the traditional aristocratic virtues. In lieu of mandatory attendance at cadet schools, however, prospective officers entered regiments as "coronets" or served with fleets as "midshipmen" at as early an age as 12 or 13 years. Thus, the conception of "honor" derived from the social code of traditional aristocracies became inculcated into a military profession whose practitioners increasingly represented a broader spectrum of the population.
3. Of course, it must be recognized that self-confident commanders have on occasion seen fit to ignore, often ingeniously, the orders of their superiors in what they presumed to be the interests of victory. The most celebrated case, perhaps, is that of Admiral Nelson's convenient inability to see a flag signal that would have prevented his destruction of the Danish fleet in Copenhagen. Grant, during his campaigns in the West, was known to have cut his own communications so as to prevent his receipt of recalls from his superior, Halleck.
4. I am tempted to use a contemporary illustration for this point. I should think the regime of Idi Amin in Uganda, of lamentable recent memory, fits most precisely this definition of both depravity and intra-societal predation, and no officer of his forces could be morally bound to support him even as the personification of sovereignty.
5. It is true that courage, fortitude, and even passionate anger have been elements that have swayed the course of battle. In that crucial engagement of the Thirty Years War, Lutzen, the death of Gustavus Adolphus occasioned a tumultuous spontaneous charge of the Swedish infantry (some Imperial soldiers were actually strangled in rage), but the victory was the consequence, rather, of Gustavus' preparations, technical and tactical; the tide was turned by his innovative artillery. The most thought-provoking recent discussion of the role of generalship as against the psychological variables affecting soldiers in battle (and, in

consequence, the validity of military history as well) is provided by John Keegan in his brilliant work *The Face of Battle* (New York: Viking, 1976).

This article, substantially abridged for the present volume, originally appeared in the June 1982 issue of *Parameters*.

13

A Do-It-Yourself Professional Code for the Military

By MAXWELL D. TAYLOR

The issue of a behavioral code for the military profession is still very much alive.[1] A frequent complaint is that no visible progress is being made toward such a code, and that meanwhile career officers are left without authoritative guidance in resolving the many moral dilemmas that have been troubling them since the Vietnam War.

When asked for examples of their problems, they cite situations that arise in their daily lives and also hypothetical cases that may occur in future wars. Many deplore the decline of the reputation of the career officer for reliability in word and deed, and wonder how to restore that hallmark of the profession. Some lament that many senior officers, being mediocre themselves, prefer mediocrity around them, and assemble sycophantic officers on their staffs who withhold unpleasant facts and carefully avoid recommendations contrary to the chiefs' biases and predilections. How can a conscientious officer who does his duty and expects the same from others survive in such an environment?

As for moral problems likely to arise in future wars, a frequent question concerns the proper behavior of an officer required to serve in a Vietnam-type war which appears unjust or unjustified to a large sector of the American public. Also, there are questions about the possibility of finding oneself in a war of aggression of the kind condemned by the Nuremberg tribunal and the United Nations Charter.

Likewise, there is always the situation of the officer in combat who receives a lawful order to undertake a difficult mission with inadequate resources and certainty of failure and heavy casualties among his men. Somewhat similar is the quandary which might arise for a NATO officer ordered to use tactical nuclear weapons to repel a massive conventional attack, possibly thereby setting off a general nuclear war that might destroy humanity.

It is not easy to give satisfactory answers to sincere officers raising such questions. As these officers point out, there are no official texts or authoritative codes to which to refer, and possibly there never will be.

In this predicament, I can suggest only that they try working out for themselves a code of conduct that might help them cope with their ethical problems—one which they would consider worthy of adoption by the entire officer corps. This is the do-it-yourself approach to a professional ethic which I recommend for serious consideration.

The starting point of such an effort would be to arrive at an accepted standard of excellence for an ideal officer in the military profession. I would propose the following: an ideal officer is one who can be relied upon to carry out all assigned tasks and missions and, in doing so, get the most from his available resources with minimum loss and waste. Such resources might include men, money, weapons, equipment, allies, time, space, geography, and weather.

With this standard established, the next step would be to form a mental picture of an officer who would satisfy its terms, and then decide on his likely predominant traits. In forming this picture, we may be guided by our personal observations of admirable officers and by historical studies of outstanding military leaders.

Obviously, such an officer would be deeply convinced of the importance of the military profession and its role in the protection of the nation and its interests. He would view himself as a lineal descendant of the warrior who, in company with the king, the priest, and the judge, has performed throughout history a primal function essential to the survival and well-being of civilization. While the means and methods of arms have constantly changed over time, the need for leaders of valor and character to protect the valuables of society from predatory enemies has remained unchanged. The American officer today may properly derive great pride from belonging to a profession charged with the defense of the nation, with its rich assets, far-flung interests, and unique obligations as a world power. Recognizing this, we may expect our model officer to be endowed with a profound feeling of vocation and pride of membership in the military fraternity.

Such feelings will, of necessity, be accompanied by a determination on his part to succeed in this profession and to make a maximum contribution to its national role. He recognizes that success will depend on his ability to carry out all missions assigned by proper authority—tasks ranging from the modest duties of a platoon leader all the way to the weighty responsibilities of a senior field commander. In short, he takes the established standard for his goal and undertakes to meet its conditions.

The requirement that he get the most from his resources obliges him to begin with himself. For this purpose, he takes complete professional fitness in all of its aspects as his permanent personal goal. This means that he must not only know his current job, but must constantly prepare for the next one. He will need an orderly, well-trained mind housed in a vigorous body, the whole surmounted by an indomitable spirit that bespeaks strong character and will.

Such fitness can be obtained and retained only by sustained personal effort. Our excellent military school system, tiered in phase with increasing rank and responsibility, is of inestimable value, but it merely lays the foundation upon which the individual officer, serving as architect and engineer, may build his own career. Thus, continuous self-improvement will be a conspicuous characteristic of an ideal officer.

But important tasks can rarely be accomplished by a person acting alone. Our military paragon, regardless of his personal talents, must reinforce himself with an able staff and subordinate commanders. To accept less than the best would, in his judgment, be a neglect of duty and an injustice to his command, since the entire command would share in the disaster that mediocrity in key positions always invites. For the same reason, he would deem it unpardonable to fail to remove incompetence in any form that reveals itself within the range of his authority.

With the attainment of personal fitness and the support of able assistants, a leader has a final responsibility in the full exploitation of his resources—he must get the most out of the units and men under his command. He must do so both as a matter of moral obligation and professional necessity if his command is to be prepared for the stern test of war.

For this purpose, he must be a demanding disciplinarian, bent on instilling in his troops those habits which, learned in training, will assure a reliable performance of duty on the battlefield, despite the confusion and fear natural to all men in an environment of tension and danger. Though often obliged to appear an unfeeling martinet in training, our officer gives unflagging attention to the well-being of his men—their health, bodily comforts, and peace of mind. To the extent possible, he shares their joys, sorrows, hardships, and dangers—everything except the doubts and misgivings that at some time afflict every commander in war. These he keeps to himself.

There is a final quality that a truly superior officer should have or try to attain if he would ever imprint his name on the roll of remembered warriors. This quality I call the X-factor, the ability of a leader to inspire men in war to the point that they forget discomforts, fatigue, and fear, and at his bidding perform feats that surprise themselves and render future historians incredulous. In the homely language of Harry Truman, such a leader is "a man who has the ability to get other people to do what they don't want to do and like it." Thus, the final obligation of our model officer will be to acquire and in due time demonstrate possession of the X-factor—elusive, indefinable, and probably unteachable though it may be. Considering the character we have postulated for him, I would concede him a good chance to succeed.

With so much as prologue, it is now possible to sum up the virtues and distinguishing traits with which our model officer has been imbued. Without priority in importance, I can identify the following: justice, patriotism, reliability, integrity, sense of duty, self-discipline, human understanding, loyalty, strength of will, and inspirational power.

Bear in mind that, though he is as nearly perfect a professional officer as one can imagine, he is not a perfect man in an ethical, religious, or cultural sense. He has shown no evidence thus far of possessing many virtues often associated with some of the most venerated personages of history: piety, religious faith, charity, benevolence, humility, meekness, righteousness, forgiveness, and resignation. He may, in fact, possess many of these virtues, but the exigencies of military life rarely create conditions calling for their display. Yet, while war is a dirty business conducted in an ugly environment of violence and destruction, it has often provided the occasion for acts of courage, loyalty, abnegation, and self-sacrifice showing mankind at its most noble.

Now that we have put together this construct of a model officer, how can he serve in resolving the moral problems of the officer corps? As an experiment, let us examine how such an officer might deal with some of the questions which we have found so troubling among officers.

Our model would surely do his best to restore the tarnished reputation of the officer corps for truthfulness and integrity—both by setting a right example and by seeking to eliminate officers who fail to meet the standard. With his commitment to mission success, he could do no less, since he knows how disastrous to success in any enterprise is the presence of unreliable officers. I suspect that he would share the view that Newton D. Baker, Secretary of War in World War I, expressed in the course of defending the West Point honor system before Congress: "The inexact or untruthful soldier trifles with the lives of his fellow men and with the honor of his government, and it is therefore no matter of pride but of stern disciplinarian necessity that makes West Point require of her students a character of trustworthiness that knows no evasion."

He would react similarly with regard to senior officers who are resentful of juniors bearing ill tidings or purveying unwelcome advice. Such senior officers damage themselves and their mission by depriving themselves of factual information and independent viewpoints to the detriment of their plans and decisions. In time they will surely come a cropper before, one hopes, they can involve too many and too much in their downfall.

An ambitious officer trapped in an assignment under such a senior can only do his duty and wait for time to free him. It is still true, as I used to tell officers joining the Joint Staff, that an able staff officer capable of logical and innovative thought carries a general's star in his briefcase in much the same way that outstanding soldiers of Napoleon were said to carry a marshal's baton in their knapsacks. In the long run, no staff officer need worry about his future who passes constructive ideas to his superior and helps him avoid trouble and error.

Then we have the case of the officer who finds himself in strong personal opposition to a decision or policy of higher authority—in opposition to the all-volunter recruitment program of the Department of Defense, for example. Before undertaking to set his superiors straight, I hope he would wait until he can answer the following questions with confidence:

- Am I sure that I know all the necessary and relevant facts?
- Am I sure that my superiors are not doing everything possible to correct the situation?

Only if both answers are affirmative should he consider action, in which case he would have two alternatives. He could resign or retire and then take his case to the public. Or, he could remain at his post and submit his argument for a change of policy through official channels. Both alternatives entail sacrifice or risk, but our model is prepared to accept them in a good cause.

What he would *not* do would be to leak his views to the press, call a press conference, or write his congressman—all reprehensible actions as he views his obligation of loyalty to his superiors.

As for fear of involvement in an unjust or aggressive war, I do not feel that our man would be greatly concerned. He knows full well that there is no authoritative definition of either kind of war. Depending on the source consulted, a just war may be one waged for a just cause that can be achieved in no other way; one capable of producing a better peace than the one existing before the war; one waged in self-defense or for legal rights; one to protect a nation's natural right; one with a high probability of producing more good consequences than bad for the human race; or one conducted non-aggressively in accordance with the international laws of war and the terms of the United Nations Charter. Obviously, most of these definitions are of little practical value to our officer, merely stimulating new semantic debates over the meaning of such phrases as "just cause," "self-defense," "natural rights," "aggressive war," and "good consequences."

In the absence of authoritative means to identify an unjust war in time to avoid participation, an officer has little choice but to assume the rightness of a governmental decision involving the country in war. Having made this assumption, he is honor-bound to carry out all legal orders and do his best to bring the war to a prompt and successful conclusion. If his side wins, he knows that there will be few charges or injustice save from the vanquished; if he loses, the victors, following the precedent of Nuremberg, are quite likely to charge him with crime and aggression regardless of evidence to the contrary. For these reasons, our model officer views this contingency as a professional hazard which, along with other dangers of the military service, he took into account, or should have, when he took his oath as an officer.

Lastly, there is the dilemma which may arise if an officer receives a lawful order to undertake an impossible or prohibitively costly mission, or one likely to produce dire consequences apparently ignored by his superiors. Our model, recognizing that obedience to orders is one of the highest military virtues, one without which armies are worse than useless, will be instinctively inclined to obey any legal order. He would consider making an exception only in the rare circumstances when all the following conditions are met:

- He is sure that he understands the purpose of the order and the results desired by the issuing authority.
- He is equally sure that this authority does not understand the local situation and the disastrous consequences that would ensue from compliance.
- There is no time to appeal the order or a prior appeal has been rejected.
- He is disobeying on sound military grounds, not in compliance with the voice of a disapproving conscience, and is fully prepared to accept the legal and professional consequences.

As for his attitude toward the voice of conscience as a guide to military behavior, he has serious doubts as to its reliability. He is aware that wise men over the ages have disagreed as to the source, nature, and authority of conscience. Is it, as some think, the voice of God or at least a God-given moral sense with which we are endowed to serve as a source of higher guidance? There are skeptics who maintain that it is little more than the voice of conventional morality, of ingrained habit resisting a departure from past practice, or of self-interest in a pious guise. Then there are the cynical words of H. L. Mencken: "Conscience is the inner voice that warns us that somebody may be looking."

Despite his doubts about the universal validity of the deliverances of conscience, our model officer recognizes that there is in himself resistance to actions inconsistent with the principles of behavior he learned to follow early in his career. Perhaps this is the voice of his professional conscience; if so, he is happy to have one to keep him straight and will give it due heed. However, he is most unsympathetic with officers who use conscience as an excuse for dereliction of duty or the avoidance of dangerous or unpleasant tasks. In his view, such conduct is worthy of the disdain accorded the soldier who does not discover until the eve of battle that he is a conscientious objector.

This essay being of necessity in the nature of a monologue, I cannot judge the degree of reader acceptance of the views thus far advanced. I would expect some disagreement about the basic premise that the worth of an officer is properly measured by mission success and resource economy. This standard may appear too narrowly professional or too inflexible for equitable application to all officers.

It is quite true that in this inquiry, our attention is focused exclusively on the ethical needs of the career officer corps. It seeks to delineate not the perfect man for all seasons, but the ideal professional officer prepared for a war environment. We cannot assume that culturally he is a Renaissance type; nor can we assume that his private life is above reproach. He may be loyal to his superiors and his profession but disloyal to his wife. He may be devoted to his troops but speak to them in the profane language of a Patton. He may keep physically fit but have General Grant's weakness for strong drink. He may work hard for victory but never go to church to pray for it. However, if he has compensating professional virtues, he may still be an exemplary military leader, although that fact in itself will not qualify him for high position in government, politics, the performing arts, or the celestial hierarchy.

The standard is indeed inflexible in that it makes no allowance for inequality of advantage among officers resulting from race, sex, education, or family background. In the military, the payoff for all is necessarily based upon performance of duty, with rewards adjusted upward in proportion to the difficulty of the task. Given the importance of the factor of luck in many cases, injustices may arise in the distribution of the prizes, but all life is unfair to some degree, particularly life on the battlefield, where the bullets, like rain, fall on the just and the unjust. However, the high national stake involved in the success of our arms justifies the rigid standard we have adopted.

Another area of possible disagreement is the choice of the virtues ascribed to our model officer. It may be argued that no such Galahad ever existed in the real world and that, if he did, he would be too depressingly virtuous to live with. I must admit that I feel about our model much as General Sherman did about born generals: "I have read about men born as generals, peculiarly endowed by nature, but I have never seen one." However, I have met many officers who displayed the traits and characteristics of our model in varying degrees and combinations. In that sense, each virtue on the list is real and hence attainable, although the model who embodies the entirety remains a distant ideal.

The weakest part of our procedure has been the effort to predict the behavior of our hypothetical officer when confronted with the several moral dilemmas considered. Obviously, his responses are no better than my personal opinion of how an officer should act under the circumstances. One of the merits of our do-it-yourself methodology, however, is that it can be used by individuals, groups, and conceivably by the entire profession—anyone anywhere can participate who is seriously concerned with the ethics of the military profession. Such parallel efforts could lead to a revival of interest in a comprehensive professional code of the kind that has thus far eluded us. If such a code emerged from this procedure it would have the unique merit of being the creation of bona fide military professionals who understand the requirements of leadership in war.

In the past, we have been inclined to entrust the writing of military history, the critique of military operations, and the evaluation of the proper role of the military profession to civilian writers of varying degree of competence. In our present study, we have found no need to invoke extra-professional help to support our conclusions and judgments. Nor have we been obliged to call on any of the great names of philosophy, ethics, or religion to justify our interpretation of right and wrong in our life's work. The voice of long experience tells us that in our profession, that which favors mission success is right or good and that which works to the contrary is wrong or bad. We need not look elsewhere for confirmation of what, for a soldier, is a self-evident truth.

If indeed we are ever to have a professional code, the military must get on with its codification, whether by the route suggested herein or by a better one. Otherwise it will never be done or will be done badly by the unqualified. The determination of what constitutes right conduct in the officer corps is too serious a business to be left to those lacking intimate acquaintance with the nature of war.

NOTES

1. Refer, for example, to my article "A Professional Ethic for the Military?" *Army* 28 (May 1978): 18-21; Arthur J. Dyck, "Ethical Bases of the Military Profession," *Parameters* 10 (March 1980): 39-46; or Richard A. Gabriel, "To Serve with Honor," *Army* 30 (May 1980): 17-21.

This article originally appeared in the December 1980 issue of *Parameters*.

14

A Military Ethic in an Age of Terror

By ANTHONY E. HARTLE

National military forces throughout the world today are involved in combating terrorist activity, if only in terms of preparation. Capable organizations formulate and debate at length appropriate tactics and methods that will be effective in reducing the terrorist threat or in countering terrorist actions. As various headquarters and agencies examine the problem, a troubling issue arises for many. They must consider not only what they *can* do but also what they *ought* to do. Some measures that might be highly effective will also be highly questionable from a legal or moral point of view.

Inherent in most discussions are moral issues that are at least partly determined by the codes of conduct that govern the military forces involved. In particular, the range of permissible actions by American military forces is unquestionably limited by the uncodified professional military ethic that governs its members. The moral complexity of counterterrorist and other likely operational commitments of U.S. forces provides sufficient reason to suggest that a formally codified ethic should once again be considered. In this discussion, I am primarily concerned with revealing the moral structure within which such an ethic would be developed.

When nations employ force in international relations, civilians are almost always killed and maimed, property destroyed, and children rendered homeless; the fabric of social life for noncombatants is torn apart. Because the use of military force unavoidably affects people adversely, most military decisions have moral dimensions, whether the military decision-makers are sensitive to them or not. Thus some course of action will, on balance, be right and some will be wrong when we consider results that could and should have been foreseen.[1]

The history of South Africa provides a striking example of such moral considerations and a failure to take the foreseeable consequences of a military decision adequately into account.[2] The results were disastrous. At the turn of the century, Britain faced a particularly unpleasant war against the Boers in South Africa. The expected rapid defeat of the Boers had not come about, so to hasten that event Britain placed in command her most distinguished soldier, Lord Kitchener, the hero of Khartoum.

Kitchener was determined to end the war as rapidly and efficiently as possible, but he faced a most difficult situation. Many heads of Boer households and able-bodied men of the Boer families had left home to join the Boer commandos, leaving behind the wives, children, and infirm. Those remaining on the farms suffered great hardship as the war dragged on; however, they also provided logistical support and intelligence to the Boer fighters. Both for their own protection and to further Britain's war effort, Kitchener ordered all the families removed from the farms and placed in great concentration camps, the infamous *laagers*. Unfortunately, Kitchener and his staff failed to make adequate provisions for medical care, administration, or even food in the camps. Whether adequate care was even possible in view of the constrained resources and the ongoing war effort is in question. In the months that followed, over 20,000 Boer women and children died.

The brutal conditions in the camps were widely reported in British papers, and many people at home in England came to question the war and the actions of the British forces (a development which should have a familiar ring), making prosecution of the war much more difficult for the British government. Kitchener had made what he felt was a logical military decision in war, but he failed to give adequate consideration to the logistical and the concomitant moral dimensions of his decision. The moral cost of his decision was painfully high. In addition to damaging his own country's interests, he was responsible for the deaths of thousands of people. The point of this piece of history is that we still face the same kinds of problems in decisions about the actions necessary to defend our national interests. One notable contemporary arena is that of terrorist activity.

In the United States today, both within the American military and among those considering and criticizing national policy, we find extensive debate concerning counterterrorist measures. In this context, I want to consider the implications of the professional military ethic for the debate about the moral acceptability of various counterterrorist tactics and techniques. I maintain that specific principles that provide the foundation for the American military ethic also place limits on what U.S. military organizations can do in fulfilling their responsibilities to defend the nation.

Fundamental Values and Ethical Conduct

Western history provides a long account of attempts to govern the conduct of military forces through means other than force alone. Custom, law, and conscience were brought into play as well. Through force and the threat of punishment, a minimum level of performance by members of a military organization can perhaps be assured, but inducing an army to fight well under difficult conditions requires more than coercion. Exceptional performance comes only under exceptional leadership and through commitment to sets of values and forms of conduct.

The codes of honor that governed the conduct of medieval knights in fighting each other, however imperfectly observed they may have been in practice, combined with another historical development to produce the basis for military codes of ethics in the 17th and 18th centuries. The other development was the secularization of the concepts *jus in bello* (law in waging war) and *jus ad bellum* (law for resort to war) developed originally by church scholastics. The result was a set of concepts about when and how wars should be fought among civilized nations.

During the 19th century, a new kind of warrior arrived on the scene, the military professional. The ramifications of being a member of a profession are prominent factors in considering the moral status of a particular group such as the military. Professionals are accorded special considerations in society as a result of their status. One such consideration is the granting of authority to act in ways legally or morally proscribed to nonprofessionals.

Members of national military organizations became professionals in a technical sense during the 19th century when they developed the three characteristics of a professional organization as described by Samuel Huntington: (1) specific expertise, gained only through extended schooling and training; (2) a sense of corporateness, largely generated through society's acceptance of the organization as a distinct body having the authority to set its own standards of conduct and performance; and (3) responsibility to society in providing the profession's expertise as required.[3]

Military organizations in Western Europe solidified their status as professional groups as military tactics became more standardized and complex. Even more important were the burgeoning technical requirements of weaponry and logistics that required training and experience. Western nations became dependent upon their professional military for national security, and the military organizations became institutions within their societies. In some cases, of course, they also took over the government. All professional military organizations worthy of the name developed codes of conduct governing accession to and behavior within the professional group.

The American military has experienced the same kind of development over the last 200 years, and we have well-established standards of conduct, though a professional ethic has not been formally articulated and published. The code governing behavior has developed through custom and tradition and has been perpetuated through professional socialization and the military's schooling systems.

Because the code has not been formally articulated by the institution and because it is a product of slowly evolving custom and tradition, I can get disagreement from almost any member of the military about exactly what should be included in any fully elaborated and codified professional ethic, but reasonable agreement exists at least about the fundamental principles. Specifically, professional soldiers:

- Always do their duty, subordinating their personal interests to the requirements of their professional function. Duty here is understood both in the sense of response to immediate, specific requirements established by the organization—direct orders—and in the sense of the overarching responsibility for the security of the state under the Constitution.
- Conduct themselves as persons of honor whose integrity, loyalty, and courage are exemplary. Honesty, courage, and integrity are essential qualities on the battlefield if a military organization is to function effectively. Reports must be accurate. Actions promised must be performed. Virtues claimed must be possessed in fact. Failures in these areas mean lost battles and lost lives.
- Develop and maintain the highest possible level of professional skill and knowledge. To do less is to fail to meet their obligations to the country, the profession, and the individual soldiers they serve.
- Take full responsibility for their orders.
- Strictly observe the principle that the military is subject to civilian authority and do not involve themselves or their subordinates in domestic politics beyond the exercise of basic civic rights.
- Promote the welfare of their subordinates as persons, not merely as soldiers.
- Adhere to the laws of war in performing their professional function.

The Army is now seriously considering the formal publication of a code of professional ethics. If a code is formalized, it may not be worded just as I have presented it, but the principles above will be included. The Navy is actively engaged in formalizing a professional code of ethics, and in 1986 a conference in the Pentagon recommended to the Army Chief of Staff that a code common to all the services be considered. While that recommendation was apparently put on the shelf, the concerns that generated it still exist.

The existing professional military ethic, as encapsulated by the seven principles set forth above, results from the interaction of three primary formative influences: (1) the functional requirements of military activity itself; (2) requirements established by the laws of war; and (3) the enduring core values of American society. Obviously, the professional military ethic must be functional, that is, it must accommodate the features necessary for effective performance in battle. Just as obviously, the ethic must be legal, that is, it must conform to all established laws. And perhaps less obviously but no less important, the ethic must be culturally and politically acceptable, that is, it must conform to the dictates of American values. The product thus formed is a complex pattern of normative practice expressible in terms of principles such as the seven I listed above.

Enduring American Values

As we approach the 21st century, identifying those values common to all Americans becomes more and more difficult. Still, several sociological studies and analyses do point to a set of goods to which most Americans attach transcendant worth. The set includes freedom, democracy, achievement, individual worth, and equality. From these goods, or values, come constraints on the activity of the American military, constraints that have not always been properly observed, but constraints acknowledged as appropriate by both society and the military profession.

These characteristic social values are manifested through the concept of basic rights in our society, which in turn rest upon the nation's founding documents. While I sympathize with those who say our society has become nearly paralyzed at times in our preoccupation with nebulous rights claims, the primary sources for rights conceptions are, it is important to recall, the Constitution and the Bill of Rights, which comprises the first ten amendments to the Constitution. Not coincidentally, when officers receive their commissions, they take the following oath, which provides the basis for the existing American military ethic:

> I do solemnly swear that I will support and defend the Constitution of the United States against all enemies, foreign and domestic; that I will bear true faith and allegiance to the same, and that I take this obligation freely, without any mental reservation or purpose of evasion; and that I will well and faithfully discharge the duties of the office on which I am about to enter.[4]

This oath establishes the foundation of the concept of duty that I referred to in the first principle of the professional ethic presented earlier: a professional soldier always does his duty. In that prescription, duty means much more than following the orders of one's superiors. When we see that the duty prescribed, as the oath makes clear, is to maintain and preserve the Constitution, we recognize that duty may well at times require that orders be disobeyed if they are illegal or if the orders clearly do not serve the larger purpose for which the profession exists. Thus the loyalty and responsibility of the professional soldier are to American society *under the Constitution*, not to any particular superior or administration.

The various political principles that are embodied in American government, such as representative legislation and the system of checks and balances, are all finally concerned with creating a system in which the rights of individuals are protected. Through his commitment to the Constitution, the American officer is firmly and unreservedly committed to the principle that individual rights are fundamental concerns of his professional role.

The commitment to the Constitution invokes the other major formative influence on the existing American professional military ethic—the laws of war. When we talk of professional military ethics, we sometimes overlook this point, but we must remember that Article VI, Clause 2, of the Constitution makes all treaties and conventions to which the United States is a party the supreme law of the land. Thus the laws of war resulting from treaties bind the American military directly and without exception. By swearing the oath, the military officer is bound morally as well as legally. Orders and actions that violate the laws of war, for example, are illegal for American soldiers, and by his personal and professional commitment to the Constitution, the military officer is morally committed to ensure that such orders are not obeyed.

Principles and Our Response to Terrorism

The laws of war today are largely contained in the two Hague Conventions (1899 and 1907) and the four Geneva Conventions of 1949.[5] Those documents limit how wars can be fought, what weapons can be used, and what persons can be attacked. The laws of war, incomplete as they certainly are, can be explained on the basis of two humanitarian principles:[6] First, individual persons deserve respect as persons, using the term person to refer to self-conscious, autonomous, rights-bearing individuals. Second, human suffering ought to be minimized.

These principles are accepted by the American military as further constraints on legally and morally permissible action by U.S. soldiers, and in our tradition the first of these principles, that of granting appropriate respect to individual persons, is most clearly understood as the requirement to respect the rights of others. Thus the emphasis on rights is derived from two of the three primary formative factors that have shaped our military professional ethic: the laws of war as well as the values of American society.

In view of these boundary conditions, terrorist activity itself—that is, violence that accepts and often prefers random, innocent victims—is clearly prohibited for members of American forces.

Some suggested responses to terrorism also involve the violation or infringement of individual rights. Among those rights could most obviously be at risk in attacks on countries that host terrorists or on ambiguously defined targets are noncombatants, and the particular rights concerned, among the most fundamental of all rights, are the right of life and the right to security of the person. Because the American professional military ethic requires the recognition of human rights in moral terms as well as legal, the central question then becomes: Under what conditions can such rights be justifiably infringed or overridden?

In possible responses to international terrorism, the use of directed or controlled violence against the responsible terrorists seems justified when less radical means of effective response are not available. The rights of the terrorists are infringed in the same manner that the rights of a criminal before the court are infringed by carrying out the sentence imposed upon him. If violence is employed only as a last resort, both procedural and institutional justification are credible in such a situation in terms of inherent human rights. When noncombatants are knowingly endangered, however, even if such risk is necessary to permit effective response, the case becomes much less clear.

All moral dimensions of military decisions must be considered carefully in such cases. Military officers must ensure that actions undertaken are in accordance with the professional military ethic, which includes the commitment to individual human rights. In addition, officers must be fully aware of the consequences of contemplated actions, which must be examined both in terms of furthering national interests and in terms of effects upon the status and welfare of the persons involved. The moral rights of persons are not limited by national boundaries or ethnic origin, and, under the American professional military ethic, military decision-makers must include such considerations in their reasoning.

The nature of such considerations is hardly new, needless to say. Hamburg, Dresden, Hiroshima, Nagasaki, and other experiences in our recent past have made the issue of noncombatants and noncombatant immunity a continuing subject of concern, but the spotlighted, photographed, and media-covered stage on which counterterrorist actions are performed prompts us once again to insist on moral clarity with respect to those actions.

Under the murky moral conditions of counterterrorist activity and the prosecution of low-intensity warfare—the most likely forms of commitment for American military forces in the near future—the moral dimensions of military activity become hard to discern. We may very well have reached a point at which a formally published professional ethic would benefit the military services and the country. If a formal code were to provide a focal point for teaching and an effective guide in situations requiring difficult decisions, it would indeed be a benefit.

As a final point, consider this brief argument: To fight for freedom means to fight against oppression; oppression means violation of man's rights; hence to fight for freedom means to oppose such violations.[7] In considering this argument, if we define terrorism as "the deliberate and systematic murder, maiming, and menacing of the innocent to inspire fear for political ends,"[8] one who fights for freedom cannot with logical consistency commit such violations himself, for he would become a terrorist in the name of fighting terrorism.

To these basic arguments, the American professional military ethic provides a comprehensive reinforcing structure rooted in cultural and social values that limit in principle what is permissible in any activity that the military undertakes, including counterterrorist operations.

Having focused on limitations on counterterrorist activity in my discussion, however, let me also note that those actions against terrorism that are appropriate for our government should be carried out with maximum force and efficiency, for international terrorism is indeed a growing threat to legitimate governments—a threat more dangerous than many appreciate. Paul Johnson calls it "the cancer of the modern world."[9] If we are to prevent it from destroying the societies it attacks, we must apply drastic and radical treatment to what clearly is a malignancy. At the same time, we must ensure that our responses to terrorism do not injure the moral fabric of our society. A clear understanding of the moral structure within which we operate constitutes the most effective means to that end.

NOTES

1. A decisionmaker's act may have two moral dimensions, the interior (relating to the motivation or intent behind the act) and the exterior (relating to the consequences of the act). Thus a good decision in terms of consequences can have been made from a morally reprehensible motive. A hasty, ill-planned attack, for example, might win a battle, but if the commander ordered it primarily to make himself look good, most would agree that his character merits criticism from a professional as well as a moral point of view. The reader should be mindful of both moral dimensions during the discussion that follows.
2. Thomas Pakenham, *The Boer War* (New York: Random House, 1979), pp. xxi-xxii, 521-24. See also Edgar Holt, *The Boer War* (London: Putnam, 1958), ch. 21.
3. Samuel Huntington, "The Soldier and the State in the 1970s," in *The Changing World of the American Military*, ed. Franklin D. Margiotta (Boulder, Colo.: Westview, 1978), p. 16.
4. The oath taken by enlisted members imposes a similar duty to defend the Constitution.
5. Field Manual 27-10, *The Law of Land Warfare* (U.S. Department of the Army, 18 July 1956), and Air Force Pamphlet 110-31, *International Law—The Conduct of Armed Conflict and Air Operations* (U.S. Department of the Air Force, 19 November 1976), identify additional treaties and agreements that contribute to the law of war and to which the United States is a signatory.
6. Anthony E. Hartle, "Humanitarianism and the Laws of War," *Philosophy* 61 (January 1986), 109-15.
7. Benzion Netanyahu, "Terrorists and Freedom Fighters," in *Terrorism: How the West Can Win*, ed. Benjamin Netanyahu (New York: Farrar, Straus, Giroux, 1986), p. 27.
8. Ibid.
9. Paul Johnson, "The Cancer of Terrorism" in *Terrorism: How the West Can Win*, p. 31.

This article originally appeared in the summer 1987 issue of *Parameters*.

IV. OPERATIONAL ETHICS

15

A Soldier and his Conscience

By JAMES GLOVER

A soldier is trained to kill. He may be ordered to, or he may order others to break the Sixth Commandment. He can commit, in the course of duty, an intensely personal act the memory of which may haunt him for the rest of his days. As many of us know only too well, he may hold the enemy in the sights of his rifle and then watch him fall. He is not protected by that shell of remoteness that shields the sailor in his ship and the airman in his aircraft. In simple terms this—the act of killing—poses the soldier's ultimate moral predicament.

But, of course, the debate reaches out to embrace so many more than the infantryman with his rifle and the tanker with his gun. What about the artilleryman with his hand on the firing lever?—the trucker delivering the nuclear round?—the staff, operational and logistic, producing the orders?—the commander in the field making the decisions?—and the Chief of Staff looming behind it all? No one can escape the dilemmas, whether he be a four-star general or a rifleman, a man or a woman.

The whole poignancy of the predicament is heightened when we are committed to internal security operations within our own country. We are then no longer fighting an external, identifiable enemy; we face our own fellow citizens. The moral dilemmas are more painful (as I found to my cost in Northern Ireland). Furthermore, not only the public, but also, of course, the soldier himself is now far more aware and far better educated than in the past. He tends to be more quizzical of authority. Consequently, whether he likes it or not (and he may not), he answers to a more acute and demanding conscience.

But conscience is difficult to define. Socrates likened it to an inner voice telling him what *not* to do. Yet it is all too easy to deceive oneself. The temptation to do nothing and to sit back, or to turn a blind eye, is often irresistible. Thus, I believe that "conscience" is probably best described as a fallible moral judgment which, if acknowledged, produces action and which, if ignored, merely produces guilt.

How, then, shall we tackle this elusive but absorbing subject? First, by looking at the law, in the broadest sense, within which a soldier deploys his conscience. Second, by examining the moral pressures within these legal boundaries—in short, the conflict between morality and military necessity. Third, by assessing how the antidote, the classic soldierly qualities (or the age-old warrior virtues), impacts on this conflict. And, finally, by drawing the strands together and discussing how the whole debate impinges on the soldier's position in society today.

The Force of Law

The soldier is subject to the codes of international law and to those of the law of the land. But two critical questions have to be answered before we can define the legal boundaries within which he operates: Is there such a thing as a just war? And is obedience to superior orders a valid defense when a crime is committed?

The controversy of whether war can be "just" has raged over the centuries. In the 15th century, for instance, Calvin and Martin Luther were at loggerheads. The former warned against war and undue cruelty. But Luther was far more ruthless. He declared that "it is both Christian and an act of love to kill the enemy without hesitation, to plunder and burn and injure him by any method until he is conquered." As a nice afterthought he added: "except that one must beware of sin and not violate wives and virgins!" But the founder of modern international law is the Dutch jurist Grotius. He was a man of formidable scholarship who in 1625 published in Paris a remarkable book—*De Jure Belli ac Paris*. It shocked and fascinated the traditionalists. Grotius did not look for authority for war in church or creed, but in the conscience of the individual. He concluded with a dire warning that although war may be undertaken for a just cause, it may become unjust if it gives rise to unjust acts.

However, the whole nature of war has of course changed—utterly. The innocent are no longer immune. In insurgency the peasant by day is the guerrilla by night, and in general war the weapons of mass destruction speak for themselves. All attempts to outlaw war have failed. But the United Nations General Assembly has tried to distinguish between the legal and the illegal use of force (it was under the banner of the UN Charter—Article 51—that Great Britain went to war in the Falklands). Furthermore, at the UN's instigation, the International Law Commission has designed seven principles governing the acts of individuals in war. Number four is of critical interest to us. It states that "the fact that a person acted on the orders of his Government or of a superior does not relieve him from responsibility under international law, *provided a moral choice was in fact open to him.*"

This takes us straight into our second question: superior orders as a valid defense. The nub of the soldier's problem is not the existence of the law itself but rather whether "a moral choice [is] in fact open to him." Yet his duty demands that he obey orders instantly and without hesitation. Any legal encouragement to disobey strikes at the very roots of military discipline. But in the heat of battle, whether the enemy be a Russian, an Argentinian, or even an IRA terrorist, things are necessarily and rightly done which later, in the frigidity of a law court, may seem outrageous—for war is a rough game. The law of the land, certainly of Great Britain and the United States, usually acknowledges this. Witness the legal aftermath of some of the incidents in the Falklands, for instance, the exoneration of a Royal Marine sergeant who had deliberately shot, to put him out of his agony, an Argentinian prisoner who was literally burning to death.

In essence, then, the soldier when answering to his conscience must remember that he not only has the right, but he also has the duty, to disobey an unlawful order. It is one of his privileges for serving a democracy, as it is one of his burdens that he must answer for his own actions. We cannot have one without the other. We in Great Britain accept this. Every soldier in Ulster who accidentally kills a civilian—by mistaken identity or even by bullet ricochet—has to stand full trial in a civil court. Similarly, after the Iranian Embassy siege in London, and despite the circumstances, all those regular-soldiers who had shot the terrorist holding the hostages were put in the dock—but exonerated.

The Moral Pressures

In a letter to *The Times* (London), Laurens Van Der Post wrote that "the most urgent problem of our age is the problem of discovering a way of overcoming evil without oneself becoming a force of evil in the process." It is this very conflict between what may seem necessary and yet is in itself wrongful that highlights the moral pressures to which a soldier is exposed. His own actions may precipitate a profound feeling of guilt, which then arouses and alerts his conscience. The playwright William Douglas Home is himself a graphic example of this reaction. In the closing stages of the last war, he found he was unable to accept the moral burden of being involved in, although not directly responsible for, the killing by bombardment of innocent civilians. This led him in 1944, as a captain in the Scots Guards, to refuse to participate in the final assault on Le Havre. He was arrested, tried by court-martial, cashiered, and imprisoned in Wormwood Scrubs Gaol where (as *he* says) his "conscience found rest at last."

A soldier's refusal to conform may spring from a wide variety of motives, ranging from sheer exhibitionism to cowardice, or even to masochism. But we are talking here about his refusal to do something which he reckons to be wrong. The rarity of this deliberate refusal says much for the normal legitimacy of the soldier's orders and also for the exceptional moral courage which the actual act of refusal demands. The infrequency can also be linked to those potent *quieters of conscience* which protect the soldier, yet do not necessarily deaden his sensitivities. They include:

• First, "leadership by persuasion" which silences the soldier's misgivings. It may be no more than a simple injunction to "kill or be killed." But today the soldier's needs are different, especially in peace—he must be able to come to terms with the growing anger of the peace movements, the advocates of capital punishment for terrorists, and other such groups.

• Second, the soldier's loyalty to, and pride in, his own outfit, which convinces him that he is part of something bigger than himself, and which he cannot abandon. This is, of course, the essence of the regimental system.

• Third, the very presence of others who are doing the same thing as he without funk or complaint, whom he just cannot let down. It is this, the loyalty he has to his mates, which ultimately persuades the frightened infantryman to get up and tangle with the enemy on the other side of the hedge. In sum, these three represent the critical ingredients of high morale. They flourish in a unit with fine esprit and languish in one where morale is faltering. And it is in the latter, where the ties are not so strong, that the depths of demoralization are reached. Men can see manifest crime committed and are then so despairing of all remedy that their consciences grow numb and impotent.

On a different note, a soldier may be deterred from deliberately cutting himself off from the security and comradeship that surrounds him by the prospect of the desolate loneliness which would then be his lot. He may also reject his conscience because his efforts are so puny that in no way can he alter the course of events. For instance, many a German soldier in World War II might have screwed up the requisite courage had he thought that his action would have an effect. Yet a handful did. One such was a member of a firing party ordered to execute Dutch hostages. When a party formed up, he suddenly stepped out of rank and refused to take part. He was charged on the spot with treason, found guilty, placed among the hostages, and promptly shot by his own comrades. He had answered his conscience. And he paid a terrible penalty for doing so.

The distinction between right and wrong is probably more easily blurred when one has discarded the principle that "in the sight of God all men are equal" than by the rejection of any other ethic. That particular rejection breeds double standards—one for "them" and one for "us." Some Americans encountered it in Vietnam, and we British have done so all too frequently elsewhere. It can precipitate appalling inhumanity. Yet often it strangely fails to impact on the soldier's conscience.

Now to the last and most disputable of the moral pressures, the mandate that the end justifies the means. The arguments range between two extremes, the purist and the ruthless. Many military commanders have, over the years, subscribed to the latter, no one more confidently than General Massu who, in Algiers in 1957, openly and blatantly condoned the use of torture by the 10th Parachute Regiment. As General Massu put it, "We must accept these methods heart and soul as both necessary and morally justifiable." But what happened in Cyprus, in Malay, in Northern Ireland (in the early days), and perhaps in Vietnam too? Indeed, the controversy is at its sharpest in counterinsurgency. For it is here that "the means" impinge on the civilian population, many or most of whom may be innocent. Searches, interrogation, and resettlement may be operationally essential and morally justifiable, but the soldier of conscience must assure himself that what he is doing is within the law and is genuinely necessary. If he does not boldly reject brutality he will be lost because, first, he will be operating outside the law and will have no defense. In Belfast we had to suffer the frustration of watching known murderers of British soldiers walking the streets as free men because the law could not touch them. And we had to bite back the temptation to eliminate them in some way because we too would then have been outside the law.

Second, the soldier must reject brutality because by matching the terrorists at their own methods the soldier will only be playing into their hands. The threshold of violence will escalate. Ultimately he will find himself using methods so outrageous that not only will they revolt his own conscience but they will also attract the hatred of the very people whom he is protecting and whose support is vital to him.

Under these circumstances, the end can *never* justify the means, however expedient it may seem at the time.

Yet there will be other situations when the moral dilemma is more blurred, as anyone who has been in the intelligence game (as I have these last two years) knows only too well. But it can also be far more acute. To take an extreme, consider the need to torture a terrorist to force him to reveal the location of a hidden nuclear device set to explode shortly. What then about the balance between expediency, morality, and the law?

The Military Virtues

Let us now turn to the antidote—the military virtues and their impact. We have already discussed how once a soldier's conscience is aroused, it defines a line he dare not cross and deeds he dare not commit, regardless of orders, because those very deeds would destroy something in him which he values more than life itself. If the path of military operations and this line of a soldier's conscience collide, disobedience and mutiny erupt. It happened in the British Army in Ireland in 1914 at the Curragh; it happened to the French Army in 1917; it almost happened before Suez in 1956; and perhaps even elements of the United States Army came close to it in the early 1970s.

Conscience is a voice within a soldier long before it becomes a force. It is during this embryonic phase that it can be influenced. Although principles cannot be breached, potential collisions can be averted. And it is here that the classic soldierly qualities have their effect and can hold the pressures at bay. These, the ageless virtues of the warrior, have been well rehearsed by the great captains of the past: Napoleon, Washington, Wellington, Lee, Allenby, MacArthur, Guderian, and Slim—each has produced his own muster. But I would limit mine to five: professionalism, judgment, willpower, courage, and, above all, integrity. These represent the very stuff of leadership.

Professionalism

The need for professionalism is clear. It breeds, or should breed, the thinking man. But if the soldier is left to his own, he can misinterpret the rationale behind his orders. He may then react stupidly or blindly or, because his conscience is aroused, he may even refuse to act at all. It was to overcome this very weakness that Sir John Moore in 1809 introduced the British Army to the concept of the "thinking, fighting man." And today the *Bundeswehr* ideal of the "Citizen in Uniform," or *"Innere Fuhrung,"* reflects a similar philosophy. Its origins are the same; it too was born in a revolt against rigid, unthinking military obedience. But its aim, to develop an army of morally self-determining soldiers, is far more ambitious.

Judgment

The taking of risks is innate to the soldier. Indeed we probably put our consciences at risk more so than others—but are we not therefore less sensitive as a result? Similarly, are our consciences not sometimes dulled by the sheer professional challenges and by the hectic tempo of operations? Both can erode our judgment, and we must beware.

Willpower

The ultimate test of willpower surely is the ability to dominate events rather than be dominated by them. I refer to the leader who can stand his ground, coolly and imperturbably, when chaos surrounds him. A strong will is the function of a sound conscience. And judging from my own limited experience, the prime flaw in those commanders who have cracked under pressure has usually been a lack of willpower to stand up to the pressures of people and events—or possibly an inability to relax.

Courage

Bravery is the quintessence of the soldier, and it is a quality that happily runs richly through both the American and the British armies. But moral courage—the strength of character to do what one knows is right regardless of the personal consequences—is the true face of conscience. Sacking your best friend, facing up rather than turning the blind eye, accepting that the principle at stake is more important than your job. . . . Such actions demand moral courage of a high order. Yet courage is no longer the product of an empty mind. In particular, *effective* moral courage is now more dependent on intellectual prowess than in the past. This applies as much, in a way, to the higher echelons of command striving to maintain an army in an era of stringent economy as it does to junior commanders striving to master the intricacies of an antitank plan.

Integrity

And so to the greatest of the virtues on my list, one without which the leader is lost. Integrity, of course, embraces much more than just simple honesty. It means being true to your men, true to your outfit, and above all true to yourself. Integrity of purpose, loyalty upward and loyalty downward, humanity, unselfishness—these are its components. They come more easily to a man of conscience.

The Soldier in Society

Despite all our efforts, the chance of a clash between conscience and duty through ignorance and misjudgment is still very real. The risk is there in peace, it is probably at its height in counter-insurgency, and it smolders in general war. All the while, the soldier's actions are exposed to, and his principles questioned by, society as never before. In many ways he is closer to that society than his forebears, yet—and I believe this applies to both the American and the British armies—he is still absurdly isolated.

Both at home and abroad, the soldier is confined to military garrisons almost totally divorced from the local civil community: houses, schools, hospitals, shops, pubs—all are exclusively military. As internal pressures build up within the country, this grass roots lack of communication could breed mutual disinterest, misunderstanding, and even hostility. In turn the soldier could become unsympathetic and introverted. His conscience would then operate on false premises and jaundiced principles—it might become brittle and closed to persuasion.

Indeed, in the last resort it is the leader's ability to persuade which influences the path of the soldier's conscience and avoids the needless moral collision. A true leader must have that ability to think out what he wants and then persuade others to do it. He must impress their imagination yet impose his will, regardless of the difficulties. Remember Marshal Foch's immortal exhortation in 1917: "*Mon centre cede, ma droite recule, situation excellente—J'ATTAQUE!*" Dramatic? Yes. But it must have stifled doubts and quietened consciences.

Conclusion

Violence is deterred by four kinds of force: the force of law, the force of public opinion, the force of conscience, and, lastly, military force. Frequently these will enmesh and coincide. But it is when they do not that the soldier faces a moral, and sometimes legal, dilemma of fundamental significance. He can only resolve it if, in some way, he has been prepared or has prepared himself for the battle with his conscience.

Although the soldier may strive to change the law (as some of us have done in Ulster), he must not operate outside it, however attractive the argument that the end will justify the means may seem. Despite the necessary brutality of war and the military necessity of obedience, a soldier is responsible for his own actions even though he is in duty and in law bound to other disciplines.

A man at war fights better if his mind is at peace. And a quiet yet active conscience is most likely to be found where esprit is high, where a sustained effort is made to enlighten and educate the soldier, and where leadership by persuasion rules. If the soldier is to retain an open conscience, he rejects at his peril the society of which he is part. This is not to say that he should necessarily mirror that society's standards, but rather that he must steadfastly preserve his own discipline, professionalism, and self-respect. Yet he must resist the lure of setting up even the semblance of a praetorian state within a state.

Finally, I submit that a man of character in peace is a man of courage in war. As Aristotle taught, character is a habit, the daily choice of right and wrong. It is a moral quality that grows to maturity in peace and is not suddenly developed in war. The conflict between morality and necessity is eternal. But at the end of the day the soldier's moral dilemma is resolved only if he remains true to himself.

16

The Military Ethics of General William T. Sherman

By JOHN W. BRINSFIELD

The morality of General William Tecumseh Sherman's military campaigns—what he did and what he allowed his subordinate commanders and troops to do—has been extensively debated for more than a century. Sherman's critics charge that as a commander Sherman employed such terrorist tactics as licensing the random execution of noncombatants, destroying and pillaging private property, and even plotting Indian genocide. According to Sherman's detractors, his troops during both the Civil War and the Indian Wars, protected by the moral indifference of their commander, were guilty of murder, theft, arson, rape,[1] and the desecration of cemeteries and burial grounds.[2]

During the Atlanta campaign, for example, General W. P. Howard of the Georgia State Militia reported to Governor Joseph Brown that "the crowning act of their wickedness and villainy . . . was in removing the dead from vaults in the cemetery, robbing coffins of their silver name plates and tippings, and then depositing their own dead in the vaults."[3] Confederate General John B. Hood criticized Sherman's decision to evacuate the population of Atlanta in September 1864, writing to Sherman that his action "transcends, in studied and ingenious cruelty, all acts ever before brought to my attention in the dark history of war."[4] General Richard Taylor, son of President Zachary Taylor, wrote in 1879 that "Sherman and Sheridan, spattered with Southern blood, were throwbacks to a barbarous age."[5] Jefferson Davis, whose *Rise and Fall of the Confederate Government* provoked a newspaper debate with Sherman, wrote of the March to the Sea: "The arson of the dwelling-houses of noncombatants and the robbery of their property, extending even to the trinkets worn by women, made the devastation as relentless as savage instincts could suggest."[6] Mrs. Davis evidently did not feel that her husband had put the matter strongly enough. She offered her own moral assessment of Sherman in the *Army-Navy Journal* of 10 May 1884: "He was an inhuman monster—what he did not use he destroyed."[7]

Sherman was not slow to defend himself and his army from these piecemeal attacks. Over the course of 20 years, from 1864 to 1884, Sherman wrote letters, testified in court, gave speeches, and published his memoirs in an effort to set the record straight. In a letter to Captain J. H. Lee in 1881, Sherman explained his motivation:

> We must speak and write else Europe will be left to infer that we conquered not by courage, skill, and patriotic devotion, but by brute force and cruelty. The reverse was the fact, the Rebels were notoriously more cruel than our men. We never could work up our men to the terrible earnestness of the Southern forces. Their murdering of Union fugitives, burning of Lawrence, Chambersburg, Paducah and etc. were all right in their eyes, and if we burned an old cotton gin or shed it was barbarism. I am tired of such perversion, and will resent it always.[8]

Sherman denied that he had ever favored wanton destruction of human life in any instance; rather, he had acted throughout his military career to punish those who did not obey the law.[9] In the course of most of his major campaigns, Sherman said he preferred to conserve life and generally offered the enemy the opportunity to surrender before he set about his tasks of destruction.[10]

Sherman's problem throughout the Civil War was how to reconcile the brutal nature of modern war with the ethical values he had learned as a West Point cadet, as an Army officer, in his intermittent study of law from 1839 to 1859, and as a practicing attorney. While his primary interest as a general was undeniably directed toward strategy and tactics, there was still part of his intellectual heritage from five generations of Sherman judges that demanded a correlation between the conduct of war on one hand and the laws of warfare on the other.

In the 19th century there were many schools of classical ethics. Francis Lieber, in his 1838 edition of *A Manual of Political Ethics*, pointed out that essentially all of the schools dealt with two concepts: morals and ethics. Moral philosophy answered the question *What must I do*? Ethics answered the question *Why must I do it*?

The ethical school that most attracted Sherman was not the metaphysical or theological but the pragmatic and utilitarian, as befitted the profession of a soldier and the avocation of a lawyer. Law was a perfect sanction for Sherman's utilitarian military ethic because the law books recognized that every punishment should be proportionate to the crime. If rebellion was the highest crime against an organized society, both utilitarian ethics and the law of nations sanctioned extreme measures—such as devastation by fire and sword—as permissible expedients.

To truly understand the ethics—the rationale—for Sherman's punitive expeditions in the Civil War and after, one must approach his ideas from the standpoint of their chronological development. Sherman himself noted that his military ethics before 1862 were different than they were after that year. The detailed development of Sherman's thought from his first course in moral philosophy at West Point through the end of his military career would be a lengthy task. Nevertheless, a few comments may shed some new light on his concept of the ethics of war and support the thesis that Sherman's philosophy of war was not totally devoid of ethical and legal principle.

Ethical Education at West Point: 1839-40

The two courses that seem to have contributed most to Sherman's early ethical thought were both taught in his senior, or "first-class," year at West Point. After his summer encampment preceding that year, Sherman wrote to his brother John in August 1839:

> The encampment is now over and we are once more in Barracks and tomorrow will commence our studies. . . . This year's course of study is by far the most important of the four as well as the most interesting embracing as it does—Engineering—both Civil and Military—the construction of fortifications as well as the manner of attacking and defending them, Mineralology, and Geology, Rhetoric, Moral Philosophy, International and Common Law, Artillery and Infantry tactics.[11]

Sherman enjoyed his course in fortifications from Professor D. H. Mahan, who was probably his favorite instructor.[12] Mahan not only taught Sherman the value of the spade but also offered his opinion that the way to defeat the Indians in Florida was to destroy their food supplies.[13]

One book that Professor Mahan frequently referenced in his course was Baron Simon François Gay de Vernon's *Treatise on the Science of War and Fortification*, which had an appendix by Lieutenant J. M. O'Connor summarizing the thought of Jomini and Henry Lloyd on grand strategy. De Vernon's *Science of War* had been replaced as a textbook at West Point in 1836, but Sherman checked it out of the library in 1840 anyway.[14] It is interesting that the first chapter of O'Connor's translation of the *Science of War* offers a kind of Hobbesian analysis of society. "In the original state," the text reads, "mankind possessed mere animal sensibility, which results when a state of war between nations occurs and treaties and conventions are broken." In the condition of bestiality to which men revert in war, all civilization breaks down and even "churches may be used as redoubts."[15]

Sherman was not impressed with Jomini, whose work he said was "too dull, prosaic and didactic," but he was drawn to Mahan and to the general notion that obedience to law was the prerequisite for avoiding the chaos of war.[16] By the end of 1864, Professor Mahan stated this view even more directly by noting that "there are times in a nation's existence when the safety of the State is the highest law."[17]

The second course, which probably contributed even more to the development of Sherman's ethical thought, was a course in moral philosophy taught by Chaplain Jasper Adams. Chaplain Adams was an Episcopal clergyman who had been successively a professor of mathematics at Brown University, president of Charleston College in South Carolina, and president of Geneva College in New York before coming to West Point. He was not one of Sherman's favorites on the faculty; indeed, Sherman remarked that during his four years at West Point he was not "a Sunday School cadet."[18] But the subject matter covered in "the Chaplain's Course," as it was titled in the USMA Regulations of 1839, did capture Sherman's imagination: Adams taught moral philosophy, the law of nations, and constitutional law in the course the cadets called simply "ethics."[19]

Sherman was not the first cadet to be captivated by the readings in the Chaplain's Course. From 1816 when the regulations of the Military Academy specified that "a course of ethics shall include nautural and political law," to 1874 when the Law Department was formed at West Point, nine different chaplains taught law to the cadets using a series of textbooks ranging from Vattel's *Law of Nations* (published in 1758) to Woolsey's *Introduction to the Study of International Law* (published in 1860). Robert E. Lee told Bishop Joseph Wilmer of Albemarle County, Virginia, that had he not read Rawle's *A View of the Constitution* in Chaplain Warner's course, he would never have left the Union.[20] General Erasmus D. Keyes said he "learned more from Professor Warner in the section room than from any other teacher," and Stonewall Jackson, as a cadet in 1845, wrote to his sister Laura that his class in ethics was "preferable to any other in the course."[21] Walter L. Fleming, a professor of history at Louisiana State University at the turn of the century and an expert on early education at West Point, went so far as to state that the Chaplain's Course was one of the most important at the Academy in light of the history of the Civil War.[22] In fact, one could make a pretty good case for the thesis that the textbooks in the Chaplain's Course contained many of the operative strategic and ethical concepts of the Civil War and that these concepts, including retaliation, blockade, emancipation, and unconditional surrender, were discussed at West Point more than 20 years before the first shot was fired at Fort Sumter.

The reason so many cadets were interested in the Chaplain's Course was that it combined the study of humanities and law, which were offered nowhere else in the curriculum. In Adams' course cadets recited for two hours a day from William Paley's *Moral and Political Philosophy* and from James Kent's *Commentaries on American Law*. As Adams informed Superintendent Richard Delafield in February 1840:

> An exact knowledge of these textbooks is held to be of the greatest importance, long and patient examinations are held upon them, and the relative standing of the Cadets in the Academy is made to depend on their acquaintance with them. Not only so, but their future rank in the army, and consequently their prospects in life, are made to depend on the degree of their acquaintance with them.[23]

Adams did not approve of Paley's book because it taught "the young men that they have no conscience, diminishes their respect for truth, and perplexes, if it does not confound the distinction between right and wrong."[24] A petition by Adams to replace Paley's text was denied by the academic board, however, in part because he had already changed textbooks three times in two years and had been warned by Joel R. Poinsett, President Van Buren's Secretary of War, "to be more careful."[25]

The content of Paley's *Moral and Political Philosophy* is fascinating and worth a dissertation in itself because the textbook was studied by Jefferson Davis, Robert E. Lee, A. S. Johnston, J. E. Johnston, P. G. T. Beauregard, Ulysses Grant, and Sherman. Paley's work presents advice for daily living coupled with some reflections on the origin of government, on crime and punishment, on duty, and on the justice of warfare.

In essence Paley took a utilitarian approach to life, for "the obligation of every law depends upon its ultimate utility."[26] Rules "derive their force not from their internal reasonableness or justice but from their establishment."[27] God is the ultimate lawmaker,

> a Being whose knowledge penetrates every concealment, from the operation of whose will not art or flight can escape, and in whose hands punishment is sure; such a Being may conduct the moral government of his creation in the best and wisest manner by pronouncing a law that every crime shall finally receive a punishment proportioned to the guilt which it contains, abstracted from any foreign consideration whatever [and] by carrying this law into strict execution.[28]

It is God's will that all men should be happy, and happiness is generally the greatest good for the greatest number.[29] Therefore, one asks about any moral question, "Does it promote or diminish the general happiness?" If an action promotes happiness, it is the will of God.[30]

In spite of the utilitarian nature of Paley's work, James Kent's *Commentaries on American Law* was Sherman's favorite textbook in the Chaplain's Course. In 1829 James Kent was a professor of law at Columbia, president of the New York Historical Society, and Colonel Sylvanus Thayer's personal friend. Because Kent's book covered both the law of nations and constitutional law in one summary volume, and was thus more easily taught, it replaced the works by Vattel and Rawle that had been used intermittently from 1820 to 1832.

Kent's views of human nature and the practice of warfare were rooted in a pessimistic realism. For example, Kent begins his "Third Lecture," titled "Of the Declaration and other early measures of a state of war," by contrasting Bacon's statement that "war is one of the highest trials of right . . . put upon the justice of God by an appeal to arms," with Hobbes' view that "continual war is a natural instinct of man in a savage state."[31] Kent believed that man, without the social compact, reverted to a primitive level. War was "a dissolution of all moralities" and was fought between "all the individuals of which the other nation is composed."[32] Retaliation was allowed in such a total war to restrain the enemy from further excess.[33]

One of the best protective measures against such chaos was a strong central government. Kent observed that "the history of the federal government of Greece, Germany, Switzerland, and Holland afford melancholy examples of destructive civil war springing from the disobedience of the separate members."[34] Therefore, Kent believed, "Disobedience to the laws of the union must either be submitted to by the government to its own disgrace or those laws must be enforced by arms."[35]

Coupled with Kent's "total war" theory and his unionist sentiments was his strong aversion to slavery. Kent's solution to the slavery problem was not Christian persuasion, as Paley had suggested, but violent, though legal, confrontation. Kent noted bluntly, "Pirates can be exterminated without declaration of war and the African slave trade is declared to be piracy by the statute laws of England and the United States."[36]

Sherman's class was examined in moral philosophy as well as other subjects in January 1840. Typically, examination periods lasted for 17 days, from eight o'clock in the morning to dusk; each cadet was examined orally by the entire faculty and sometimes by members of the Board of Visitors.[37] Cadet Sherman wrote, "The results were favorable toward me as usual."[38] He placed sixth in his class in moral philosophy, better than cadets Grant, Stuart, and Davis but not as well as Lee or Jackson placed in their classes.[39] Had it not been for Sherman's average of 150 demerits a year for problems in conduct, he would have graduated fourth rather than sixth in his class.

The academic curriculum was not the only place that military ethics and discipline were emphasized, of course. The code of honor, compulsory attendance at chapel, and the USMA Regulations of 1839 all contributed to an ethical awareness. Article I, paragraph 52, of the Articles of War, which were appended to the USMA Regulations, caught Sherman's eye. That paragraph made it a capital offense for a soldier to quit his post in order to plunder or pillage. After 1862 Sherman said he ignored this "old" idea.[40]

From Florida to Tennessee: The Transformation

From the time that Lieutenant Sherman joined the 3d Artillery Regiment in September 1840 until the Civil War began, he never really saw a battlefield. He was one of the few major commanders in the Civil War who had no combat experience in the Mexican War. His letters to his brothers and sisters from Fort Pierce, Florida, in 1841 show a relatively conservative view of military ethics. He discussed the treaties broken by the Indians and the suffering of their women and children, which was borne "with fortitude."[41] In his single engagement against the Seminoles, Sherman rode alone into an Indian village after instructing his troops to "revenge" him if he were killed. He talked the Indians out of their weapons and marched them back to Fort Pierce.[42] It was a bloodless victory that Sherman would try to repeat at Atlanta in 1864, but with less success.

Sherman did study law during his Army assignments in Florida and South Carolina. It was perhaps natural that he considered law as a possible second profession, as did Stonewall Jackson and J. E. B. Stuart. Yet he practiced law for only one year at Leavenworth, Kansas, before the Civil War began. Years earlier, Sherman had written to his brother John that although "everybody" in his class studied law at West Point, he did not believe he was enough of an orator to make it his profession.[43] He preferred the thought of retiring to a good farm in Iowa.

Sherman's career from his Army resignation in 1853 to the beginning of the Civil War appears to have had a marked effect on his outlook on life, but an analysis of his psychological development in the face of personal banking and business failures exceeds the scope of this discussion. Certainly his decision to abandon his post as superintendent of the Louisiana State Seminary and Military Academy in order to stay in the Union "as long as a fragment" of the "Old Constitution" survived was a monumental decision for him.[44] The turning point in Sherman's concept of military ethics, however, came between his service in Virginia in 1861 and his service in Tennessee in 1862.

Sherman's attitude in 1861 toward pillage and destruction can be seen in a letter to his wife, Ellen, after the first Battle of Bull Run:

> Then for the first time I saw the carnage of battle, men lying in every conceivable shape and mangled in a horrid way . . . No curse could be greater than invasion by a voluntary army. No Goths or Vandals ever had less respect for the lives and property of friend and foes. . . .[45]

These comments were not directed at just any volunteer army but at his own in particular. Sherman wrote to his wife in August 1861:

> Our soldiers are the most destructive men that I have ever known. It may be that other volunteers are just as bad, indeed the complaint is universal, and I see no alternative but to let it take its course. . . . My only hope now is that a common sense of decency may be inspired into the minds of this soldiery to respect life and property.[46]

Even though Sherman had given up making "any friends in Virginia," he did try to maintain some discipline among his troops, who were "straggling for water, blackberries, or any thing on the way they fancied."[47]

Sherman's determination to keep his troops in line was further manifested during his service in Kentucky in the winter of 1861–62. He issued strict orders preventing his soldiers from taking any fresh food on the march, from sleeping in any vacant houses, and even from using Kentucky fence rails for firewood.[48] As a result, one regiment under his command, the Thirty-third Indiana, had more than half of its men in the hospital and suffered 62 deaths in a single month from exposure and from insufficient rations. When two citizens of Lexington, Kentucky, asked Sherman in October 1861 if he would arrest Southern sympathizers as a "retaliatory" measure, Sherman replied that he would arrest no one merely for holding an opinion as long as that person committed no overt criminal act.[49]

In carrying out these policies, Sherman was obeying the orders of the War Department for operations in the border states. In spite of the fact that Jefferson Davis had written a personal letter to Abraham Lincoln on 6 July 1861 threatening random retaliatory executions of Union prisoners in Richmond if Confederate sailors captured by the Federal Navy were hanged as pirates, the

War Department, through General Henry Halleck, had been holding to a very strict policy respecting the sanctity of private property and individual constitutional rights, and it continued to do so until mid-1862.[50] Sherman soon discovered, however, that the enemy did not operate under such constraints:

> I would not let our men burn fence rails for fire or gather fruit or vegetables though hungry. . . . We at that time were restrained, tied by a deep-seated reverence for law and property. The rebels first introduced terror as a part of their system. . . . Buell had to move at a snail's pace with his vast wagon trains. . . . Bragg moved rapidly, living on the country. No military mind could endure this long, and we were forced in self-defense to imitate their example.[51]

The genesis of Sherman's conversion from a proponent of warfare by the rules of courtesy to warfare by the rules of survival, therefore, was not the result of a deliberate policy rooted in intellectual theory. It was a reaction to the conditions he encountered in the field. Twenty years after the Civil War, Sherman reflected on his shift in thinking:

> I know that in the beginning, I, too, had the old West Point notion that pillage was a capital crime, and punished it by shooting. . . . This was a one-sided game of war, and many of us . . . ceased to quarrel with our own men about such minor things, and went in to subdue the enemy, leaving minor depredations to be charged up to the account of the rebels who had forced us into the war, and who deserved all they got and more.[52]

From his observations in 1862 in Kentucky and Tennessee, it was a short step for Sherman to begin to rationalize his changing views of warfare in terms of the darker side of the West Point curriculum of his cadet years and to see the conduct of war as involving, to a large measure, retaliation, punishment, revenge, and devastation.

Sherman was not alone in these observations, of course. Independently of Sherman, Colonel Ulysses S. Grant wrote in 1861 of his men of the Twenty-first Illinois on a march from Camp Yates to Missouri: "The same number of men never marched through a thickly settled country like this committing fewer depredations."[53] Yet Grant told his wife, Julia, "The people are inclined to carry on a guerrilla warfare that must eventuate in retaliation, and when it does commence it will be hard to control."[54]

By the summer of 1862 both the U.S. Congress and the Lincoln administration had become convinced that more stringent measures were necessary to subdue the rebels, who had fought so fiercely in the Peninsula Campaign and at Shiloh. On 13 July Brigadier General Steinwehr ordered Major William Steadman to arrest five citizens of Page County, Virginia, to be held as hostages and to suffer death in the event that any of Steinwehr's troops were killed by "bushwackers."[55] On 17 July Congress passed the famous Seizure Act, which provided for the confiscation or condemnation of all personal property belonging to persons engaged in rebellion.[56]

The Confederate government responded in kind by issuing General Order Number 54 on 1 August 1862, declaring the adoption of "just measures of retribution and retaliation as shall seem adequate to repress and punish these barbarities." Among other measures ordered by General Samuel Cooper, the Confederate States Inspector General, was the warning that the Confederate government would hang Union officers then held as prisoner of war in "a number equal to the number of our own citizens thus murdered by the enemy."[57]

In retaliation for increasing guerrilla activities in Mississippi and the number of "murders" committed by Southern "irregulars," Union General Henry Halleck, on 2 August 1862, ordered General Grant at Corinth, Mississippi, to

> clean out West Tennessee and North Mississippi of all organized enemies. If necessary, take up all active sympathizers, and either hold them as prisoners or put them beyond our lines. Handle that class without gloves, and take their property for public use. As soon as the corn gets fit for forage get all the supplies you can from the rebels in Mississippi. It is time that they should begin to feel the presence of war on our side.[58]

Within four days of the receipt of this order, General W. L. Elliott, Rosecrans' chief of staff at Corinth, ordered General James D. Morgan at Tuscumbia to move rebel women and children beyond his lines, seize their property, and burn their homes.[59]

At Memphis, Sherman reflected on this development in a letter to Secretary Chase, dated 11 August 1862, in words reminiscent of Kent's "total war" theory:

> The Government of the United States may now safely proceed on the proper rule that all in the South are enemies of all in the North; and not only are they unfriendly, but all who can procure arms now bear them as organized regiments or as guerillas. There is not a garrison in Tennessee where a man can go beyond the sight of the flagstaff without being shot or captured.[60]

Grant, in turn, reflected later that the "Constitution was therefore in abeyance for the time being, so far as it in any way affected the progress and termination of the war."[61]

With constitutional interpretation replaced by congressional law and the principle of military necessity, Sherman was free to suppress rebellion with almost any amount of force necessary. On 1 October 1862 he wrote to his brother John:

> Even on the Mississippi the boats are fired on daily. I have been compelled to burn down one town and resort to retaliation. For after eighteen months of war the enemy is actually united, armed, and determined. . . . [The] northern people have to unlearn all their experience of the past thirty years and be born again before they will see the truth.[62]

The truth, for Sherman, was that by arming all of its citizens, the South, not the North, had plunged the nation into total war. If the Union was to survive, the people of the North would have to adjust themselves to fight on the terms that the South, Sherman charged, had dictated.

On 4 October 1862, Sherman underscored this belief in a letter to Major General Grant at Jackson, Tennessee. Sherman told Grant,

> Guerrillas have twice attacked boats near Randolph—the Forest Queen and J. J. Roe—on both of which were many lady and children passengers. The attacks were wanton and cruel. I caused Randolph to be destroyed, and have given public notice that a repetition will justify any measures of retaliation such as loading the boats with their captive guerrillas as targets (I always have a lot on hand), and expelling families from the comforts of Memphis, whose husbands and brothers go to make up those guerrillas.[63]

Evidently this "new" turn of events in Memphis—and in his own command, for that matter—took Grant by surprise. On 18 October, when Sherman proposed to "expel ten secession families for every boat fired on," thereby visiting "on the neighborhood summary punishment," Grant sent a one-sentence endorsement to General Halleck:

> Respectfully forwarded to Headquarters of the Army for information of the General-in-Chief, embodying as it does a policy, which I approve but have given no order for, in regard to treatment of rebel families as punishment to prevent firing in to boats.[64]

Five days later, Colonel William S. Hillyer, Grant's aide-de-camp, wrote Sherman: "The general heartily approves your course in expelling secession families as a punishment and preventive example for guerrillas firing into boats."[65] For the first time in the Civil War, Sherman had a commander who understood the concept of retaliation to restrain the enemy, who had witnessed the effects of total war in Texas, and who, for that matter, was also once a student of the same West Point curriculum.

From Atlanta to the Sea: The Application

That Sherman, Grant, and Sheridan translated the will of Congress and the ideas of President Lincoln into a war of devastation aimed at total victory is not a fact requiring detailed proof. Sherman himself estimated that his March to the Sea cost the State of Georgia 15,000 first-rate mules, 5,000 head of cattle, and 2,000 horses, in addition to 34,979 Confederate casualties.[66] The question is not, however, what homes, towns, railroads, colleges, churches, or government buildings were destroyed. After all, Grant had instructed Sherman to "get into the interior of the enemy's country as far as you can, inflicting all the damage you can against their war resources."[67] The question is, to what extent did Sherman leave the West Point ideas behind in his quest for victory?

Sherman maintained in 1864 that he tried on many occasions to persuade his enemies to surrender and thereby to end the destruction his army was causing in the South:

> I contended at first, when we took Vicksburg, by all the rules of civilized warfare, they should have surrendered, and allowed us to restore Federal power in the land. But they did not. I claim also when we took Atlanta, that they were bound to every rule of civilized warfare to surrender their cause. . . .[68]

During the Georgia and Carolina campaigns, Sherman certainly used his authority under the law of nations, congressional law, Army regulations, and the directives of Lincoln and Grant to offer generous terms of surrender that were not only in accord with the precepts of Vattel but also in the finest Napoleonic tradition.[69] Yet, when he submitted to Governor Brown of Georgia an offer to "spare the State, and in our passage across it confine the troops to the main roads and . . . moreover, pay for all the corn and food we needed," the Georgia Legislature rejected Sherman's proposal, called for a levy en masse of all white males aged 16 to 45, released the prisoners from the state penitentiary, and even pressed all ministers not actively serving a church or synagogue into the Confederate forces.[70] In light of this response, Sherman told Colonel Joshua Hill, one of the emissaries to Governor Brown, "There is nothing left for me to do but to proceed."[71]

Of the conduct of his troops during the March to the Sea, Sherman wrote in 1875:

> No doubt many acts of pillage, robbery, and violence were committed by these parties of foragers, usually called "bummers"; for I have since heard of jewelry taken from women, and the plunder of articles that never reached the commissary; but these acts were exceptional and incidental. I never heard of any cases of murder or rape; and no army could have carried along sufficient forage for a march of three hundred miles; so that foraging in some shape was necessary.[72]

When Sherman arrived in Savannah he placed the city, including its schools and churches, under his protection with the warning "If any person shall abuse these privileges by communicating with the enemy, or doing any act of hostility to the Government of the United States, he or she will be punished with the utmost rigor of the law."[73] Sherman claimed that the disposal of property in and around Savannah was in accord with the "laws of nations and the practice of civilized governments."[74]

Sherman's campaign in the Carolinas was marked with charges of pillage and arson, just as had been the case in Georgia. The ethical maxim he had recommended to his commanders on the March to the Sea was the principle of retaliation by degree and that principle was to be pursued, in effect, throughout his military career:

> In districts and neighborhoods where the army is unmolested, no destruction of (private) property should be permitted; but should guerrillas or bush wackers molest our march, or should the inhabitants burn bridges, obstruct roads, or otherwise manifest local hostility, then army commanders should order and enforce a devastation more or less relentless, according to the measures of such hostility.[75]

Sherman kept the responsibility for damages squarely on the shoulders of the Southern leadership. If they cooperated with him, he could be generous; if they opposed him, he was unrelenting in punishment.

Sherman's conduct in allegedly burning Columbia out of sheer malice and revenge for South Carolina's part in starting the Civil War seemed to his generation to mark the apex of his cruelty. Yet Sherman told the veterans of the Army of the Potomac in 1881, "I saw with my own eyes cotton bales which had been set on fire by the Confederate cavalry. Without Logan's troops not a house would have escaped."[76] If there were a few troops who got out of hand it was because, Sherman claimed, they found whiskey in the town the Confederates had made a liquor depot. Furthermore, the fire spread because "God Almighty started the wind that carried it."[77] "If I had made up my mind to burn Columbia, I would have burnt it with no more feeling than I would a common prairie dog village," Sherman testified, "but I did not do it."[78]

Sherman noted in 1881 that after 329 pages of testimony in 23 legal cases brought against him, an international commission of judges disallowed the claim that "Columbia was wantonly fired by General Sherman."[79] What he did at Columbia, as reflected partly in his pocket diary, was to deliberately destroy only the public buildings. Then he left behind 500 beef cattle and 100 muskets for the citizens "to arm a guard to maintain order after we should leave the neighborhood."[80] Sherman consistently maintained, "Personally, I had not malice or desire to destroy that city or its inhabitants."[81]

The proof of such personal intent to avoid wanton injury in the Carolinas is in Sherman's continuing offer of peaceful terms to his enemies. In public and largely for propaganda purposes, Sherman would threaten to turn his army loose; in his words, the soldiers were "burning to avenge the national wrong which they attach to large cities which have been so prominent in dragging our country into civil war."[82] Thus he emphasized on one occasion that he would make North Carolina "howl"; but he also told his cavalry commander, General Kilpatrick, to deal "as moderately and fairly by North Carolinians as possible, and fan the flame of discord already subsisting between them and their proud cousins of South Carolina."[83] Finally, to General Joseph E. Johnston, Sherman wrote on 14 April 1865:

> I am fully empowered to arrange with you any terms for the suspension of further hostilities between the armies commanded by you and those commanded by myself. . . . General Stoneman is under my command, and my order will suspend any devastation or destruction contemplated by him. I will add that I really desire to save the people of North Carolina the damage they would sustain by the march of this army through the central or western parts of the State.[84]

Sherman's comment to Johnston is not at variance with his famous letter of 12 September 1864 to Atlanta Mayor James M. Calhoun, in which Sherman promised, "When peace does come, you may call on me for anything. Then will I share with you the last cracker, and watch with you to shield your homes and families against danger from every quarter."[85]

An Integrated Theory

With the surrender of Johnston's Army in North Carolina under terms other than those generously proposed, General Sherman's combat experience came to an end.[86] He had evolved an ethical theory of warfare, however, that would influence the conduct of the Indian Wars in the West for the next 20 years.

Sherman believed that society without law was chaotic. In 1860 he wrote, perhaps reflecting some of the old West Point ideas he had studied two decades before:

> The law is or should be our king; we should obey it, not because it meets our approval but because it is the law and because obedience in some shape is necessary to every system of civilized government. For years this tendency to anarchy had gone on till now every state and country and town . . . makes and enforces the local prejudices as the law of the land. This is the real trouble, it is not slavery, it is the democratic spirit which substitutes mere opinions for law.[87]

The South violated the law first, Sherman believed. Southerners willingly participated in the 1860 election, but "because that election did not result as they wanted, they refused to abide by the result and appealed to war."[88] That decision, according to Sherman, was folly, madness, treason, and "a crime against civilization."[89] It left the South free to treat with foreign powers against the interests of the United States as a whole.

Sherman came to believe that the civil war the South was waging was a rebellion; therefore, under Vattel's old definition, the unjust and lawless rebels were subject to severe punishment.[90] Further, Sherman's theory of punishment leaned heavily on the ideas of collective responsibility and retaliation to prevent further cruelty by the enemy.[91] He instructed General Edward R. S. Canby, for example, to hold Southern civilians accountable for guerrilla outrages, "for if they fire on boats with women and children in [them], we can fire and burn houses with women and children."[92] This was possible, of course, because warfare was waged between "all the individuals" on one side and "all the individuals" on the other. Eventually the enemy would tire and peace would return.

Sherman realized that war was not an end in itself, but a means to an end. "The legitimate object of war is a more perfect peace" under the authority of a lawful, democratic government.[93] Toward that end Sherman believed that warfare must be waged on a psychological as well as a military level. Thus many of Sherman's public statements during the Georgia campaign were designed to make the enemy "fear and dread us" and may have accounted for the fact that Sherman's armies suffered fewer campaign casualties in 1864 than his Confederate opponents.[94] General Grant, as a matter of fact, characterized Sherman's occupation of Atlanta as a "political campaign."[95]

On another level, however, Sherman saw war in somewhat metaphysical terms. He told the graduating class at West Point in 1876 that "wars are only the means to an end—not necessarily inhuman, barbarous, abhorred by God." Indeed, he suggested that "war is of divine origin," like lightning which strikes the just and the unjust alike. "We were born in war, baptized in war, and we have had wars of aggression and defense," Sherman told the cadets, but there is still "a Divinity that shapes our ends."[96]

How could war be of divine origin? Sherman wrote to Major Henry Turner two years after his West Point address:

> I believe God governs this world, with all its life, animal, vegetable and human, by invariable laws, resulting in the greatest good, though sometimes working seeming hardships. The idea of a vocation from God seems to me irreligious and I would look for the inspiration of a vocation in the opposite quarter (the Devil). When anybody assumes ''vocation'' their reason and all sense ceases and man becomes simply a blind animal. My idea of God is that he has given man reason, and has no right to disregard it.[97]

Presumably the abandonment of reason brought on war, which was its own punishment in Sherman's view. Since punishment for the crime of unrestrained passion is part of the invariable law of God, war is punishment of divine origin which affects both the guilty and the innocent. The best one could do in such circumstances was to end the war as quickly as possible.

Sherman, in his Civil War years, did not abandon his attachment to the law or to some of the ethical concepts he may have learned at West Point. Rather, he placed the laws of warfare on a continuum of expediency. The important thing was not the means but the end, and to this point Sherman was clearly a utilitarian thinker. What the South learned to fear was not Sherman's aggression nor his lack of mercy. It was his revenge.

Yet Sherman's job was not to philosophize, but to destroy the roots of serious rebellion, Southern and Indian, and he spent his entire military career to that end. His doctrines of collective responsibility and retaliation were rationalizations for ending a destructive war. They should be fully understandable rationalizations to those who are heirs not only of Atlanta and Columbia, but also of Dresden, Hiroshima, and Nagasaki.

In the last analysis, Sherman may have contributed something relatively important in the field of military ethics. Foreseeing the death and destruction that war would bring, he wept on hearing of the secession of South Carolina in 1860.[98] Nineteen years later, he would tell a Michigan audience: ''It is only those who have neither fired a shot nor heard the shrieks and groans of the wounded who cry aloud for blood, more vengeance, more desolation. War is hell.''[99] Yet even in hell Sherman tried to show that when circumstances allowed, there should be a regard if not for chivalry at least for the laws of nations. He was not the author of either the theory or the ethics of total war, but, in his generation, he may have been the leading intellectual apologist for both. To that extent he was not a total warrior completely devoid of principle.

NOTES

1. John B. Walters, *Merchant of Terror: General Sherman and Total War* (New York: Bobbs-Merrill, 1973), pp. 137-38, 200.
2. Cited in Elizabeth H. McCallie, *The Atlanta Campaign* (Atlanta: The Atlanta Historical Society, 1939), p. 26.
3. Ibid.
4. John B. Hood, *Advance and Retreat* (New Orleans: G. T. Beauregard, 1880), p. 230.
5. Cited in Thomas C. Leonard, *Above the Battle* (New York: Oxford Univ. Press, 1978), p. 13.

6. Jefferson Davis, *The Rise and Fall of the Confederate Government* (New York: D. Appleton and Co., 1881). II, 570.
7. "J. David' Opinion," *Army-Navy Journal*, 10 May 1884.
8. W. T. Sherman to Captain J. H. Lee of Spottswood, N.J., 14 June 1881, in The Papers of William T. Sherman, Letterbook 95, USMA Archives Microfilm Collection (Hereinafter cited as Sherman Papers).
9. Robert G. Athearn, *William Tecumseh Sherman and the Settlement of the West* (Norman: Univ. of Oklahoma Press, 1956), pp. 69-70; and Lloyd Lewis, *Sherman: Fighting Prophet* (New York: Harcourt, Brace, 1932), p. 597.
10. Athearn, pp. 69-70; and Lewis, p. 598.
11. W. T. Sherman to John Sherman, 31 August 1839, Sherman Papers.
12. William T. Sherman, *Memoirs* (Bloomington: Indiana Univ. Press, 1957), II, 396.
13. George P. Winton, Jr., "Ante-Bellum Military Instruction of West Point Officers and Its Influences upon Confederate Military Organization and Operations" (Ph.D. dissertation, Univ. of South Carolina, 1972), p. 46.
14. USMA Library, "Entry of Books Issued to Cadets on Saturday Afternoons 1840-1843," in the USMA Archives, shows that Cadet Sherman checked out the *Science of War*, two volumes with plates, on 2 March 1840.
15. John Michael O'Connor, trans., *Vernon's Science of War and Fortification* (New York: J. Seymour, 1817), I, 10, 362.
16. William C. Brown, "General Sherman and the Infantry and Cavalry School," *Journal of the United States Cavalry Association* 16 (July 1905): 124.
17. D. H. Mahan to the Hon. Gouverneur Kemble, 26 September 1864, in Edward Holden's *Library Manual*, II, 59, USMA Archives.
18. Lewis, p. 56.
19. USMA Academic Board Minutes, 5 November 1838, USMA Archives.
20. Cited in Wilbur Thomas, *General George H. Thomas* (New York: Exposition Press, 1964), p. 63. See also Douglas S. Freeman, *R. E. Lee: A Biography* (New York: Scribner's Sons, 1934), I, 78-79.
21. E. D. Keyes, *Fifty Years Observation of Men and Events* (New York: Scribner's Sons, 1884), p. 77; and Thomas Jackson Arnold, *Early Life and Letters of Stonewall Jackson* (Richmond, Va.: Dietz Press, 1957), p. 73.
22. Walter L. Fleming, "Jefferson Davis at West Point," *Metropolitan Magazine*, 1908, p. 282.
23. Jasper Adams to Major R. Delafield, 3 February 1840, in the Jasper Adams Papers, USMA Archives, Drawer F.
24. Ibid.
25. USMA Academic Board Minutes, 28 October 1839 and 15 November 1839, USMA Archives.
26. William Paley, *The Principles of Moral and Political Philosophy* (Boston: West and Richardson, 1815), p. 463.
27. Ibid., p. 465.
28. Ibid., pp. 386-87.
29. Ibid., p. 64.
30. Ibid.
31. James Kent, *Commentaries on American Law* (New York: O. Halstead, 1826), I, 45.
32. Ibid., I, 53.
33. Ibid., I, 89.
34. Ibid., I, 199.
35. Ibid.
36. Ibid., I, 179.
37. Jasper Adams to Major R. Delafield, 3 February 1840, in the Jasper Adams Papers, USMA Archives, Drawer F.
38. W. T. Sherman to John Sherman, 14 January 1840, Sherman Papers.
39. Lee placed second in "Natural and National Law and Ethics" in 1829; Jackson was fifth in 1846. Grant was below average in ethics, and Sheridan had to spend a fifth year at West Point because of problems in conduct. It is interesting to note that Sherman, Grant, and Sheridan all graduated from West Point as cadet privates due to excess demerits.
40. Lewis, p. 442.

41. W. T. Sherman to "My dear Sister," 16 January 1841, Sherman Papers.
42. Lewis, p. 68.
43. W. T. Sherman to John Sherman, 7 March 1840, Sherman Papers.
44. Photographs of Sherman's letter of resignation dated 18 January 1861 are in the USMA Library.
45. Walters, pp. 20-21.
46. Ibid, p. 22.
47. Ibid., p. 21; and W. T. Sherman, *Memoirs*, II, 181.
48. Lewis, p. 188.
49. *The War of Rebellion: A Compilation of the Official Records of the Union and Confederate Armies* (Washington: GPO, 1887), series 2, vol. 2, p. 814. (Hereinafter cited as *Official Records*).
50. Jefferson Davis, *Rise and Fall of the Confederate Government*, II, II; *Official Records*, series 1, vol. 17, part 2, pp. 16-17.
51. W. T. Sherman to James Guthrie, 14 August 1864, cited in Lewis, p. 398.
52. Lewis, p. 442.
53. William S. McFeely, *Grant* (New York: W. W. Norton, 1981), p. 81.
54. Ibid., p. 78.
55. Thomas Jordan, *General Orders from Adjutant and Inspector General's Office, C.S. Army in 1862* (Charleston, S.C.: Evans and Cogswell, 1863), p. 66.
56. John F. Callan, *The Military Laws of the United States* (Philadelphia: George W. Childs, 1863), p. 521.
57. Jordan, p. 68.
58. *Official Records*, series 1, vol. 17, part 2, p. 150.
59. Ibid., pp. 154-55.
60. Walters, pp. 57-58.
61. U. S. Grant, *Personal Memoirs of U. S. Grant* (London: Sampson Law, Marston, Searle and Rivington, 1886), II, 507.
62. W. T. Sherman to John Sherman, 1 October 1862, in the USMA Library, LAC 11541 [Library of American Civilization, on microfiche], p. 166.
63. *Offical Records*, series 1, vol. 17, part 2, pp. 261-62.
64. Ibid., p. 280.
65. Ibid., p. 307.
66. W. T. Sherman *Memoirs*, II, 132, 208.
67. Cited in Archer Jones, "Jomini and the Strategy of the American Civil War, A Reinterpretation," *Military Affairs* 34 (December 1970), 130.
68. Lewis, p. 424.
69. Vattel held that "the right to make war ceases upon the offer of just terms." Charles G. Fenwick, ed., *The Law of Nations* (Washington: Carnegie Institute, 1916), p. 254.
70. W. T. Sherman, *Memoirs*, II, 138; and Charles C. Jones, *The Siege of Savannah* (Albany, N.Y.: Joel Munsell, 1874), p. 13.
71. Lewis, p. 423.
72. W. T. Sherman, *Memoirs*, II, 182-83.
73. Ibid., II., 223.
74. Ibid., II., 267.
75. Ibid., II., 175.
76. W. T. Shernan, "Address to the Army of the Potomac," *Army-Navy Journal* 11 June 1981, p. 945.
77. Lewis, pp. 506-07.
78. Ibid., p. 508.
79. W. T. Sherman, "Address to the Army of the Potomac," p. 945.
80. W. T. Sherman, *Memoirs*, II, 287.
81. Ibid., II, 286.
82. Ibid., II, 211.
83. Lewis, pp. 509, 514.
84. W. T. Sherman, *Memoirs*, II, 347.
85. Ibid., II, 127.
86. Sherman proposd that the Confederate armies deposit their arms in their own state arsenals, that the officers and legislatures of the several states be recognized by the executive of the

United States upon taking an oath to support the Constitution, and that the people be guaranteed their political rights and franchises under a general amnesty. Sherman saw these terms as effecting the will of Abraham Lincoln. The assassination of Lincoln led to their disapproval by President Johnson and Secretary Stanton. See Philemon Tecumseh Sherman, "Address to the Society of the Army of the Tennesse," p. 20, in the USMA Archives.

87. Lewis, p. 134.
88. Lewis, p. 332.
89. Lewis, p. 138; and W. T. Sherman, *Memoirs*, II, 152, 167.
90. Philemon T. Sherman, p. 18.
91. W. T. Sherman, *Memoirs*, II, 179-80; Athearn, pp. 69-70, 131, 279; and Lewis, pp. 579-99.
92. Lewis, p. 332.
93. W. T. Sherman, *Memoirs*, xii. The quotation is the inscription on Sherman's statue in Washington. See also W. T. Sherman, *Address to the Graduating Class of the U.S. Military Academy, June 14, 1876* (New York: Van Nostrand, 1876), p. 26.
94. Cited in Archer Jones, "Jomini and the Strategy of the American Civil War," p. 130. See also Timothy H. Donovan et al., *The American Civil War* (West Point, N.Y.: USMA Department of History, 1980), p. 325.
95. McFeely, p. 188.
96. W. T. Sherman, *Address to the Graduating Class . . . June 14, 1876*, p. 29; and W. T. Sherman, *Memoirs*, II, 126.
97. Cited in Joseph T. Durkin, *General Sherman's Son* (New York: Farrar, Straus, and Cudahy, 1959), p. 53.
98. Lewis, p. 138.
99. W. T. Sherman, "An Address Before the Graduating Class of the Michigan Military Academy, June 19, 1879," in *Bartlett's Familiar Quotations*, ed. Christopher Morley (New York: Little, Brown, 1957), p. 366.

This article originally appeared under the title "The Military Ethics of General William T. Sherman: A Reassessment" in the June 1982 issue of *Parameters*.

17

In War, in Prison, in Antiquity

By JAMES BOND STOCKDALE

The best education, the best preparation for a full and successful life, surely entails a proper blend of classical and contemporary studies. While we pursue the keys to the kingdom of modernity—studies in political science and economics and high technology—we need to understand the importance of a broad background in the readings of antiquity, those readings that form the basis of our civilization. In time of duress, in war especially, is that classical background important.

Achieving that magical combination of ancient and modern grounding took me half a lifetime to improvise. I grew up as a veritable prince of modernity; as a young man I was a test pilot, flying supersonic fighters when they were headline news and sharing a schoolroom with future astronauts. Then, at 37, too late for graduate school in high tech, a turn in my life took me to the quite different atmosphere of the study of moral philosophy. By that I mean old-fashioned philosophy—Socrates, Hume, Mill—mixed with literature with moral overtones—Shakespeare, Dostoyevski, Camus, and the like. I was deeply exposed to the thoughts and actions of men of the ancient past, of mankind dealing with Ultimate Questions.

In the course of my study of moral philosophy I have been privileged to have wonderful mentors. One was Phil Rhinelander at Stanford. He introduced me to the great stoic tract by Epictetus, *The Enchiridion*, and explained that Frederick the Great never left on a campaign without having a copy in his knapsack. Three years later I was slapped in a political prison for four years of solitary confinement—in the very world of Epictetus. Another mentor was Joe Brennan of Columbia. He came to the Naval War College when I was its president to help me introduce moral philosophy there. For ten years he has taught a course in "Foundations of Moral Obligations." He has taught a generation of Navy and Marine Corps leaders, and they are better leaders for having taken his course. Those two mentors, despite their differences, had a great deal in common; each had one foot in modernity, one in antiquity. They gave me much. They led me to a treasure of striking insights such as this one by Mark Van Doren: "Being an educated person means that given the necessity [after doom's day, so to speak], you could re-found your own civilization."

The Stoics said that "Character is fate." What I am saying is that in my life, education has been fate. I became what I learned, or maybe I should say I became the distillation of what fascinated me most as I learned it. Only three years after I left graduate school, I participated in the re-founding of my own civilization after doom's day, when the giant doors of an Old World dungeon had slammed shut and locked me and a couple hundred other Americans in—in total silence, in solitary confinement, in leg irons, in blindfolds for weeks at a time, in antiquity, in a political prison.

That re-founded civilization became our salvation. Stripped to nothing, nothing but the instincts and intelligence of the ancients, we improvised a communication system dredged up from inklings of a distant past (actually the tap code of Polybius, a second-century Greek historian with a flair for cryptography), and lived on comradeship in a polity that would have been a credit to Polybius' Athens. The spiritual power (not necessarily religious) that seeped into us as we surreptitiously joined forces against our common enemy came as a surprise.

In my solitude the impact of this unexpected spiritual power sometimes caused me to wonder. Does modernity (post-Enlightenment life under big governments and big bureaucracies, constantly competing to remake the world in the image of the new) deaden our noblest impulses? Does it smother or atrophy the power of the human spirit, the power of human nature? Do the readings of ancient times, the classics, serve merely to give us insight into the events of the past? Or do not the texts of those self-contained cultures of antiquity portray human power in all its vibrant potential? Do they not contain evidence of a more imaginative and fundamental grasp of the essence of being human than can be found even in 20th-century texts that have since joined the classics on the humanities shelves?

In Homer's immortal epic, *The Iliad*, as Hector is about to leave the gates of Troy to fight Achilles—knowing, as he must have known, that he would lose and he would die—he says goodbye to his wife and baby son at the gates, and the baby starts to cry, frightened by the nodding of the plumes on his father's shining helmet. Some would think the tale of the Greek-Trojan war to be an irrelevant relic of bygone days. Some would think it should be stricken from the reading list because it glamorizes war. Some think that now at last, with reason to guide us, we can scoff at a warrior's suicidal obligations. But others of us react quite differently, seeing in that scene a snapshot of the ageless human predicament: Hector's duty, his wife's tragedy, Troy's necessity, the baby's cry. . . .

My reaction, of course, is the latter, not only because I am a romantic by nature, but because by the time I first read *The Iliad* I had lived in antiquity (and I am not referring to the lack of electricity or plumbing). I had lived in a self-contained culture, a prison culture I watched grow among men of good will under pressure. I knew what it was to be a human being who could be squashed like a bug without recourse to law, and I knew that the culture, the society, that preserved me had to be preserved or nobody had anything to cling to. I knew that civic virtue, the placing of the value of that society above one's personal interests, was not only admirable, it was crucial to self-respect, and I knew that to preserve that culture, sometimes symbolic battles had to be fought before real battles could start. I knew that obligations, particularly love and self-sacrifice, were the glue that made a man whole in this primitive element, and I knew that under the demands of these obligations being "reasonable" was a luxury that often could not be afforded.

I also knew during this prison existence that I was being shown something good—life can have a spiritual content one can almost reach out and touch. I suppose it can always have that, but I was used to the idea of it being fuzzed up, powdered, fluffed, and often ridiculed here in man-made modernity, where changing the world takes precedence over understanding it, understanding man himself.

The same message comes through in the writings of Fyodor Dostoyevski, Arthur Koestler, and Aleksandr Solzhenitsyn. They've been where I've been. So had Miguel Cervantes. This future author of *Don Quixote* was a young officer in the Spanish army taken prisoner after the Battle of Lepanto in the 16th century. He spent seven years in an Algiers political prison. Same story: "Confess your crimes," "Discredit yourself," "Disavow your roots." He was tortured to disavow Christianity; he could get amnesty and go home if he would disavow it. I was made much the same offer. I was to disavow "American Imperialism." Good boy, Cervantes, you hung in, too. You knew how this age-old game is played. Political prisons are not just sources of fables of the past. They could just as easily inspire the literature of the future. Unable to tolerate dissent, totalitarian governments must have them. How else to suppress and discredit their enemies within?

You know, the life of the mind is a wonder—the life of the mind in solitude, the life of the mind in extremis, the life of the mind when the body's nervous system is under attack. If you want to break a man's spirit, and if your victim's will is strong, you've got to get physical. Sometimes you might think that you can unhinge strong people with psychological mumbo jumbo. Sorry, there is no such thing as brainwashing. But even physical hammering will not alone change all hard-set attitudes. The real method to jellify those attitudes, that is, to extract those seemingly heartfelt "confessions," is the artful and long-term imposition of fear and guilt. Solitary confinement and tourniquet-tight rope bindings are mere catalysts for the fear and guilt conditioning. Remember, I'm talking about strong-willed victims. They're going to make you hurt them. They know from experience that the compliance extracted by brute force is in no way so spiritually damaging as that given away on a mere threat. And they have learned from experience that in the end it is a spiritual battle. The leak in the dike always starts from within.

How does the mind of the victim respond to these challenges? How did we respond in those North Vietnamese prisons? Realize the situation here: They've got man in a laboratory test that no university in the United States could set up. They're not going to leave him in a room just to fill out a bunch of questionnaires, or give him some innocuous maze to work his way out of. They're going to boil the *essence* out of him as a chemist would heat and pressurize a specimen to study its properties, its nature, in a laboratory. What is the nature of man? What surprises does human nature have in store under these conditions?

First, regarding the loneliness, the solitude: It's not as bad as you think. Don't forget, the time factor is stretched out way beyond most psychological experiments. There was a professor at Stanford who got national attention several years ago for locking some students in the basement of a library for a few days, and then writing a book about his observations on their behavior. I laughed when I read it. You don't know the first thing about a person until he has been in the cooler for a couple of months. He has to first go through the stage when he is preoccupied with going insane. That's a normal prelude without lasting significance. Figure on that phase lasting for the first three to four weeks. It ends when it suddenly dawns on him that he'll have no such luck; he's stuck with himself. Almost everybody then sets himself up in a ritualistic life. Something deep-seated in human nature likes, feels safe with, repetition—a time for this, and a time for that, repeated regularly every day. You get to thinking about how liturgies of worship must have gotten started in some prehistoric clan.

Your mind drifts to many anthropological questions. How do institutions and governments get started? Are they the product of a man on a white horse? Does some powerful person impose rule: "We gotta get organized; here are the tribe's rules; break 'em and I'll cave your skull in." I doubt it. When you're scared (and that's probably why people grouped into those first crude polities—fear of predators, human or otherwise), you don't feel the urge to take charge. And when you're expected to, by virtue of heredity in clan or tribe, or seniority, for sure, among military prisoners, on first contact you seem compelled to say something becoming a well-brought-up American boy, like: "In these circumstances when you are being threatened or tortured to do things that offend your very being, I can't bring myself to order you to do this or that. Everyone must have the autonomy to choose the best of the alternatives facing him. Do the best you can and God bless you."

How civilized and compassionate! But it will never sell. Those fine young people in trouble won't let you get away with that. Their response is sure to be something like this: "You have no right to piously tell us each to seek out the good, and then back out of the picture. You are in charge here and it's your duty to tell us what the good *is*. We deserve to sleep at night, feeling that at least we're doing *something* right in all hewing to what our leader says. We deserve the self-respect that comes with knowing we are resisting in an organized manner. We expect you to tell us to take torture before we comply with any of their demands. Give us the list!" There's nothing rational about such a reaction. Anybody could see that we probably weren't going to win the battle. But on the other hand, as the veteran prisoner Fyodor Dostoyevski aptly noted, "Man's most deep desires in life under pressure are not for a rationally advantageous choice, but for an independent choice."

On the parade ground, all the rankers vie for leadership, to be out front; but in a political prison, being the boss means you're the first guy down the torture chute when the inevitable purge starts. In that place, the drive for discipline and organization starts at the bottom and works its way up. Maybe it always does when lives and reputations are at stake.

How about the handling of fear and guilt? Those are determining forces in any life. You can't accomplish anything without a little of both ("fear of failure" can keep you going once you get started), but if you let them get out of control, they'll tear the very core out of your being.

Did I say a little guilt—a feeling of inadequacy with regard to your duties—was a good thing? Most modern psychiatrists would have us float around on a pink cloud of emotional tranquility, free of conscience's nagging, but you've got to have a goad if you're going for anything big. In Arthur Koestler's *Arrival and Departure*, the brain of a restless young southeast European exile, who is determined to get back into the fighting of World War II, is given a spring house-cleaning by a female psychiatrist, who finds him hiding in Portugal in 1940. "What's eating him?" his friends all want to know; "He's seen enough war," they conclude. Predictably, the psychiatrist finds the problem in his past, a troubled childhood, and after clearing him of his hangups (she thinks), she awaits him on a ship with tickets that will take them both to a safe, carefree life in America. At that point he runs aboard the ship only to divulge the shocking news that he has just signed up with British Intelligence to be parachuted as an agent behind enemy lines. Old prisoner Koestler writes him a notable farewell speech: "The prosperity of the race is based on those who pay imaginary debts! Tear out the roots of their guilt and nothing will remain but the drifting sands of the desert."

There's power in feelings of guilt.

Yet there's devastation when it rises to such levels that it consumes you (remember, in your wartime prison cell you're waiting to be picked off by the first vulture to interrogate you), or when it creates self-delusion ("After all, I *was* tortured; maybe something came over me; my poor performance must not have really been my fault; I must have been broken or brainwashed"). Such rationalizations won't play well in the cold light of day when you're edging yourself out on the thin ice separating you from a nervous breakdown. And a nervous breakdown you cannot afford in this place. So there you are, wretched, about to sink into the Slough of Despond—bow first or stern first, depending on which crutch (consuming yourself or deluding yourself) you elect to use. Either will guarantee you the loss of your self-respect; that being all you have left, you have to learn to just sit there in your solitude and throw away both crutches and heal yourself—there's no outside professional help available. You have to deal with guilt, eat it, if you will. You can learn to use its fire for what it was intended, a flame that cauterizes your will to make you stronger next time. Of all the challenges guilt brings in a political prisoner's life, working off the feeling of having brought harm to a fellow inmate is the most demanding.

Later, out in public, you have no recourse but to join in the inevitable discussion of your so-called "agony" in prison: "How was the food?" "Did you get any fresh air?" "Were you warm enough all the time?" "Did you have any feelings of friendship for your captors?" "How was the mail service?" But when you get one old political prisoner alone with another, they exchange tales of a quite different nature, of nervous exhaustion, uncontrollable sobbing in solitude, the wages of fear, and the feelings of inadequacy, of guilt. It doesn't do to discuss these matters with strangers; they put you down as some kind of wacko.

But believe it or not, as time wears on in solitary you get better at dealing with these matters. The ultimate accommodation with them comes from focusing intensely on leading a very, very clean and honest life, mentally and otherwise—and you find yourself being consumed in a strange, lasting, and unexpected high-mindedness. By this, I don't mean "joyfulness," and I particularly don't mean "optimism." (In *Man's Search for Meaning*, Viktor Frankl makes the point that babbling optimists are the bane of existence of companions under stress. I totally agree with him—give me a pessimistic neighbor every time.) What I mean by the setting in of high-mindedness is the gradual erosion of natural selfishness among people of good will facing a common danger over time. The more intense the common danger, the quicker the "me-first" selfishness melts. In our situation, at about the two-year point, I believe most of us were thinking of that faceless friend next door—that sole point of contact we had with our civilization, that lovely, intricate human thing we had never seen—in terms of love in the highest sense. By later comparing notes with others, I found I was not alone in becoming so noble and righteous in that solitude that I could hardly stand myself. People would willingly absorb physical punishment rather than let it fall to their comrades; questions arose in my mind about the validity of the much-talked-about instinct of self-preservation. Solzhenitsyn describes his feelings of high-mindedness in his Gulag writings in words like these:

> It was only when I lay there on the rotting prison straw that I sensed within myself the first stirrings of good. Gradually it was disclosed to me that the line separating good and evil passes not between states nor between classes nor between political parties but right through every human heart, through *all* human hearts. And that is why I turn back to the years of

my imprisonment and say, sometimes to the astonishment of those about me, "Thank you, prison, for having been in my life."

Was I a victim? Not when I became fully engaged, got into the life of unity with comrades, helping others, and being encouraged by them. So many times, I would find myself whispering to myself after an exhilarating wall-tap message exchange: "I am right where I belong; I am right where I was meant to be."

In all honesty, I say to myself, "What a wonderful life I have led." No two of us are the same, but to me the wonder of my life is in escaping the life Captain McWhirr had programmed for himself in Joseph Conrad's *Typhoon*: "to go skimming over the years of existence to sink gently into a placid grave, ignorant of life to the last, without ever having been made to see all it may contain of perfidy, of violence, of terror." And the author adds, "There are on sea and land such men thus fortunate—or thus disdained—by destiny. . . ."

Phil Rhinelander, my philosophy mentor at Stanford, died not too long ago. We were preparing a book together, and consequently I was with him almost every day at the last. He sat up in his bed at home, surrounded by his books and papers, writing on a yellow legal pad, never mentioning the cancer in his liver which he knew would take him in a matter of weeks (he was nearly eighty). One of the last things we talked about was our agreement on a point we had each separately stated publicly: "The challenge of education is not to prepare a person for success, but to prepare him for failure." It is in disaster, not success, that the heroes and the bums really get sorted out.

Always striving for true education—with its emphasis on moral reflection—is the best insurance against losing your bearings, your perspective, in the face of disaster, in the face of failure. I came home from prison to discover something I had forgotten; in my old Webster's collegiate dictionary I had pasted a quotation from Aristotle: "Education is an ornament in prosperity and a refuge in adversity." I had lived in the truth of that for all those years.

This article originally appeared in the December 1987 issue of *Parameters*.

About the Editors and Contributors

COLONEL HARRY G. SUMMERS, Jr., U.S. Army Retired, is military affairs commentator for the *Los Angeles Times* and a contributing editor with *U.S. News and World Report*. Prior to retirement from the Army, he held the General Douglas MacArthur Chair of Military Research at the Army War College. A combat infantry veteran of the Korean and Vietnam wars, Colonel Summers is the author of *On Strategy* (1982), regarded as a classic work on the Vietnam War. He is also the author of the *Vietnam War Almanac* and the forthcoming *Korean War Almanac*.

COLONEL LLOYD J. MATTHEWS, U.S. Army Retired, is editor of *Parameters*: *U.S. Army War College Quarterly*. He holds a B.S. from the U.S. Military Academy, an M.A. from Harvard University, and a Ph.D. from the University of Virginia. Colonel Matthews served as an infantry officer in the Vietnam War during 1964–65, later commanding a battalion at Fort Ord, California. He was director of philosophy instruction at the Military Academy during 1971–79, serving as chairman of the Superintendent's Honor Review Committee during academic year 1978–79. Colonel Matthews was the associate dean at the Military Academy from 1981 to 1984.

CAPTAIN DALE E. BROWN, U.S. Army, is an assistant operations officer with the 31st Air Defense Artillery Brigade, Fort Hood, Texas. He was assistant editor of *Parameters*: *U.S. Army War College Quarterly* from 1984 to 1988. Captain Brown earned an M.A. in history from the Ohio State University and has served in a variety of air defense assignments in the United States and Europe, including command of a missile maintenance company.

★ ★ ★

PROFESSOR WILLIAM BARRETT was educated in philosophy at Columbia University, New York, where he received his Ph.D. in 1939. He taught philosophy at New York University for 29 years and was a visiting professor of philosophy at the U.S. Military Academy. Professor Barrett is the author of nine important books in the fields of philosophy and ethics.

CHAPLAIN (MAJOR) JOHN W. BRINSFIELD, U.S. Army, is assigned

to the staff and faculty, U.S. Army Chaplain School, Fort Monmouth, New Jersey. He received the Master of Divinity degree from Yale (Connecticut), Ph.D. from Emory University (Georgia), and D.Min. from Drew University (New Jersey). He is a graduate of the Armed Forces Staff College and served from 1980 to 1984 as an assistant professor in the department of history at the U.S. Military Academy.

MAJOR GENERAL CLAY T. BUCKINGHAM, U.S. Army Retired, is a graduate of the U.S. Military Academy (1949) and the U.S. Army War College. During the Korean War, he was a tank platoon leader and company commander in the 3d Infantry Division. In Vietnam he was a sector adviser in Hau Nghia province. Thereafter, General Buckingham enjoyed a succession of important command and staff assignments in the United States and Germany. During the last six years of his career, General Buckingham occupied all the Army's principal positions in the management-information and computer systems fields. He retired from the Army in 1982 and is currently president of the Association of Military Christian Fellowships.

COLONEL JAMES L. CARNEY, U.S. Army Reserve, is the Army Reserve senior adviser to the Army Materiel Command. He is a graduate of Spring Hill College in Mobile, Alabama, and of the U.S. Army War College. Colonel Carney also holds a J.D. degree from Harvard Law School. He served in Vietnam in 1968–69.

DR. JOHN W. COFFEY received his Ph.D. in 1971 from Stanford University, where he was a Woodrow Wilson Fellow. His book, *Political Realism in American Thought*, was published by Bucknell University Press in 1977, and his articles on national security affairs and American politics have appeared in numerous journals and newspapers. Dr. Coffey served in the Office of the Secretary of Defense from 1986 to 1988 and is currently an associate professor of political science at Rockford College in Illinois.

DR. ARTHUR J. DYCK is professor of Population Ethics at the Harvard School of Public Health. He is also co-director of Harvard's Kennedy Interfaculty Program in Medical Ethics, a member of the Harvard Center for Population Studies, and a faculty member of the Harvard Divinity School. Dr. Dyck is a graduate of Tabor College, Hillsboro, Kansas, and has earned two M.A. degrees in psychology from the University of Kansas and a Ph.D. in Religious Ethics from Harvard University. Dr. Dyck is the author of *On Human Care: An Introduction to Ethics* and is co-editor of *Ethics in Medicine*.

GENERAL SIR JAMES GLOVER, KCB, MBE, retired from the British Army in 1987. His final assignment was as commander in chief of the United Kingdom Land Forces. General Glover's assignments have included tours in Malaya, Cyprus, Hong Kong, West Germany, and Northern Ireland. He is now a director of the British Petroleum Company.

COLONEL ANTHONY E. HARTLE, U.S. Army, is the director of the philosophy program at the U.S. Military Academy. A 1964 graduate of the academy, he has served in a variety of assignments, including operations officer for the 2nd Infantry Division and battalion commander in the 101st Airborne Division (Air Assault). He holds an M.A. degree from Duke University (North Carolina) and a Ph.D. in philosophy from the University of Texas, Austin. In 1986, Colonel Hartle served as a staff member of the Presidential Commission investigating the Space Shuttle *Challenger* accident.

DR. JAMES TURNER JOHNSON is a professor in the departments of religion and political science at Rutgers University (New Jersey). He is the author of four books dealing with the morality of war, including *Can Modern War Be Just?* and *Just War Tradition and the Restraint of War*. Dr. Johnson received his Ph.D. from Princeton (New Jersey) and is currently directing a project comparing Western and Islamic religious and cultural values on war, peace, and politics.

CHAPLAIN (MAJOR GENERAL) KERMIT D. JOHNSON, U.S. Army Retired, was chief of Army chaplains from 1979 to 1982. He was commissioned in the infantry from the Military Academy in 1951 and saw combat in Korea. Chaplain Johnson received his divinity degree from Princeton in 1960 and is the author of *Realism and Hope in a Nuclear Age* (1988).

DR. STEPHEN M. MILLETT is manager of Forecasting and Strategic Planning Studies at Battelle Institute, Columbus, Ohio. A 1969 graduate of Miami University (Ohio), he received the Ph.D degree in history from the Ohio State University in 1972. Dr. Millett served as an officer in the U.S. Air Force from 1973 to 1979. Since joining Battelle in 1979, he has conducted numerous national security projects and has published several papers on Soviet-American defense issues. He is also a senior faculty member of the Mershon Center of the Ohio State University.

LIEUTENANT COLONEL JAMES L. NAREL, U.S. Army, teaches philosophy and ethics at the U.S. Military Academy. In addition to his command and staff assignments in air defense, he has served on the headquarters staff of the Combined Arms Center at Fort Leavenworth, Kansas; in the office of the Deputy Chief of Staff for Operations and Plans at the Pentagon; and as special assistant to the commanding general of the Training and Doctrine Command. He is a 1969 graduate of the Military Academy and holds a master's degree in literature from the University of Massachusetts.

VICE ADMIRAL JAMES BOND STOCKDALE, U.S. Navy Retired, served for 34 years as a Navy officer, most of them at sea as a fighter pilot aboard aircraft carriers. Shot down over North Vietnam in 1965 during his second combat tour, he was the senior Navy prisoner of war in Hanoi for eight years. He was tortured on 15 occasions, was in leg irons for two years, and was in solitary confinement for four. He is a former president of the Naval War College and is currently a senior research fellow at the Hoover Institution, where he has published widely. Among his combat decorations is the Medal of Honor.

GENERAL MAXWELL D. TAYLOR, U.S. Army Retired, was a

graduate of the U.S. Military Academy (1922) and the U.S. Army War College. His service during World War II included duty with the 82d Airborne Division in the Sicilian and Italian campaigns. General Taylor served as commanding general of the 101st Airborne Division (1944–45), the Eighth Army in Korea (1953–54), and U.S. Army Forces, Far East (1954–55). From 1945 to 1949, he was superintendent of the Military Academy and from 1955 to 1959 the Army Chief of Staff. General Taylor retired in 1959 but was recalled to active duty in 1961 as Military Representative of the President, following which he served as Chairman of the Joint Chiefs of Staff from 1962 to 1964. He was the U.S. Ambassador to South Vietnam in 1964–65; from then until his retirement in 1970 he served in such roles as presidential consultant on diplomatic and military affairs and chairman of the President's Foreign Intelligence Advisory Board. General Taylor was the author of four books, the most prominent of which was the *The Uncertain Trumpet* (1960). General Taylor died in May 1987.

PROFESSOR TELFORD TAYLOR received his LL.B from Harvard in 1932, thereupon embarking on a legal carreer that led him to influential positions in government, the military, and academe. These have included U.S. Army General Staff Corps membership in 1943, U.S. Chief of Counsel for war crimes prosecution (1946–49), and, presently, Nash Professor of Law (Emeritus) at Columbia University Law School and professor of law at the Benjamin Cardozo Law School. His military honors include the Distinguished Service Medal, the Order of the British Empire, and the French Legion of Honor. He has held fellowships with Churchill College, Cambridge, and is a member of the American Academy of Arts and Sciences. Professor Taylor's books include *Grand Inquest* (1954), *The March of Conquest* (1958), *Nuremburg and Vietnam* (1970), and *Munich: The Price of Peace* (1979).

PROFESSOR MICHAEL WALZER received his B.A. at Brandeis (Massachusetts) in 1956 and a Ph.D. from Harvard in 1961. After teaching political theory at Princeton for four years, he joined the department of government at Harvard, remaining there until 1980. In 1981, he joined the school of social science of the Institute for Advanced Study at Princeton. Professor Walzer is the editor of one book and the author of nine others. His recent writing has focused mainly on questions of political and moral philosophy, a prime example being his widely acclaimed book *Just and Unjust Wars*, appearing in 1977.

PROFESSOR DONALD ATWELL ZOLL is a well-known political philosopher and commentator on military affairs. Among his books are *Reason and Rebellion* (1962), *The Twentieth Century Mind* (1967), *The American Political Condition* (1973), and *Twentieth Century Political Philosophy* (1974). Formerly professor of philosophy at the University of Saskatchewan and professor of political science at Arizona State University, Professor Zoll left academic work in 1974 to write and lecture.